The Kingdom
of Matthias

The Kingdom of Matthias

Paul E. Johnson

and

Sean Wilentz

Updated Edition

OXFORD UNIVERSITY PRESS

New York   Oxford

Oxford University Press

Oxford University Press, Inc., publishes works that further
Oxford University's objective of excellence
in research, scholarship, and education.

Oxford   New York
Auckland   Cape Town   Dar es Salaam   Hong Kong   Karachi
Kuala Lumpur   Madrid   Melbourne   Mexico City   Nairobi
New Delhi   Shanghai   Taipei   Toronto

With offices in
Argentina   Austria   Brazil   Chile   Czech Republic   France   Greece
Guatemala   Hungary   Italy   Japan   Poland   Portugal   Singapore
South Korea   Switzerland   Thailand   Turkey   Ukraine   Vietnam

Published in 1994 by Oxford University Press, Inc.,
198 Madison Avenue, New York, New York 10016-4314

First issued as an Oxford University Press paperback, 1995
Updated edition published by Oxford University Press, 2012.
Oxford is a registered trademark of Oxford University Press

Library of Congress Cataloging-in-Publication Data
Johnson, Paul E., 1942–
The kingdom of Matthias : a story of sex and salvation
in 19th century America / Paul E. Johnson and Sean Wilentz.
p.   cm.   Includes bibliographical references and index.

ISBN 978–0–19–989249–5 (Pbk.)

1. Matthews, Robert, b. 1788.   2. Kingdom of Matthias (Cult)—Biography.
3. Kingdom of Matthias (Cult)—History.   4. Cults—New York (State)—History—
19th century.   5. Impostors and imposture—New York (State)—History—19th
century.   6. Sex customs—New York (State)—History—19th century.
I. Wilentz, Sean.   II. Title.
BR1718.M3J64   1994
277.3′081′092—dc20
[B]   93–50727

Frontispiece: Matthias, the Spirit of Truth, the Prophet of the God of the Jews, from
*Memoirs of Matthias the Prophet, with a Full Exposure of His Previous Impostures and of
the Degrading Delusions of His Followers* (New York, 1835).

11 10 9 8
Printed in the United States of America

To our children
Molly Johnson
James Wilentz
Hannah Wilentz

CONTENTS

THE KINGDOM OF MATTHIAS

Matthias (Robert Matthews), The Spirit of Truth, Prophet of the God of the Jews

Elijah Pierson

Sylvester Mills

Isabella Van Wagenen

Catherine Galloway

Ann Folger

Benjamin Folger

Lewis Basel

Henry Plunkett

Anthony the Dutchman

Mr. Thompson

Elizabeth Thompson

Isabella Matthews Laisdell

Elizabeth Pierson (Elijah's daughter) and possibly her half-sister, name undisclosed

Catharine, Edward, and Mary Ann Folger (Ann and Benjamin Folger's children)

William, James, and John Matthews (Matthias's sons)

Thompson children, names undisclosed

Galloway child or children, names undisclosed

LIST OF ILLUSTRATIONS

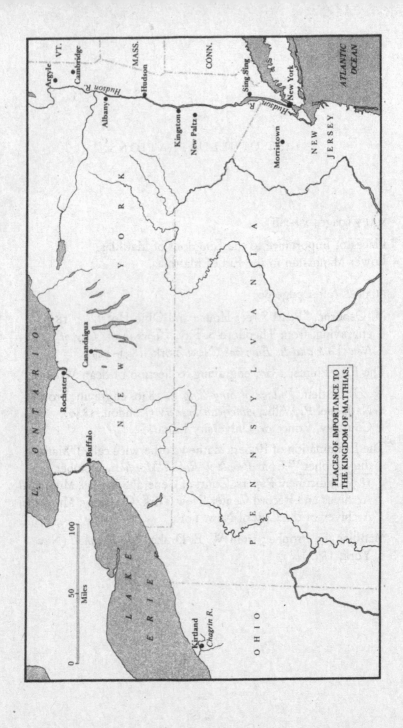

PLACES OF IMPORTANCE TO
THE KINGDOM OF MATTHIAS.

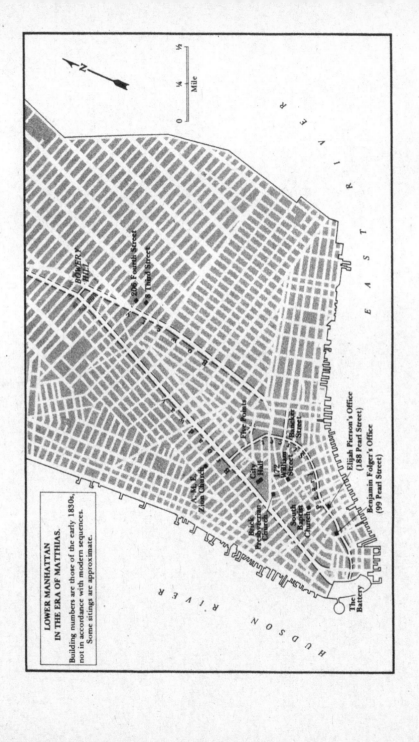

LOWER MANHATTAN
IN THE ERA OF MATTHIAS.

Building numbers are those of the early 1830s,
not in accordance with modern sequences.
Some sitings are approximate.

N

0   ¼   ½
Mile

HUDSON RIVER

EAST RIVER

BOWERY HILL

206 Fourth Street
8 Third Street

A. M. E.
Zion Church

Brick
Presbyterian
Church

City
Hall

Five Points

Thacker
Street

172
William
Street

South
Baptist
Church

Elijah Pierson's Office
(188 Pearl Street)

Benjamin Folger's Office
(99 Pearl Street)

The
Battery

The Kingdom
of Matthias

Prologue:
Two Prophets
at Kirtland

EARLY IN NOVEMBER 1835 the Prophet Matthias, four months
out of jail, traveled the roads of Ohio's Western Reserve, headed
for the pioneer Mormon settlement at Kirtland. The Christian
gentlemen of New York City had failed to convict Matthias of
murder and theft, but they had found him guilty of lesser charges:
contempt of court (true enough, he was contemptuous of their
courts) and malicious assault on his own daughter. Most of Matthias's followers had turned against him; the others had dis-
persed. Now he journeyed by himself to the banks of the Chagrin
River, looking for his fellow prophet, Joseph Smith.

Kirtland, about twenty miles northeast of what is today the city
of Cleveland, turned out to be a colony of rude buildings scattered on a hill that led down to the river—half-formed, like the
Mormon Church itself. When Matthias arrived on November 5,
workmen were braving cold weather to plaster the outside walls
of a structure that the Mormon Prophet Smith called his chapel. It
was a worthy effort, blending Gothic and Greek Revival styles,
but it was also a far cry from the grand and mysterious temples

that Mormons would build further west—in their first city at Nauvoo, Illinois, and, after 1847, in Utah Territory. Matthias was almost certainly unimpressed; Smith's chapel was no match for the great golden temple that *he* had long contemplated, and that he still expected to build when his luck returned.

Matthias sought out the Mormon Prophet and announced himself as Joshua, the Jewish Minister. (There was no need to reveal himself as the infamous Matthias, whose name had appeared in all the newspapers; Joshua, he would explain, was his priestly name.) Smith took the visitor seriously. Early in the conversation, with his scribe writing furiously at his side, the Mormon Prophet revealed details of his early sacred history in Palmyra, New York: his first vision at age fourteen, when two personages (he later identified them as Jesus and God) appeared to him in a column of white fire; the second vision, three years later, when an angel ordered him to keep the Ten Commandments and told him of a sacred record hidden near his father's farm; and finally, his visitation by the Angel Moroni, who, after severe testing, led him to golden plates that translated into the *Book of Mormon*. The recovered scripture revealed that in ancient America there had been light-skinned peoples who were literal descendants of Abraham, and whose epic history had included a visit from Jesus Christ following the Old World Crucifixion.

Smith invited the Jewish Minister to stay for mid-day worship and for lunch. In the afternoon the two resumed their interview, with the visitor now doing most of the talking. Matthias spoke from the Biblical Prophet Daniel's dream of the golden image, with which Daniel had awed King Nebuchadnezzar and won a kingdom for himself (perhaps a clue to what Matthias planned in Kirtland). As described by Daniel, it was a terrible image with a head of gold, arms and chest of silver, belly and thighs of brass, legs of iron, and feet of iron and clay. The image, according to Daniel, foretold a succession of earthly kingdoms that would precede the Kingdom of God. As Matthias explained, the last kingdom (the feet of iron and clay) was the American republic. The United States, he said, had promised union, freedom, and equal rights but in fact produced political and religious confusion—a nightmare world where the wicked spirit separated what God had joined and joined what God had split apart. Now, however, the first resurrection prophesied by Daniel was at hand: the spirits of the Fathers that had been cut down were waking up, Matthias warned, and it was time to get out of Babylon.

Such rambling exegesis had worked on others, particularly on Matthias's chief follower, the now-deceased New York merchant and Christian reformer Elijah Pierson, and on Pierson's womanish Christian friends. It worked less well on Joseph Smith. The Prophet Joseph told his visitor that he did not understand his remarks about the resurrection of the spirits of the Fathers that had been cut down. According to Joseph's scribe, the Jewish Minister replied that "he did not feel impressed by the spirit to unfold it further at present, but perhaps he might at some other time."

After sundown, at the Prophet's invitation, Matthias preached to the Mormons from the book of Genesis: "God said, 'Let there be light and there was light.'" Joseph granted that his visitor made some excellent points, but concluded that "his mind was evidently filled with darkness." Later that night, the visitor, after equivocating, admitted what the Mormons had already figured out: that he was in fact the accused swindler and murderer Matthias of New York. Unembarrassed, Matthias showed up for yet another meeting with Smith the next morning, when he described some of his own spiritual history. He proclaimed himself a direct descendant of the Hebrew prophets and patriarchs, of Jesus Christ, and of Matthias the Apostle. He possessed the souls of all these Fathers, for that was the way of everlasting life: the transmigration of spirits from Father to son. He was, in short, the incarnate Spirit of Truth.

The Mormon Prophet had heard enough and after announcing that an evil spirit governed Matthias he banished the miscreant from Kirtland. "I told him," he recorded in his diary, "that my God told me that his God is the Devil. . . ." (A local newspaper would report that *both* prophets had discerned devils in the other.) Joseph Smith, who, like Matthias, had the power to cast out devils, was gratified: "I for once cast out the Devil in bodily shape and I believe a murderer."[1]

THE MEETING OF the Prophets Matthias and Joseph Smith was one of hundreds of strange religious events that occurred all across the United States from the 1820s through the 1840s. These were the peak years of the market revolution that took the country from the fringe of the world economy to the brink of commercial greatness. They were also (not coincidentally) years of intense religious excitement and sectarian invention, the culmination of what historians have called the Second Great Awakening. While revivals reshaped the landscape of mainstream American Protestantism, smaller groups went beyond evangelical orthodoxy into direct and often heretical experience of the supernatural. Young women conversed with the dead; male and female perfectionists wielded the spiritual powers of the Apostles; farmers and factory hands spoke directly to God; and the heavens opened up to reveal new cosmologies to poor and uneducated Americans like Matthias and Joseph Smith. Building on more than two centuries of occultism and Anglo-American millenarian speculation, the seers of the new republic set the pattern for later prophetic movements down to our own time and gave birth to enduring religious institutions, including Smith's Church of Jesus Christ of Latter-day Saints.[2]

Matthias was almost certainly drawn to Kirtland because he knew that, amid this nationwide spiritual ferment, he and Joseph Smith shared certain enemies—the comfortable, pious entrepreneurs who commanded the market revolution. Matthias and Smith, poor men who were rooted socially and emotionally in the yeoman republic of the eighteenth century, had been diminished by that revolution; both of them detested the emerging Yankee middle class and its new moral imperatives. They thus fell outside of what respectable northern opinion considered the main currents of religious change in the decades before the Civil War, currents most closely identified with the evangelical reformism of Yankee revival preachers like Charles Grandison Finney.

Finneyites were largely drawn from the new, up-and-coming northern entrepreneurial classes—men and women who, in Finney's terms, had rejected sin and made their own new hearts.[3] Having abandoned the gloomy Calvinist determinism of their parents' generation, they understood that every human being was a moral free agent, and that individuals could overcome inherited human selfishness and be saved through repentence and prayer. Revivals, the mass conversion of sinners by preachers skilled at the task, were the major instruments of Finneyite piety. But with their championing of personal autonomy, Finneyites also reassessed all aspects of everyday life. The reassessment began at home. In the wake of the great Finneyite revivals, businessmen whose fathers and grandfathers had assumed unquestioned control of their households began to pray with their wives and to give themselves over to a gentle, loving Jesus. Finneyite men worked honestly and hard, prayed for release from anger and passion, used their money for Christian purposes, and willingly delegated day-to-day authority over child-rearing and other household affairs to their wives. Evangelical women, for their part, taught their children (and very often their husbands) how to pray, how to develop an instinctive knowledge of right and wrong, and how to nurture the moral discipline that would prepare them for conversion and lifelong Christian service. Reordered in these ways, Finneyite households became models for what would eventually emerge as American Victorian domesticity.

Untold thousands of Finneyites also became social reformers; indeed, by the time that Matthias and Joseph Smith met, the Finneyite revivals had led to ambitious efforts to translate northern middle-class religion into a national culture for the United States. The reformers' personal improvements, in business as well as in spiritual matters, told them that history was not the unfolding of a Calvinist God's Providence. On the contrary, history was made by morally accountable human beings. Good moral choices hastened the millennium—the thousand years of Christian social perfection that (they believed) would precede Christ's Second Coming. Sinful choices pushed the millennium further into the future. And so middle-class evangelical reformers sought to transform society as they had transformed themselves, by removing obstacles to spiritual independence and voluntary submission to God. They built militant temperance and Sabbatarian crusades; their interdenominational societies showered the country with Bibles and tracts; their missionaries showed up on doorsteps throughout the northern and western states (and increasingly in places like Hawaii, China, and India); their Sunday schools sanctified countless American childhoods; their spiritual egalitarianism led some to oppose social hierarchies based on race; their fervor and organizational skills turned the Whig party in revival-soaked regions into an arm of Finneyite reform.

A brave and uncompromising minority among the reformers followed Finneyism to its furthest anarchist and perfectionist conclusions. If perfection began in individual autonomy, they reasoned, then *all* coercive human relations were sinful. Fathers who terrified their children into unthinking obedience stunted the children's ability to make their own godly choices. A similar sinfulness drove rum sellers who enslaved drunkards to the bottle. Whites who treated blacks as lesser beings were ungodly tyrants. Prostitution, with its ungoverned passions and its selling of human flesh, robbed prostitute and customer alike of self-ownership; indeed, to some perfectionists, the entire traditional sexual order, with its fixations on male power and endless procreation, was unholy. Very quickly, this logic led radical reformers to attack two of the nation's central institutions. Southern slavery, they argued, interposed a despotic power between slaves and a loving God. Traditional marriage and the patriarchal family committed the same soul-destroying crime against women.

In contrast to the Finneyite inventors of Yankee middle-class culture, the two prophets at Kirtland may look like marginal men—cranky nay-sayers to the economic, domestic, and social progress of the nineteenth century. Against the Finneyites' feminized spirituality of restraint, Smith and Matthias (each in his own way) resurrected an ethos of fixed social relations and paternal power. Yet as they saw things, they were defenders of ancient truth against the perverse claims of arrogant, affluent, and self-satisfied enemies of God. And a majority of those Americans who were exposed to Finneyite evangelicalism apparently shared their anti-Finneyite views, if not their spiritual inventions and revelations. Southern evangelicals of all classes and colors were either untouched by the Finneyite revivals or actively hostile to them. And in the North, as historians have only begun to discover, the great democratic revivals of the early nineteenth century emerged primarily not from the new middle class but from Americans whom the market revolution had either bypassed or hurt.[4] These plebeian Christians—including most Methodists, Baptists, and Disciples of Christ, the members of smaller evangelical sects like the Freewill Baptists, and prophets like Matthias and Joseph Smith—resented the Finneyites' wealth, their education, their aptitude for organization, and their self-assigned roles as the cultural vanguard of market society and moral reform. So did the relatively tiny groups of American free-thinkers and deists, along with uncounted other Americans who were indifferent to any form of religion.

Hostility to Finneyite reformers contributed to numerous outbursts in the late 1820s and 1830s, ranging from good-natured heckling of Sabbatarian ministers to violent mob assaults on religious abolitionists, blacks, and their supporters. But many (perhaps most) of the plebeian Christians detested above all the Finneyites' tinkering with the traditional father-centered family and the customary, scripturally approved roles of men and women. These anti-Finneyites remained grimly committed to the Old Testament patriarchy of their fathers—a hallowed family form that had dominated rural America when they were children, and that both market society and the Finneyite revivals seemed determined to destroy. While they barred their doors to middle-class missionaries and shored up paternal authority within their own households, their leaders often proclaimed the old patriarchy with public dramas of fatherly power and filial respect: the Disciple Alexander Campbell, who placed his white-haired father in the seat of honor while he debated a well-known infidel; the Baptist William Miller, a disobedient son who after reading a sermon entitled *Parental Duties,* began studies that led to eschatological prophecies and, ultimately, the founding of the Seventh-Day Adventist Church; the Mormon Joseph Smith, who gave his broken, alcoholic father the honorific position of Patriarch of his new church, insisting that he be addressed as Father Smith; the Prophet Matthias, who would crown the all-powerful Father (and not the Son) as king of a restored patriarchal world.[5]

The meeting at Kirtland has left only the faintest trace in the annals of this large but little understood populist revival, mainly because the Prophet Matthias, unlike Joseph Smith, failed and left no ecclesiastical legacy. Yet on the day they met, it would have been difficult to say which of them was the more notorious. In 1834 and 1835 Matthias was one of the first penny-press sensations in American history—the main protagonist in a deeply disturbing scandal that received unprecedented national attention. With its whispers of murder and sexual crime, the Kingdom of Matthias made good copy. But Americans also sensed that the Matthias cult spoke with strange eloquence to the social and emotional upheavals in which they lived their own lives—particularly their struggles to redefine what it meant to be a woman or a man in the new world of the nineteenth century. For Matthias was not content, as some other prophets were, to convert a few members of his own social class and then hide out with them. He was angrier and more ambitious than that: he launched a mad (and for a time successful) mission among some prominent New York City Finneyite reformers, converting, humiliating, and ruining evangelical businessmen who had tried to assume social and religious dominance over better men. The result was a sustained and singularly well-documented encounter between well-to-do Finneyites and a mysterious prophet who hated them and all they stood for.

The story of Matthias and his Kingdom fascinated contemporaries. In the newspaper accounts, each of the Kingdom's major characters appeared to be emblematic of a more general social type; and almost every twist in the plot seemed indicative of some larger cultural trend. The story was shocking (and the newspapers made sure to play up its shock value) but it was also significant—"a bitter satire upon the age and country," one writer observed, an eccentric but dead-serious commentary on the contests over family life, sexuality, and social class that accompanied the rise of market society, with continuing resonance for Americans today.[6] This book tells that story.

ONE

Elijah Pierson

ELIJAH PIERSON WAS a supremely unlikely candidate for membership in the cult of Matthias. In the 1820s he was one of New York's best-known religious reformers. He helped inaugurate the Sabbatarian campaign, the key evangelical political initiative of the day. He joined in the Free Church movement and in missions to blacks and Jews. He gained special notice as a tireless worker in the Finneyites' efforts to reclaim the souls of the city's prostitutes. "No layman in New-York," a loyal journalist friend remarked, "exerted a more salutary and holy influence" than did Elijah Pierson.[1]

Pierson's private affairs matched his exemplary reformist career. At home, Elijah and his wife Sarah fashioned a simple life, a paragon of the loving, prayerful domesticity that middle-class evangelicals were inventing for themselves and spreading around the country. Indeed it was the joy of romantic union with Sarah that propelled Elijah into a life of missions and perfectionist reform. And it was her death that deranged his faith and prepared him for the Prophet Matthias. In its odd and touching way, the life of Elijah Pierson is a love story.

I

Nothing in Elijah Pierson's youth portended perfectionist religious experiments, much less his later involvement with the Prophet Matthias. The surviving evidence shows that he passed his boyhood in a quiet corner of rural New Jersey, where social hierarchy and domestic order were as unproblematic as such things can be. Men inherited family farms, sired large families of their own, and ruled their households unopposed; the wealthier and more judicious fathers cooperated in governing society at large. Underwriting everything was a stern Yankee Calvinist faith, very different from the optimistic evangelicalism that Elijah and Sarah would one day practice together.

Elijah descended from one of the more important families in the history of American Puritanism. His great-great-great-grand-father was the Reverend Abraham Pierson, the strict Connecticut divine who, in protest of the liberalizing Half-Way Covenant, led the Puritan migration out of New Haven Colony to Newark, New Jersey, in 1666. In Newark, Abraham created the spiritual framework for what one historian later called "the last Puritan theocracy"; his descendants pioneered settlements across northern New Jersey, helping to make that part of the state a virtual extension of New England. In the 1720s, Benjamin and Elijah Pierson, two of Abraham's grandsons, settled farms next to each other at Convent Station, near the new village of Morristown. Here Elijah Pierson was born in 1786, the second son in a family of seven children, on the 178-acre farm that his forebear Benjamin had cleared three generations earlier.[2]

Visitors to Morristown in the late eighteenth century spoke of the stateliness (a few said "haughtiness") of the town and the beauty and prosperity of the surrounding countryside. For young Elijah Pierson, the whitewashed houses and gentle green hills composed a living map of family history and inherited rules. On two sides of the farm where he grew up lived heirs of his great-grandfather's brother, Benjamin. Scattered through the township were the households of Elijah's grandparents, aunts and uncles, and uncounted distant kin.[3]

At the center of the family map stood the Piersons' spiritual bulwark, Morristown's First Presbyterian Church. The Piersons had been founding members, and through most of his childhood Elijah's father, Benjamin, and his uncle, Silas Condict, served as trustees.[4] In the pulpit, the Reverend James Richards preached the New Light divinity he had learned in his native Connecticut and in his studies at Yale. (First Presbyterian remained a self-consciously New England institution and recruited its minister from the Yankee homeland.)

The Reverend Mr. Richards's Calvinism was free of the super-natural terrors known to some country congregations, and contained hints about human abilities to attain grace that more ortho-dox preachers would have branded heresy. But it was Calvinism nonetheless. Young Elijah learned early in life that God had placed men and women into families and social ranks, then governed their destinies according to His inscrutable Providence. Elijah was not to question this visible, worldly order. He had only to apprehend his station within it and then follow the rules of that station. As a child this meant fearing God, denying his own sinful will, and obeying his father and mother. (Later, it would mean being a father and family governor himself.) Elijah grew up knowing that he was a corrupt being and that even perfect outward adherence to God's rules would not assure him a place in heaven. But he also knew that if he misbehaved or if the local fathers allowed others to misbehave, God would do terrible things to Morristown.[5]

Sitting in church while Richards preached his Sunday lessons, Elijah could scan the room and see what the minister meant by God's social ranks. The Piersons always sat in the same place, with the father at their head, in the pew for which he paid rent. In front of him, near the minister's family and the old folks who were hard of hearing, Elijah saw richer families that rented the more expensive pews near the pulpit. Behind Elijah sat families that paid less than his. In the back of the church and up in the gallery sat poor people, who paid nothing at all.

The boy could not mistake the local hierarchy of wealth, but he also learned that wealth did not count for everything in Morristown. Although his father did not rent a front pew, he was an important man nonetheless: a lifelong church member, an elected church trustee, and a descendant of one of the church's founders. And in a town as small as Morristown, family ties inevitably connected the rich people of the congregation to poorer kin. As Elijah looked around he could spot the faces of relatives in every part of the room. Among those at the very front was his Uncle Silas, who had been a delegate to the Continental Congress during the Revolution and who, during most of Elijah's youth, served as the speaker of the lower house of the New Jersey state legislature. In the gallery, Elijah's destitute uncle, Usual Crane, was in charge of taking up the collection.[6]

The social primacy of kin ties and fatherly authority extended to the Pierson fireside. Elijah's father spent most of his time working the farm he had inherited from his grandfather and father, which he would pass on to one of his sons. He labored not in isolation but as the head of a household work team that included his wife, two daughters, five sons, and a black slave. As a patriarch he was responsible for the well-being and behavior of everyone in his household; as neighbor, church officer, and member of a thick and busy network of kin he extended those responsibilities beyond his domestic circle. In 1796, for instance, Benjamin Pierson and the other church trustees disciplined the wife of a Mr. C because everyone knew she took too much opium. The trustees threatened to shoot the pigs that careless owners allowed to browse on church property; they talked with the town officers about a Mr. Hyer, who, for reasons that no one recorded, had fired a musket ball through the church steeple; they provided widows of the congregation with winter firewood and took up collections for Morristown's poor and for Presbyterian missions to the frontier. In addition, Benjamin Pierson helped give Usual Crane, his poor and ailing brother-in-law, his little position of authority gathering donations in the church gallery, even as the family prepared to take care of Crane's wife in the event of his death.[7]

By standards that Elijah Pierson would later adopt, the immutable inequality of this tight-knit patriarchy was a perfect model of injustice. That women, slaves, and propertyless men should stand subordinate to the likes of Benjamin Pierson—or any other mortal—would one day look to Elijah like the negation of Christ's Word. But for those raised within it, Morristown's regime held out the example of mutual care and obligation: under the rule of fathers, widows stayed warm in winter, deaf people took the best seats in church, and men like Usual Crane kept their dignity. For generations of Piersons it had been a workable formula for decency and order in this world. Almost certainly, Elijah carried that formula in his head when, while still a young man, he left Morristown and set off to take a job as an apprentice clerk in New York City.

2

Nobody noted exactly when Elijah departed for Manhattan, probably because there was nothing exceptional about the move. During the early nineteenth century thousands of country boys (particularly younger sons, who would not inherit farms) made the trek from New England and the rural Middle States, hoping to earn their fortunes in the nation's fastest growing seaport. Elijah Pierson was one of the success stories of that migration. An acquaintance later remembered that he was "an amiable, intelligent, and pious" youngster, who performed his duties "much to the satisfaction of his employers." Elijah lived simply and saved his money, and he postponed the comforts and responsibilities of marriage. It was the prescribed path for young men on the make, and in Elijah's case it worked. In 1820, at the age of thirty-four, Elijah Pierson and a partner named John Steinbrenner opened their own mercantile firm on Pearl Street. By working hard, delaying gratifications, and leading an upright life, the farm boy from Morristown had reached an enviable place in mercantile New York.[8]

Pierson and his fellow Pearl Street merchants were a new breed of urban businessman. The established salt-water elite (old New York families that owned ships, wharves, warehouses, and much of the city's real estate) occupied the import-export counting houses that overlooked the harbor on South, Front, and Water streets. Most Pearl Street merchants, by contrast, were specialized wholesalers and jobbers who bought imported goods at auction and sold them in smaller lots to country storekeepers who made yearly buying trips to the city. The fortunes of Pearl Street were tied less to established mercantile networks of transatlantic shipping and the coasting trade than to the market revolution in northeastern agriculture and the growing appetite for finished goods in the hinterland. Many of Pearl Street's leading merchants, like Elijah Pierson, were themselves migrants from New England and from rural Yankee colonies elsewhere. Newly successful and set in their small-town habits, they were a self-consciously middle-class Yankee enclave within the Manhattan business community. In ways that others found abrasive, they nurtured a part of their separate identity by making unfriendly moral judgments about their fellow New Yorkers.[9]

Like others on Pearl Street, Elijah Pierson probably attributed his success to the moral code he had learned on his father's farm. But the lessons of country churches and patriarchs only carried so far in helping young men fashion Christian lives in New York City. Elijah and his colleagues were a decided minority; classes of people above and below them cared nothing for the old rural pieties. The richest men in New York drank wine and courted women who wore jewelry and silks; the worst of them even kept mistresses. The few who went to church attended elegant Episcopalian and Dutch Reform establishments that, to Elijah's way of thinking, were mere social clubs for the rich. When asked about God, they seemed to think He was a warm-hearted gentleman like themselves.

The poor were different, too. There were untold thousands of them, and they occupied their own neighborhoods and lived beyond the reach of Christian influence and paternal benevolence. Elijah had seen nothing like them: brutal men with whiskey bottles, children who ran loose and seemed to have no homes, gaudily dressed girls who strolled the sidewalks and smiled at gentlemen who passed them by—a mass of unclean desperation that clearly needed more than firewood and positions in the gallery. Faced for the first time with such squalor and disorder, Elijah Pierson and other pious, upwardly mobile migrants struggled to stake out social and emotional ground between the thoughtless rich and the vicious poor. It was an enterprise for which their fathers' examples provided incomplete lessons at best.

Country patriarchy and Calvinist determinism provided even fewer hints about how to translate mercantile success into marriage and domestic life. Morristown's social arrangements depended on large families, inherited land, and cooperation between generations. Elijah's great-grandfather, the Puritan patriarch who first settled at Convent Station, fathered ten children; his grandfather married at twenty-four and fathered a daughter and seven sons; his father took a sixteen-year-old bride when he was himself twenty-two, and raised seven children on the family homestead.[10] But in New York City such arrangements made no sense. Elijah's fortunes were now tied not to an inherited farm set within a network of kin but to individual ambition, risk-taking, and the accumulation of money. Early marriage, a large family, and the assumption of fatherly pretensions would have doomed him to failure. Given the choice, Elijah kept to himself. Perhaps the personal discipline that shaped his success had congealed into habits of bachelorhood. Perhaps the meekness that others counted among his Christian virtues did not serve him well with women.

Thus Elijah Pierson arrived in his middle thirties, affluent and alone. He was, as any of his Pearl Street colleagues could have testified, one of New York's rising young men. But after work he walked through threatening streets to a house in which he lived by himself. He had his business associates but no relatives in the city. It is almost certain that he steered clear of the girls on the streets, and that at thirty-five he remained chaste. Elijah's rise from farm boy to merchant had gone well. His passage from youth to manhood was deferred and confused.

3

Like many others in his situation, Elijah looked to his religion for sustenance. In July 1819 (about the time he entered business with Steinbrenner) Elijah became a full member of the Reverend Gardiner Spring's Brick Presbyterian Church, one of the leading congregations for Yankee newcomers; by the time Elijah joined, the Reverend Mr. Spring had also turned the church into a center for an emerging network of evangelical lay missionary societies.

When one of these groups—the Female Missionary Society for the Poor of New York and Its Vicinity—approached Brick Church looking for a male elder for its mission church to the black slum on Bancker Street, Elijah volunteered.

It was a fateful step. As an aide to the missionaries, Elijah found himself immersed in the new evangelicalism. Although he could not have fully realized it at the time, he had encountered a religious life that questioned the entire formula about fatherhood and God he had taken with him from Morristown. Out of that encounter he would form his marriage, his closest friendships, and his life as a new kind of Christian man.[11]

The women of the Female Missionary Society were pioneer emissaries to New York's poor. They had begun as a fund-raising organization for male missions, and had sent the Reverend Ward Stafford, their first full-time missionary, into the East Side slums in 1817. Stafford saw things that appalled him: the laboring classes, he reported, were drowning in a sea of Sabbath-breaking, laziness, promiscuity, drunkenness, and utter ignorance of the Christian religion. Earlier charitable societies, operated by the salt-water elite, had seen the same things, and interpreted them as part of the permanent order of the world—fit objects of police action and patrician noblesse oblige, not of religious proselytizing. But the alarming increase in poverty that accompanied the trade disruptions of the Napoleonic Wars had overwhelmed the alms-giving capacity of the old merchant families. Middle-class missionaries—Ward Stafford and his female colleagues—took their places with an entirely different approach to the problem. As evangelicals they preached that poverty and disorder resulted neither from original sin nor God's design but from failed families and bad moral choices. "The sufferings of the poor in this, and other cities," Stafford insisted, "are the immediate effect of ignorance and vice." Charity was useless among men who drank, avoided work, and brutalized their families. The poor did not need handouts. They needed preaching, moral instruction, and the spiritual support of godly friends.[12]

The new missionary movement demanded nothing less than the moral reformation of the poor, and to that end its adherents called for a permanent missionary presence in poor neighborhoods. In 1817 male missionaries built a church among the sailors' boarding houses and waterfront dives near the East Side docks at Corlear's Hook. A year later the Female Missionary Society, extending its efforts to the poorest and most despised New Yorkers, opened its mission church amid the destitute blacks of Bancker Street. The F.M.S. chapel was a preaching station with an ordained male minister in charge. But in practice it was headquarters for middle-class women who visited the poor and prayed with them in their homes.

Home visits were at the center of evangelical missions. And in making these visits a matter of moral education, the missionaries tied their work to their emerging notions of domestic life—notions that pointed away from traditional patriarchy and toward what would become the spiritualized, mother-centered interiors of the Victorian era. In evangelical homes the primary moral teachers were no longer fathers who laid down the law; they were loving mothers who prayed with their children and taught them right from wrong. When evangelicals turned from their own homes to the slums, the roots of poverty seemed clear: the sufferings of the poor began with the brutality—the deformed patriarchy—of their family lives. "Like us," said a preacher to male missionaries, "they *might* exercise parental authority, while they felt all the yearnings of parental love. Like us, they *might* be benefited by parental correction, whilst they clung in filial submission, at the parent's feet. But among *them*, parental authority is only the consciousness of exertion of *Power*; and filial affection is but the dread and hatred of its coercion."[13] Absent, ignorant, and cruel fathers had degraded poor women and children and left a moral void. City missions would fill that void, mainly (in the case of the Female Missionary Society) through the ministrations of middle-class women.

The Reverend Elihu Baldwin occupied the pulpit at the female mission on Bancker Street; Elijah Pierson assisted him as elder; no doubt there were other men in positions of formal authority. But the mission was staffed by pious women, and its success rested on their visits to the poor. Male missionaries acknowledged that women gained entry into sinful households much more easily than did men. Once inside, they worked effectively with their unfortunate sisters and "the children of poor and careless parents" who were the chief targets of reform. Working in pairs, the women left Bibles and tracts, prayed with the sick, made note of children who belonged in Sunday school, and coaxed destitute, frightened mothers and daughters out of their houses and into church. In the process, they provided poor people, the men of their own class, and (just as important) each other with demonstrations of the dignity, competence, and spiritual courage of an emerging evangelical womanhood.[14]

Clergymen who supported the Female Missionary Society knew that city missions conferred new responsibilities upon the female rank and file. They also knew that experiments could get out of hand, and they mixed their encouragement with stern reminders of the limits that God had placed upon the female sex. Preaching to the women missionaries as they began their work in 1817, the Reverend Matthew LaRue Perrine reminded them that God still governed the world through fixed relationships of dominance and subordination. Christians, he insisted, must honor the "respective duties of old and young, rich and poor, rulers and ruled, ministers and people, *males* and *females.*" Any upright woman could join societies, collect funds, visit families, and work for the conversion of her own domestic circle. But she also had to perform her expanded labors "knowing her true dignity and usefulness consist in filling that station marked out for her by the God of nature and of grace . . . , satisfied in being an *assistant* of man." In the same year that Perrine cautioned the women, a preacher to male missionaries insisted that the goal of missions was to unite "that holy family, of which God is the Father and Christ the Elder Brother." Always, clergymen addressing the new lay missionaries spoke the language of patriarchy—the language Elijah Pierson had learned as a boy.[15]

Behind the clergymen's injunctions lay an awareness that something potentially disturbing was taking place. Brick Presbyterian Church and the Bancker Street Chapel held out the possibility that sinners could be educated, and that some could gradually grow in grace. Moderate evangelicals like Matthew Perrine and Gardiner Spring—men loosened from the presumptions of both noblesse oblige and Calvinist determinism—hoped that such conversions would build ties of benevolence across the God-given boundaries of rich and poor, male and female. At the same time, however, ministers attached to city missions sensed the dangers of radically new spiritual possibilities, and that is why they lectured so carefully to the women. If conversion was ultimately a matter of voluntary prayer and submission, one might logically conclude that humankind could overcome sin one soul at a time. And if sin could be completely vanquished, then all rationales for hierarchy and government would dissolve.

The ministers' fears came to pass. Although most of the women and nearly all of the men in the new missions went about their labors within familiar boundaries, a few realized the anarchic implications of a life of prayer. Experiencing their own transcendence of sin, they envisioned a world without selfishness, a world governed by perfect Christian love. To such persons God revealed that the corrupt human nature that supposedly justified worldly power was really an authoritarian mirage. The power of laws, husbands, fathers, and ministers, along with prescribed customs and social divisions, was not only needless but harmful, for it interposed human force between individuals and God's tender mercies. Worldly power, in their eyes, was not a defense against disorder. It was disorder's principal cause.

By the mid-1820s a few city missionaries had traveled out of Gardiner Spring's and Matthew Perrine's orbit and into a smaller perfectionist community where social boundaries and social power dissolved before the prayer of faith and perfect love of humankind. At the forefront of that perfectionist community, writing many of its manifestos and leading many of its crusades, was Elijah Pierson.

4

Every perfectionist walked an intensely emotional spiritual path into a sinless life.[16] Elijah Pierson began on the most crowded of these paths: engagement in lay missions and a willingness to be governed by God through prayer. But in Elijah's case prayer and missions were also tied to friendships with radical women missionaries, and to his marriage to one of the most pious and perfect of those women.

When Elijah Pierson took up the work on Bancker Street, he probably approached the ladies in the missionary community with more than ordinary curiosity. Among the most interesting was Sarah Stanford. Sarah was the eldest daughter of the Reverend John Stanford, the official chaplain to New York's charitable and penal institutions, and one of the most respected evangelicals in the city—preacher to the inmates of hospitals, debtors' prisons, insane asylums, orphanages, almshouses, jails, and penitentiaries. Her mother had died in 1798 (when Sarah was only four), victim of a yellow fever epidemic; her father had not remarried. Sarah had grown up strong, the caring, competent woman of her busy father's house. By the time Elijah met her she had been briefly married, then widowed, and she was the mother of a small daughter.

Sarah was not pretty. But her face radiated sincerity and Christian love, and she carried herself with a sureness that came from faith in God. A friend talked with her for four years, and never heard a hint of envy, peevishness, or mean-spiritedness. She was remarkably intelligent and well-informed, and she spoke with quiet confidence in the company of both men and women. As much as any of her missionary colleagues, Sarah Stanford embodied the virtues of the new evangelical woman.[17]

Elijah Pierson had met few women like Sarah. She was more substantial than the silly girls that some merchants chased and married; more cultivated, self-assured, and openly loving than the farm wives he had known in Morristown. Doubtless his attraction to Sarah stirred confusion as well as joy in Elijah, but he worked up his courage and courted her. They married in May 1822.[18]

Elijah's wedding ended years of searching and uncertainty. Sarah and her father introduced Elijah into the inner circles of New York evangelicalism, and Sarah quickly assumed a gentle control over his domestic and spiritual development. Shortly before the wedding Elijah left Brick Presbyterian (thereby breaking his family's old ties to the Presbyterian Church) and joined Sarah's congregation, South Baptist Church, where they held their wedding. Charles Sommers, the minister at South Baptist, was a close friend of the Stanfords who preached from a Bible and prayer book presented to him by Sarah's father. (When John Stanford died in 1834, Sommers edited his memoir.) In the middle and late 1820s, Elijah Pierson became a leading New York evangelical while serving as deacon of Sarah's South Baptist Church.[19]

Late in 1823 the Piersons left Elijah's bachelor abode on Greenwich Street and bought a three-story brick townhouse on William

Street. The building's graceful curved front, its twelve-inch-thick walls, its ample living space, and its $7000 price tag attested to Elijah's continuing success in business.[20] The move put him into a substantial home that was about as close to his Pearl Street store as the old one. Perhaps significantly, it was also closer to Bancker Street and the home of John Stanford.

Elijah spent his days with his business deals and his missionary labors; at night he returned to William Street, prayed with Sarah, and experienced a peace that he had never known. The Piersons, like other young evangelicals, were learning to raise marriage to new spiritual levels. Available evidence suggests that sex, particularly the straightforward procreative sex that took place in Morristown farmhouses, was unimportant to that process. When he married, Elijah was almost certainly a virgin. Sarah's sexual experience was limited to an early marriage that had ended after a few months. In eight years together Elijah and Sarah produced one child. A friend remembered that Sarah kept her own sleeping apartment in the house on William Street.[21]

The marriage of Elijah and Sarah Pierson was not based on inherited property, large families, or patriarchal assumptions. It was a spiritualized union between partners: it began in a shared vocation in Christian missions, and it thrived on prayer and feminine influence. Like other evangelical wives, Sarah became her husband's guide in matters of the spirit. Elijah admitted that she was more prayerful than he; unlike him, she seldom had to ask God to remove anger and self-righteousness. She truly loved Christ, and she took good care of Elijah. After her death, Elijah would ask Jesus for guidance in areas that suggest that Sarah had mothered him in the smallest details of his life: Should he move or stay in the same house? Where should he send the children to school? Which foods should he eat or avoid? Was it cold outside? Should he wear his coat? Must he take his medicine? The questions suggest male foibles and male dependence within a loving, mother-centered household. They were not questions that the patriarchs of Morristown would have thought to ask.[22]

Elijah's spiritual path took another radical turn in 1825, when Sarah began attending prayer meetings led by a woman named Frances Folger. The daughter of a Presbyterian minister and the wife of a Wall Street broker, Folger was among the Christian women who, not content with simply rearranging her domestic life, had begun to attack male authority and religious rules in public. Her chief cause was "retrenchment," the ultra-evangelical movement to avoid luxury in diet, clothing, and home furnishings.

Our one informant on Frances Folger is the journalist William Leete Stone, and he disliked her intensely. Stone and Folger were both members of Brick Presbyterian Church, and Folger won her first taste of notoriety in an attack on Stone's wife, Susannah. One Sunday, Frances upbraided Susannah Stone for wearing a feathered hat to church; Mrs. Stone fought back, and the ensuing argument split the Brick Church congregation. At the height of the controversy, Mrs. Folger descended on the house of Gardiner Spring, demanding that the minister take a stand against ungodly ostentation. Deeply offended at the woman's presumption, the Reverend Mr. Spring quietly asked his wife and daughters to dress more modestly, then responded to Mrs. Folger with an attack of his own. In keeping with his moderate evangelicalism, he publicly condemned luxury and applauded the new domestic influence of women (though he insisted that women's "natural and amiable timidity" should keep them out of the sphere of "the stronger sex"). He insisted, however, that church-going ladies could find clothes that were both fashionable and modest. Mrs. Folger's extreme demands for plain dress were to his mind "preposterous or anti-Christian."[23]

Before it ended, the affair of Susannah Stone's hat alienated Frances Folger from her minister father and damaged her husband Reuben Folger's relations with the church. But none of that worried her, for she knew that true piety was now at war with worldly power. In 1822 she organized a band of women who traveled in pairs and entered respectable houses unannounced, then prayed for conversions "whether the inmates would hear or not." The campaign (Stone later branded it "wild and ill-judged") brought praying women into direct confrontation with the power of husbands and fathers—not just the neglectful drunkards of the slums but outwardly pious, well-regarded men of their own class. Folger herself led a second assault on Gardiner Spring's beleaguered household: while his astonished wife and children looked on, Folger knelt and prayed for Spring's conversion to true Christianity.[24]

Folger launched a less direct but more successful attack on the house of her husband's cousin, a handsome, mannered (and, some said, shallow) young hardware merchant named Benjamin Folger. Stone tells us that Benjamin (whom he had known as a boy in Hudson, New York) did not trust his overzealous relative. In 1823 Benjamin told Frances that she was welcome in his house only if she left her missionary work at the door. Frances agreed, but then began paying private visits on Benjamin's elegant and articulate wife, the former Ann Disbrow, a daughter of one of Manhattan's old families. By 1825 Ann Folger was fasting regularly, wearing the simplest of clothes, and inviting Frances Folger's followers—including Sarah Pierson—into her parlor for prayer meetings. Benjamin Folger sat in another part of the house he no longer fully governed, listening to the rise and fall of female prayer.[25]

Elijah Pierson followed Sarah to the meetings at Ann and Benjamin Folger's house in 1825. He found thirty or forty praying Christians, "for the most part well-informed and highly respectable persons, of both sexes," who were exploring the limits of personal holiness. Most were Methodists who had discovered the perfectionist implications of Wesleyanism. (The profane called them the Holy Club; it was the name John Wesley had given to his earliest religious society.) They were joined by like-minded members of other Protestant churches. Anyone—man or woman—could speak at meetings, but only if she or he felt the direct inspiration of the Holy Ghost. Some claimed the gift of interpreting prophecy. Some worked miracles through the prayer of faith. Some knew the meaning of visions and dreams. Others could heal the sick (and in fact presided over ceremonies in which the sick were healed). All denied the sanctity of marriage, believing that only the single, celibate life encouraged holiness; the more insistent Holy Club members proclaimed that all earthly marriage bonds were dissolved.

Frances Folger and her friends were perfectionists, literally living in apostolic times, gaining spiritual gifts through unmediated experience of the Holy Ghost. They rejected the reality of final judgment and the holiness of the Sabbath: to them, all time was holy, and women and men were being judged every day. One man announced that he had not experienced temptation in ten years. A woman claimed that she was at that moment standing upon a sea of glass and talking directly with God. "This is the final judgement-seat of Christ," wailed an inspired female preacher as she careened across the room. "The Judge is now on the throne, and he is judging every one of you *now*."[26]

Elijah and Sarah prayed with the Holy Club for three years, and in 1828 Elijah began talking with the Holy Ghost. He had always been a man of prayer, and had always asked God for help when he had to make some decision. But it was only in 1828 that God began answering him in English. Elijah started to record what He said.[27]

Beginning in 1828, Elijah Pierson's prayers with Frances Folger, his conversations with the Holy Spirit, and his ever-deepening union with Sarah shaped a private experience of Christian perfection. At the same time, his personal mission expanded. The evangelical community first learned of Pierson's new energies when he called a meeting of the city's ministers to discuss plans for the immediate conversion of New York City. Most judged Pierson's project unwise, and many thought he was insane—but Pierson had additional unsettling proposals in store. In 1828 he denounced Sunday collections and the annual auctioning off of pews at South Baptist Church, claiming that the exchange of money desecrated the Sabbath and that pew rents reinforced worldly hierarchy, making the poor feel unwelcome in God's house. Pierson submitted a long written argument explaining his case. The journalist Stone, always on the lookout for female encroachments on male territory, later noted that two-thirds of the manifesto was written in Sarah Pierson's hand.[28]

In December 1829, Elijah and Sarah left William Street and moved to Bowery Hill, a spot of high ground north of the heavily built sections of the city. It was a pleasant patch of greenery that overlooked lower New York, with views of the Hudson and the East River on either side. The controversy over pew rents and collections at South Baptist may have encouraged Elijah's move. But more important was the opportunity to join a nascent perfectionist community. As early as 1822 the Methodist reformer Margaret Prior had operated a school for poor children on Bowery Hill, and in the late 1820s the neighborhood attracted some of the city's leading evangelicals. Frances Folger was there, and she was calling upon Christians—with Sarah and Elijah Pierson at the head of the list—to abandon all sensual extravagances and false hierarchies and to join her in living as simply as Christ had lived.[29]

Under Folger's direction, the Bowery Hill perfectionists formed themselves into a Retrenchment Society. They got rid of fashionable clothing, ornaments, and jewelry and dressed strictly for modesty and warmth. They sold off their expensive furnishings—all upholstered furniture, pictures, mirrors, curtains, carpets, and everything made of mahogany or brass. They also simplified their diets: no cakes, pastries, sweetmeats, or butter, no coffee or tea. Often they subsisted on bread and water, and sometimes they fasted for days on end. (William Leete Stone, who tells us these things, portrayed Bowery Hill as another manifestation of the fanaticism and strange power of Frances Folger.) Among the wealthy young Christians who moved to Bowery Hill were Benjamin and Ann Folger. In 1829, Benjamin had made arrangements to buy a house downtown, but the Holy Spirit told Frances Folger that Ann and Benjamin were to join her on Bowery Hill. The Folgers dutifully moved north with their three small children, and Benjamin watched as his fine possessions—each of them a hard-won trophy of some commercial triumph—went out the door. In their place came water pitchers, plain bread, pine tables, bare floors, and fasting and prayer without end.[30]

Elijah Pierson began to preach shortly after his move to Bowery Hill, and he soon applied for formal orders as a Baptist preacher. Rejected by the Baptists, he quit South Baptist Church and, in February 1830, organized an independent church on Bowery Hill. The community entered a full-time religious frenzy. At one point Pierson's followers met fourteen times in a single week; at another they met continuously for three weeks, pausing only for naps and light refreshments. They fasted regularly: Elijah himself never ate during the twenty-four hours following sundown on Thursday, and often he fasted for two days and three nights straight, claiming that it "gave him great light in the things of God." From his makeshift pulpit Elijah preached the religion of the Holy Ghost. His sermons included all of the prophesying, visions and direct revelations that had originally inspired the Holy Club. Now, though, Elijah added findings from the Book of Revelation: the first resurrection was near, the second was not far behind, and through the prayer of faith believers might attain perfect holiness—perfect love of humankind flowing from perfect love of God.[31]

5

More cautious evangelicals shook their heads at the antics on Bowery Hill. But they did not denounce Pierson and his enthusiastic friends outright—for in the religious excitements of the late 1820s, who was to say what was excessive and what was not? The Retrenchment Society's orgies of self-denial may have been a bit silly. Yet they also bespoke a more general anxiety among the whole church-going middle class about defining proper standards of material decency and comfort. Likewise, although the power wielded by Frances Folger, Sarah Pierson, and other women on Bowery Hill was almost unprecedented, it was tied to an evangelical movement that everyone knew would result in expanded spiritual and domestic roles for women. Even Elijah Pierson's chats with the Holy Spirit, although troublesome to some of his friends, made sense in an evangelical world where everything began with the prayer of faith, and where no orthodoxy had yet drawn limits to where those prayers might lead. The Bowery Hill community was not, as some of New York's more conservative Christians were beginning to mutter, a dumping ground for religious lunatics. On the contrary, it was a scouting expedition at the edges of a new experimental evangelicalism that had gripped a large segment of New York's up-and-coming merchant families.

Both before and after their move to Bowery Hill, Elijah Pierson and his friends built alliances with more mainstream downtown evangelicals, including some of the nation's leading reformers. With financial help from more moderate believers, the perfectionists constructed a school to educate poor children for the ministry. They organized a mission to the Jews; as part of that, Sarah

Pierson and the other women formed a sewing circle and used the proceeds to train converted Jews as Christian ministers. Late in 1829, Benjamin Folger joined with other evangelical worthies, including the celebrated Lewis Tappan, to found the First Free Presbyterian Church of New York. (The Free Church realized Elijah's dreams of democratic congregations without collections or pew rents; in time, the church became the headquarters for the reform work of Lewis Tappan and his brother Arthur.) A year earlier, Pierson had joined Arthur Tappan and three others to found the General Union for Promoting Observance of the Christian Sabbath—the uncompromising Sabbatarian organization that, with its petition campaign to halt Sunday postal service, introduced Americans to the politics of evangelical reform.[32]

While occupied with all these new efforts, Elijah and Sarah found time to help start a mission to New York City's prostitutes. Like his new faith, his perfectionist friends, and every other good thing in Elijah Pierson's life, the project stemmed from his marriage. In 1828 Sarah's father, the Reverend John Stanford, asked the Piersons to teach at his Sabbath school for prostitutes at the women's prison. They accepted the call, and from the beginning they knew the work was God's. Elijah preached and prayed with Sarah at his side, then watched the light of Jesus enter the faces of the most hopeless, despised, and degraded of His creatures.

Elijah, Sarah, and some of the other teachers were powerfully drawn to the new mission, and soon they were following the women home after their release from jail. The journeys took them to the Five Points, the most notorious slum neighborhood in North America. Passing through crowds of dirty children and idle men, stepping over passed-out drunks and heaps of garbage and excrement, Sarah and Elijah confronted fallen women on their own territory. Sometimes they preached and prayed before hostile crowds in the streets. More often they visited prostitutes in their homes, where they stared into the squalor of basement rooms, felt the threat of the streets outside, and listened as girls told them how they had descended into sin.

The majority of the girls were not full-time professionals; they were young runaways and vagrants who sold sex as a temporary means of making ends meet. But they were learning to tell their potential benefactors from the middle class exactly what they wanted to hear. Sarah and Elijah and the other missionaries returned home with stories that invariably began with mean fathers and ended with vile seducers. Many of the girls claimed to have sold themselves in confusion and desperation after being abandoned by bad husbands or fathers. Some told of applying for jobs as domestic servants, only to be "sent into a room with some man, or rather monster in human shape, and compelled to submit to his vile purposes." Others were daughters of respectable families, who said they had been coaxed into places of assignation by charming, nattily dressed men and then seduced and abandoned. (These cases often required the use of drugs.) Once violated, the ruined girl was shunned by good society. She continued to submit to evil men until she utterly relinquished control of herself, moving step by step into irreversible degradation, disease, and an early death.

Sarah and Elijah Pierson knew they had discovered another contest between male power and Christian love. The new mission sped them along their spiritual path and drew them closer together. Early on, Elijah talked it over with the Holy Ghost: "Prayed for the harlots at Five Points. . . . The Lord said, *'You must go and fetch them out.'* The Lord said, concerning the two witnesses, *'Thou art one and Sarah the Other.'*" God had given Elijah and Sarah another work to do together.[33]

The Piersons and their missionary friends knew how to interrupt the deadly sexual pattern: they would remove the younger harlots—those who were soiled but still redeemable—from the clutches of ungodly men, put them into a Christian house of refuge, pray with them, and change their hearts. In January 1830 the missionaries formed themselves into the Female Asylum Society. Staffed almost entirely by Sabbath-school teachers from the jail, the society set up a storefront preaching station and Sabbath school at the Five Points. There they identified the most hopeful and repentant of the girls and sent them uptown to the Female Asylum House.

It may have been Elijah Pierson who suggested putting the asylum on Bowery Hill. (He and Sarah rented the place in December 1829, and may have moved to the Hill partly in anticipation of running it.) In any case, the Piersons, with the financial backing of their downtown friends, had chief control of the asylum's operations from the start.[34] The downtown benefactors may not have known at first that Elijah made the mission a branch of his Bowery Hill church. The original matron of the house was a woman named Phoebe Carpenter, who would soon become the bride of the moral reformer John McDowall. Pierson replaced her with a reformed prostitute named Mrs. Bolton—a camp-meeting devotee whose extravagant jerkings and hysteria were the talk of New York City Methodists. She had come to Bowery Hill to do sewing for the Piersons and then stayed on; at the time of her appointment as the asylum's matron, Bolton was one of Elijah's spiritual advisers and a member of his church.[35]

Another new resident of Bowery Hill was a black servant named Isabella Van Wagenen, the ex-housekeeper for the perfectionist sectarian James Latourette. A Manhattan fur merchant, Latourette had broken with the Methodist Church to lead New York's little band of Wesleyan perfectionists. He proclaimed the imminence of the Second Coming and claimed apostolic sinlessness for himself and some of his followers; he also believed in "signs and wonders and mighty deeds by prayer." Isabella, Latourette's co-believer as well as his servant, had been talking with God since her childhood as a slave in upstate Ulster County.

When Latourette's wife and another woman invited her to a prayer meeting at the Five Points mission, Isabella went along. At the meeting, the crush of believers pushed Isabella to the floor; enthusiasts assumed that God had thrown her down, and they would not let her get back up. While she avoided the Five Points mission thereafter, Isabella left the Latourette household, joined the Piersons' church, and kept house for the Piersons when their regular housekeeper left town.[36]

For prostitutes who came to Bowery Hill looking for peace and a chance to change their lives, the goings-on at the Female Asylum House must have come as an unsettling surprise. But for Elijah Pierson the work was a continuing triumph of the spirit. Through prayer and submission, he and Sarah (now gaunt and hollow-eyed from her fasting and labors) had attained perfect holiness and a circle of perfect friends. Through their work with fallen girls, they had turned their prayers and their union outward into universal Christian love. Later, Sarah would speak to Elijah from beyond the grave: "The last work we did together [Five Points] brought us nearer to God than we ever were before."[37]

6

On June 20, 1830, Elijah traveled downtown and boarded an omnibus. He had been neglecting work, and he was going to spend a day on Pearl Street. But as he looked out the window his thoughts went to Sarah. She had taken sick over the previous winter, and had spent the entire spring in bed. The doctors now told him there was nothing they could do. Their diagnosis was consumption brought on by exhaustion and malnutrition: Sarah had literally worked and fasted herself to the edge of death.

As the horse car turned and rattled onto Wall Street the sights blurred and the sounds of hooves and iron wheels, of voices and countless footfalls, ran together and quieted and moved into the distance, and Elijah heard the voice of God: *"Thou art Elijah the Tishbite—gather unto me all the members of Israel at the foot of Mount Carmel."*

It was the second such message. The night before, God had told Elijah, *"I have named thee this day Elijah the Tishbite, and thou shalt go before me in the spirit and power of Elias, to prepare my way before me."* With the message on Wall Street it was confirmed: Elijah Pierson of Morristown had become the Prophet Elijah of Tishbe, and his handful of followers were now the Elders of the true Israelite church. He would prepare the world for the coming of the Lord; as part of the preparations (God was good) he would go among the sick and heal them.[38]

Three days later, Elijah gathered the principal members of the Bowery Hill Kingdom—Frances Folger, Ann Folger, the servant Isabella, and a few others—and arranged them at Sarah's bedside. Sarah, delirious with fever, heard her husband read from the Epistle of James: "Is there any sick among you? Let him call for the elders of the church: and let them pray over him, anointing him with oil in the name of the Lord. And the prayer of faith shall save the sick, and the Lord shall raise him up." Elijah then poured oil over Sarah's body and spread it, while he and others prayed over and over for the Lord to raise her up.

Sarah Pierson hung on for six more days, and on June 29 she died.[39]

About two hundred persons, most of them women, attended the funeral of Sarah Pierson on the first of July.[40] It would be no ordinary ceremony: Elijah the Tishbite had announced that he would raise his Sarah from the dead. A physician who attended the funeral found the house crowded and excited: "The hall and rooms being filled, I stood upon the piazza, which opened by a large raised window into the parlour where the corpse lay in a coffin, clad in grave-clothes. Soon after I took this position, where I could hear and see the anticipated ceremonies, I was questioned by several persons whether I believed that she would be raised. As I saw they were followers of Mr. Pierson, and addressed the same question to others who looked sceptical, I evaded a direct answer." Elijah sat in an adjoining room. He was quiet and utterly composed, and he held an open Bible in his lap. At length he rose and walked into the parlor and stood before the coffin.

Elijah read again the passage from James, ending with a solemn "THE LORD SHALL RAISE HIM UP!" He looked across at the mourners. "This dear woman," came his measured hollow voice, "has been anointed in the name of Israel's God, and in obedience to this divine command; and I believe that God will fulfill his promise." Elijah's voice grew louder as again and again he chanted "THE LORD SHALL RAISE HIM UP!"—always with the emphasis on "shall." He paused and caught his breath, then told the mourners about the revelation on the omnibus and the healing service at Sarah's bedside. Sarah, he said, had died in the faith that she would rise again.

Elijah spread his hands over the coffin and closed his eyes and prayed: "O Lord God of Israel! thy own word declares that if the elders of the church anoint the sick and pray over him, the Lord shall raise him up. We have taken thee at thy word; we have anointed her with oil, and prayed the prayer of faith, and thou knowest in this faith the dear woman died, and in this faith we thy children live. Now, Lord, we claim thy promise! God is not man that he should lie, and if this dear woman is not raised up this day, thy word will fall to the ground; thy promise is null and void; and these gainsaying infidels will rejoice, and go away triumphing in their unbelief. Lord God! thou canst not deny thyself. Thou knowest we have performed the conditions to the very letter. O Lord, now fulfill thy promise—now, Lord—O let not thy enemies blaspheme—show that thou hast mighty power—thou canst raise the dead—we believe it Lord. Come now, and make good thy word, and let this assembly see that there is a God in Israel!"

As Elijah spoke, women stood beside the coffin. Among them was Frances Folger, who turned now and then to touch Sarah's hands and face, feeling for signs of returning life.

Elijah preached and prayed for an hour, then sank exhausted into a chair. The room fell silent. Shocked mourners stared at each other or at their feet. Believers fixed their eyes on the coffin. After a long and awful time one drop of thick dark blood appeared at Sarah's nostril. There were gasps, and two women ran to the physician. Was Sarah coming back? The doctor could take no more of it. No, he said; the drop of blood did not mean that Sarah Pierson was returning from the dead. It meant that her corpse was rotting before their eyes.

The doctor approached a clergyman who stood among the mourners and begged him to stop the proceedings. The minister rose and firmly told the audience, "Yes, this beloved and lamented Christian SHALL rise again—AT THE RESURRECTION OF THE JUST! For it is the promise of God, that all those who are Christ's he will bring with him at his coming. . . ." "The Lord will raise her up," he went on, "but not to-day, nor tomorrow; yet dying in the Lord, she shall have a part in the first resurrection."

Elijah sat quietly as friends closed the coffin, then followed them as they carried Sarah out and buried her in the churchyard on Amity Street. Close friends walked him home. He said goodbye at the door and entered his desolate house. He called his servant Katy (like Isabella, a black ex-slave) and told her to clean Sarah's bedroom, change the linens, and lay out her night clothes. Then he sent out for plates of her favorite foods. He spent the night in Sarah's room, waiting for her knock at the door.

The next day a jubilant Elijah recorded that Sarah had appeared to Katy, "sitting in the coffin, top off—looking well." She directed Katy to straighten the house, and she left advice about the children for Elijah. Then she gave Katy some stockings and a robe that had belonged to her.

Sarah returned to Katy three days later, and Elijah transcribed what she said: "She showed how we were living before we were married. We were like two trees dug up by the roots and planted together, and we were covered by one mantle. At that time we conversed together about the work the Lord gave us to do, and it has been carried on ever since. I now had the whole of it on me. . . .. Our union was an everlasting covenant never to be broken." Five days later, Sarah reappeared, wondering "'How the children were.' 'Have you got all your things?' she asked. The Lord will do for him (me) what He sees best before he goes away. Tell him to go to the Penetentiary, State Prison, Almshouse, and Five Points, if it be only once or twice. . . . She says the mantle, or covering, is still over us, and we are both together in it, and shall never be separated." Surely this was Elijah's Sarah: sharing concern for the children, urging Elijah to continue the missions to the poor, affirming an eternal marriage in Christ.[41]

On July 4, Jesus spoke directly to Elijah: *"If thou wilt preach my Gospel, thou shalt have thy wife."*[42]

Elijah accepted Christ's offer with all his heart. Retaining his powers as Elijah the Tishbite, the grieving prophet returned to the work that he and Sarah had begun, preaching and missionizing with new vigor and hope. He made plans to quit business and devote himself to a full-time ministry. He preached, prayed, and studied the Bible. At night, lost in solitary mourning, he talked with Jesus.

The holy conversations turned always on the covenant of July 4, 1830: Elijah would throw his whole being into gospel labors, and Jesus would return Sarah to Elijah. Elijah asked for new powers to carry out his commission: "Now, Lord, grant me all the graces, gifts, and qualifications, both of mind and body, which thou didst give to thy Son Jesus for the fulfilling of his ministry. . . ." It was a tall order, but God granted it willingly: *"Son, all that I have is thine; that which thou hast asked is freely granted unto thee, and thou shalt have every good and perfect gift, that I may be glorified in thee. We will be with thee in this work. We in thee, and thou in us, and be fellow-workers together; and this work shall be carried on till the world shall end."*[43]

That was at the end of August. Two months later, after many more conversations with God, Elijah was at his morning prayers. Jesus appeared in the flesh, stood at Elijah's right hand, and laid hands upon his head. *"Peace be unto you,"* said Jesus. *"Receive ye the Holy Ghost—as my Father hath sent me, even so send I you. Whosoever sins ye remit, they are remitted unto them; and whosoever sins ye retain, they are retained. Go into all the world, and preach the Gospel to every creature. Teach all nations, baptizing them in the name of the Father, Son, and Holy Ghost—teaching them to observe all things whatsoever I have commanded you, and lo I am with you always, even unto the end of the world."*

The talks continued through December. Elijah preached during the day and prayed at night, and sometimes Jesus appeared to Elijah, gave him further instructions, and granted him new powers to carry them out. Through it all, the talks (as Elijah recorded them in his journal) never strayed far from the revelation of July 4 and Christ's promises about Sarah:

August 25, 1830. "O Lord, some days since . . . in the silence of the night thou didst ask me, 'Wilt thou have thy wife?' O Lord, my heart replied, yea Lord, I will. Now, Lord Jesus, grant me the desire of my soul, and let us be together in all thy work in the building up of thy kingdom. Lord Jesus, take this thing into thine own hands, and bring it to pass, and herein glorify thyself, and take [away] my reproach. Asked the Lord if I had any thing more to do about it. He said, *'Thou hast committed it to me. I will bring it to pass—wait patiently'.*"

September 22, 1830. "This morning, while in prayer, I had in the Spirit a full view of the Father and the Son, Sarah standing between them. The impression made on my mind was, that the Lord was preparing her for her return. This view continued most of the day."

October 3, 1830. "Had a season of earnest prayer for Sarah's resurrection in the body; though the Lord appeared displeased with me in other things, and rebuked me, yet he said concerning this, *'Thy prayer is heard.'*"

October 5, 1830. "During the meeting, while one was in prayer and mentioned the grave, the Lord said to me, *'This is nothing to thee . . . for thou hast triumphed over it by faith'* (conquered it). This seemed spoken in relation to Sarah."

November 13, 1830. "This evening the Lord said, *'This is my covenant with you,'* saith the Lord; *'thou shalt have Sarah thy wife, and she shall be with thee in all thy work, and shall bear thee a son, and thou shalt call his name James. Thou shalt have Abraham's blessing.'*"

December 11, 1830. *"'As I live,'* saith the Lord, *'thy companion shall be raised up, and shall be with thee in the work, and shall bear thee a son, and thou shalt call his name James. When you have done my work, you shall ascend up to me, and not pass through the grave.'*"

December 19, 1830. *"'Thou shalt prophesy to many nations, and thy wife shall be with thee; and when you have finished your work, you shall both of you together ascend up to heaven like Elijah of old.'*"

December 27, 1830. "Prayed concerning Sarah; asked the Lord to show whether I had rightly understood his promise to raise her up in the body, and if she would be with me in the work. The Lord said, *Did I ever give you a stone for bread, or a serpent for a fish.*"

7

Over the year after Elijah's attempt to raise Sarah, his old evangelical friends abandoned him one by one.

John Stanford rejected Elijah immediately after the funeral. Stanford had loved his daughter dearly, but he was not a man to wallow in grief. After his own wife's death more than thirty years earlier, he mourned, then quickly straightened himself out and returned to his duties. ("The will of the Lord be done," he wrote in his diary.) He had visited the Piersons often during Sarah's illness, both to comfort her and to prepare himself for her death. On his last visit he "found her in her last agonies, insensible & speechless." When a messenger arrived at his house and announced that Sarah was dead, Stanford once again reached for his journal: "The Lord gave and the Lord hath taken away. Blessed be the name of the Lord."[44]

Stanford attended his daughter's funeral, unprepared for what Elijah had in mind. Standing among his ministerial colleagues and family friends, he watched in disbelief as Pierson began his chanting. Stanford may have been the minister who intervened and ended the service. At home, he wrote, "Still there is every reason to believe that she sleeps in Jesus and will partake of the resurrection of the just." He concluded with a veiled prayer for Elijah: "May the Lord sanctify this bereavement to me, and to all my children." Stanford's diary never again mentioned Elijah Pierson.[45]

Three months later, in the fall of 1830, downtown reformers revived the mission to the prostitutes, and faced a decision about what to do with an obviously deranged Elijah Pierson. The mission was now in the hands of John McDowall, a Princeton seminarian who came to the Five Points in September 1830 to establish Sabbath schools for poor children. McDowall took a pious interest in the prostitutes he encountered, and with the help of Arthur Tappan and other reformers he opened a storefront preaching station, two Sabbath schools, and a halfway house for prostitutes fresh from jail. There the young women received moral instruction and a safe place to stay, promises of employment, and simple meals. (McDowall was a retrencher who admitted that "Having eaten until I am full, lust gets the control of me.")

McDowall soon felt the need to place prostitutes in a more isolated, long-term residence, and he traveled to Bowery Hill to see what could be done. By now, Pierson's Asylum House contained only two inmates, and it is safe to say that the sight of Elijah would have worried John McDowall. Still, McDowall sent prostitutes to the house on Bowery Hill.

In the spring of 1831 the newly formed New-York Magdalen Society absorbed Pierson's Asylum House and renamed it the Magdalen House of Refuge. Arthur Tappan was president of the new organization; among the founding directors was Elijah Pierson.[46]

Later in 1831, Arthur Tappan claimed that he quit the Magdalen Society because he had spent a lot of money on it and could see no results. Others hinted that public opposition to the society had driven Tappan into an un-Christian, selfish concern for his reputation. Neither Tappan nor his accusers mentioned what may have been a principal cause of his defection: Elijah the Tishbite, wielding apostolic powers and talking about Sarah's return, retained direction of the asylum's day-to-day operations.[47]

John McDowall developed doubts about Pierson early on, and on April 1831 he broke his ties with the entire Magdalen enterprise. "I have become dissatisfied with the asylum," he said. McDowall's biographer explained: "Mr. Pierson, who first established the house, he believed was a very godly man, but inculcated some doctrines with which he could not accord. . . ." In December 1831 the Magdalen Society ceased its work, transferred its houses to Elijah Pierson, and announced that Pierson was choosing his own helpers and associates. Henceforth, Pierson would bear full responsibility for what remained of the mission. McDowall and his friends promised to establish their own asylum when circumstances grew more favorable.[48]

All along, Jesus was telling Elijah to ignore the scoffers and lukewarm Christians and to follow Him alone. At the end of 1830, Pierson formally accepted Christ's promises and spiritual gifts, and grew strong in his new identity as the Prophet Elijah—John the Baptist—Elias. He would preach and work wonders and baptize in the name of Jesus. And in that work he would have Sarah, resurrected in the flesh, united with him—like Barnabas and Paul—in the most holy of Christian missions.

At the beginning of 1831, Pierson quit his Pearl Street business once and for all. In May, a month after young McDowall's defection, he left Bowery Hill and rented a house on Fourth Street near the Bowery with Frances Folger and her husband Reuben. Elijah took up preaching, as he put it, "in his own rented house"—just like (he explained) the Apostle Paul. Pierson and Folger outfitted the largest room as a chapel; old friends drifted back into the fold. The mystic Isabella stayed on as housekeeper; she and her friend Katy were seldom absent from Pierson's meetings. Mrs. Bolton was there, and so were Benjamin and Ann Folger. The enthusiastic sessions on Fourth Street also produced a few converts: a carpenter named Beauman; Mrs. Rosetta Dratch, an elderly Jewish widow from Newark; Sylvester Mills, a merchant who had, like Pierson, lost his wife, and who suffered from deep and seemingly insurmountable bouts of depression.

Elijah Pierson's gifts now went uncontested. His duties on Pearl Street, which had demanded a businesslike demeanor at least part of the day, ended at about the time he made his pact with Jesus. His formal missionary work, which called for similar behavior among the downtown evangelicals, crumbled during the following year. Now Pierson's social contacts shrank to Jesus and the members of his church. The congregation on Fourth Street prayed and fasted as they had on Bowery Hill. Pierson continued to preach against pew rents, collections, and salaries for ministers, and he demanded long seasons of fasting and prayer. The days of the Apostles had arrived, he proclaimed, and through the prayer of faith his adherents could gain apostolic gifts: they could heal the sick, cast out devils, and (of course) raise the dead. Mrs. Bolton and some of the others fanned through the city advertising Pierson and his powers, distributing tracts, inviting the city to "come and hear Elijah the Prophet."[49]

So it went for exactly a year, until the first Saturday in May 1832, when the servant Isabella answered a knock at the door, withdrew to find Elijah, and announced that a man named Matthias was waiting in the parlor.

TWO

❧❧

Robert Matthews

SATURDAY, MAY 5, 1832. The Prophet headed uptown from his rooming house near the Battery. A direct route would have taken him along Pearl Street, past Elijah Pierson's old office, through Chatham Square near the Five Points slum, to the Bowery, the workingmen's boulevard—a trip across Manhattan's highs and lows in search of a rare holy rich man. His street preacher's clothing was nearly worn out. An immaculate, gray-flecked beard covered his chest.

Like Elijah Pierson, the Prophet had first come to New York as a pious boy, eager to make good. But his talents and his fear of God could not fend off terrible misfortunes, which led him on a prolonged and erratic religious journey. One sacred profession led to another, from Calvinism to Hebraic prophecy, while his home life degenerated into a nightmare of wife-beating and child abuse. A failure in trade, rejected by his friends and neighbors, forced to wander in search of work, he lost everything save his solitary faith—the same improvised, misogynist faith that drew him up to Fourth Street, where he turned, located the correct address, and rapped on Elijah Pierson's door.

I

Robert Matthews was born in 1788 to a Scots immigrant family in the farming village of Cambridge, in Washington County, New York. Tucked in the bounteous Owl Kill Valley, midway between the Hudson River and the Green Mountains of Vermont, Cambridge had been founded as a permanent white settlement twenty-five years earlier by some land-hungry New England squatters. Soon after, the Scots began arriving, part of the great migration from Scotland that lasted from the mid-1760s until the eve of the American Revolution.[1]

Clustered in their farms and shops about a mile from the village proper, the Cambridge Scots mostly kept to themselves and to their old ways in their new home. They named their little neighborhood Coila, probably a variation of *coil* or *coilie,* the Scots Celtic words for haystack. They spoke English with a Lowlands burr that made their conversation difficult for outsiders to understand. The few associations they sustained with others came mainly with their fellow immigrants in the surrounding New York and Vermont country towns or with those who chose to live in Manhattan. Above all, they clung to their uncompromising Scots Calvinism, nursing ancient ecclesiastical grudges unknown to the rest of the world.[2]

Coila's strictest believers (including, it seems, Robert Matthews's mother) attended the Anti-Burgher Secession Church, a sectarian splinter of a militant faction from within Scots Presbyterianism.[3] Some of the Anti-Burghers' ancestors had fought in the bitter Covenenter struggles from 1660 to 1690, ignited by Charles II's attempts to transform Scotland's prebyteries into an episcopal church subordinate to English civil law. After a generation of bloody resistance, most of the opposition died down (although a group of unreconciled Coveneters would form a Reform Presbyterian Church in 1743). But tensions remained strong within the Church of Scotland.

In 1733, a group of dissenters seceded from the church to protest the leadership's alleged moderation and rationalism. Fourteen years later, these so-called Seceders divided against each other, when one group, thereafter called Anti-Burghers, spurned the Burgess Oath that was enforced in the wake of the Jacobite rebellion to bar Roman Catholics from office. Although fiercely anti-Catholic, the non-swearers could not bring themselves to acknowledge (as the oath demanded) that the Church of Scotland professed "the true religion." For their pains, they incurred heavy fines and civil penalties. Simon-pure believers in John Knox's Calvinism, the Anti-Burghers would not lightly forsake their heritage of devotion to the tiniest points of religious principle.[4]

In 1769, the first Scots settlers in Cambridge established a Reform (that is, Seceders') kirk without reference to the Burgess Oath dispute, on the assumption that the controversy was irrelevant in the New World. But the congregation could not forever contain sectarian strife. Dissatisfied with the congregation's choice of psalms, Coila's Anti-Burghers left to form their own Associate Presbyterian Congregation in 1785, and acquired the ministerial services of the Reverend Thomas Beveridge, a leading Anti-Burgher doctrinaire. According to one chronicler, Cambridge's Burghers and Anti-Burghers were the best of neighbors on weekdays but acted like members of separate tribes on the Sabbath, "haughtily looking down their noses, without salutation," when they passed each other on the way to services. The divisions persisted, handed down from parents to children, through the middle of the nineteenth century—long after the Burgess Oath had been lifted and most of the Burghers and Anti-Burghers back in Scotland had reunited.[5]

It would have been hard to find, anywhere, more dedicated adherents to Calvinist orthodoxy. Cambridge's Anti-Burghers read their Bibles literally and debated their scriptural understandings. They rejected Romish, priestly ritual (although, like other Scots Presbyterians, they retained a heavily modified version of the Eucharist). They sang psalms without any instrumental accompaniment and without the aid of hymnals, in imitation of the primitive Christians; they guarded against any perceived government interference in their religious affairs; they demanded strict observance of the Sabbath and enforced a personal code of righteous temperance every day of the week.

Appalled by the doctrinal laxness of mainstream Presbyterians, the Anti-Burghers sustained an absolute belief in predestination along with a certainty that God's will could be studied in every twitch of daily life. A story comes down about one Coila farmer who forgot about an announced day of fasting and tried to light a fire in his hearth; after discovering his error in a supernatural sign, the sinner gathered his family and had everyone spend the rest of the day in reading the Bible, singing psalms, and repeating the catechism. The social life of Cambridge, New York, was simple, a later resident remarked: no one with pretensions to respectability ever danced.[6]

Piety in Coila, as in other Scots Presbyterian settlements, followed cycles of humiliation and thanksgiving, centered on the annual communion, or Lord's Supper, held in late summer—an event the faithful likened in importance to what Passover was to the Jews. Preparations for the sacrament began months ahead of time, when the church elders fixed a date and the membership undertook continuing exercises in self-examination, devotional reading, personal covenanting, and other acts of spiritual cleans-

ing. Over the week before the Supper, the worshipping inten-
sified, with fasting, public psalm singing, family prayer, sermons
on Christ's love, and (on the eve of the Supper) the distribution of
tokens to all deserving communicants. Finally, on the day itself,
the membership stood, sang, and prayed before long benches,
while the minister "fenced the table"—that is, solemnly debarred
a long list of those characters whom God deemed unworthy
(thieves, gluttons, promiscuous dancers, liars, backbiters; contemporary accounts of Scots evangelical services noted that it
could take an hour or more for the minister to finish this part of
the service). Suddenly, the mood then changed from exclusion to
loving invitation, as the penitent took their seats, received the
consecrated bread and wine, and shared it all around. Long weeks
of abnegation and self-reproval gave way to tears of joy; tears
flowed again the next day at the thanksgiving service that closed
the sacramental season.[7]

Young Matthews would have attended his first Lord's Supper
at about the age of twelve, but for years before that he took part
in the household services that preceded the big event. And
throughout the year, he would have witnessed the Coila church's
vigilance in regulating its members' behavior. Whenever even
the slightest transgression became public knowledge, the minister
and his leading local laymen investigated. Anyone suspected of
drunkenness or adultery, the most common infractions, could
expect a visit from one of the elders, who would demand a public
confession. The surviving Coila church record book contains
numerous notations about other proceedings, against the likes of
the farmer William Taylor ("charged with profane swearing")
and one Esther Musket ("concerning a report she was said to
have spread about Margaret Graham's being with child").[8]

It was hard to get away with sin in watchful Coila; it was even
harder to make any gestures toward religious unorthodoxy. In
1804 the vexed elders issued a warning to several church mem-

bers who "had of late practiced, some more some less, to hear preachers of other denominations"—a practice, the elders alleged, that made the Anti-Burghers seem like "Narrow-minded Biggots," who held their beliefs "as merely their own without a persuasion that they are warranted in the word of God." The message's conclusion reminded the congregation of a cardinal rule, that the Associate Church "decline[d] communion with other churches."[9]

During Robert's early boyhood, Coila's chief spiritual overseer was the Reverend Mr. Beveridge, a man much admired by the observant majority. Trained in Edinburgh by the highly regarded Reverend Adam Gib, Beveridge had arrived in America in 1784, settled in Philadelphia, and drafted the doctrinal testimony that became the American Anti-Burghers' theological platform. After a brief stay in New York City (where he organized a Seceder congregation), Beveridge moved to Cambridge and remained as Coila's pastor until his sudden death from dysentery in 1798.[10]

Beveridge was an energetic cleric who evangelized constantly—catechizing and exhorting from house to house, bolstering the faithful in the nearby Scots settlements. People in Coila remarked that he had much secret fellowship with the Father, and with His Son, Jesus Christ; his parishioners especially appreciated his abiding interest in catechizing Coila's children, exercises the Anti-Burghers took with utmost seriousness. Among his favorite pupils, apparently, was Robert Matthews, who, at about the age of seven received a special blessing from the minister.[11]

From Beveridge and the church elders, young Matthews learned to live in an anxious world, where humankind was innately corrupt and where the thunder claps of the Hudson Valley sprang from the mouth of the Lord. From the theater of the Lord's Supper, he learned additional lessons about purity and pride. In both metaphorical and material ways, the Scots Presbyterian sacramental season was an unrelenting process of self-purification, "a holy revenge upon the Flesh or Body for its former excesses," one eighteenth-century writer remarked. Only those who had purged themselves could sit at the benches alongside the communion table, symbolically covered with immaculate bleached linen. As part of the congregants' role in the performance, all were supposed to wear plain, neat clothing, the best clothing they owned, laundered spotless and impeccably arranged. Anyone in dirty clothing betrayed a lack of inner devotion.[12]

Both the Suppers and the ordinary family services further instructed Matthews about the admixture of equality and patriarchy that undergirded the Anti-Burgher faith. Unlike the weekly Presbyterian services that Elijah Pierson attended as a boy in Morristown (with their carefully graded pew assignments), the Scots' Suppers mixed everyone in a communal body, dissolving the differences in wealth and power that marked off one Coila household from another. Riches and status stood for nothing before the Anti-Burghers' Christ; one Scots writer noted that the Lord's Supper bore "some faint resemblance" to "the heavenly city of the New Jerusalem." At the same time, however, the ceremonies reinforced distinctions *within* households between men and women. Scots evangelical fathers, the masters of their households, led their wives, children, and servants in morning and evening prayers before meals, thus helping to ensure, one saint wrote, that each father's charges would be "more observant of his other commands." At the Lord's Supper, the presiding ministers and elders, who controlled admission to the sacrament, were always men; their constant invocations of how the saints had gathered at the Father's table to hear the Father's testament ratified on a public stage the domestic presumptions of paternal authority.[13]

The one potentially destabilizing element in this stylized order was the appearance of voices and visions to individual church members. During the long weeks of anxious fasting and prayer, it was hardly surprising that believers lapsed into ecstatic trances. Reports from various congregations show that for some, especially young women, the experiences may have contained sensual, even erotic metaphors, connected to a belief in the Lord's Supper as a marriage and consummation between Christ and the soul in a divine, cleansing love—far different from, and greater than, human love. (One Scots writer recorded a woman's disclosure that she had "earnest longing desires immediately to be Unclothed and to be with Christ.") Visionaries told of interviews with the Redeemer, of promises of Salvation, of seeing bread and water shower down like manna from heaven, or seeing Christ's wounds gushing blood. The Scots clergy, wary of these sights and sounds as possible threats to scriptural authority (as well as their own authority), tried to minimize the episodes; almost certainly they went under-reported in church records. But the ministers, whose own sermons offered graphic descriptions of Christ's passion, never entirely denied the possibility of genuine visionary experiences.[14]

In 1835, an enterprising Manhattan journalist disclosed that, as a boy, Robert Matthews had his own conversations with supernatural spirits and impressed his friends with feats of clairvoyance.[15] The source is highly suspect and no such report appears in the Coila church records. It is just possible, however, that the visions did appear and that the worried Coila churchmen suppressed the fact. It is even more likely that when the adult Matthews began having visions years later, he would have instinctively trusted that they came from God.

What is certain is that Matthews, along with Coila's other boys and young men, grew up trying to handle sharp polarities of assurance and uncertainty. Every day of the year, especially communion days, brought reminders that he might eventually gain a secure place as an independent household head within the community of saintly fathers. Yet that hope, like salvation itself, remained contingent on the Lord's unknowable will. Earthly existence, as the Reverend Mr. Beveridge preached, was a series of trials and disappointments, for the elect as well as for the wicked: "It is through much tribulation," he told his listeners, "that all the saints enter into the kingdom of God." The tests got no easier as one grew older, endlessly searching for some clue about God's design. "The tempest sometimes ceases, the sky is clear, and the prospect is desirable," Beveridge sermonized, "but by the by the gathering clouds threaten a new storm; here we must watch, and labor, and fight, expecting to rest with Christ in glory, not on the way to it."[16]

2

Matthews's trials started early. In about 1795 (roughly the same time that the Reverend Mr. Beveridge blesssed him), both of his parents died, leaving him along with his four brothers and five sisters to the care of kin and neighbors. John Maxwell, a future ruling elder of the church, agreed to keep Robert and instruct him until he was twenty-one, in exchange for the boy's farm labor.[17]

Robert grew tall (to five feet, ten or eleven inches), with a well-proportioned build—but he would not be a farmer. He continually fell sick: one writer later claimed that, at age sixteen, he was still too feeble to work a plow; another, that he began suffering from chronic nervousness, perhaps as a result of his childhood sorrows. In about 1806, Robert left the Maxwell household to live with Edward Cook (like Maxwell, a future church elder), who taught him the carpenter's craft. A year or two later, Robert struck out on his own. The sources are silent about why he departed so abruptly, or whether some quarrel or other trouble had arisen. Clearly, though, he had learned his woodworking lessons extremely well. He turned up in Manhattan in 1808, a skilled journeyman carpenter living in a backhouse dwelling on Henry Street on the city's plebeian East Side.[18]

Straightaway, Robert sought out some reliable hometown companions, the Wrights. Andrew Wright, a cabinetmaker, had emigrated from Scotland to New York, where he served as an elder in the same Nassau Street Seceders' church that the Reverend Mr. Beveridge had founded in 1785. During the yellow fever epidemic in 1798, Wright moved his family upstate to Cambridge and safety; after five years in Coila, the Wrights returned to New York, just as a fresh outbreak of the fever was subsiding. They were happy to pick up their acquaintance with Robert Matthews when he arrived in the city some years later. The Wrights' fifteen-year-old daughter Margaret remembered the Matthews children as orphans, and Robert as a boy highly praised by his neighbors. Now that he had reached the border of manhood (she later wrote), Robert unfailingly attended Sunday services at the Seceders' church. On weekdays, he attended faithfully and skillfully to his work, "bidding fair to become a useful member of society."[19]

More than a hundred miles from Coila, Matthews had managed to find, in the Seceders' congregation, a semblance of his boyhood community. Unfortunately, that community collapsed once he stepped an inch outside of his small circle of friends. All around lower Manhattan, aspiring apprentice clerks like Elijah Pierson walked nervously through the streets, past prostitutes and drunkards. Robert Matthews, the precocious journeyman carpenter, viewed the same city scenes with the righteous fervor of a devout Anti-Burgher, which quickly got him into trouble.

It was not that Robert lacked for respect: a carpenter of his skills had little difficulty finding jobs in rapidly expanding New York. But keeping those jobs proved to be a problem. He could not, evidently, refrain from proselytizing his workmates, urging them to quit their sinful habits (especially their drinking) and warning them to act more like the good people of Coila. It all must have come easily to Robert, warning others to obey God's laws much as his surrogate fathers, the elders of Cambridge, instructed the wayward back home.

Robert soon discovered some of the rougher facts of Manhattan working-class life. Carpenters, like other New York workingmen, liked to drink, at all times of the day, in stupefying quantities. Drink made them men and, they thought, gave them strength. They despised holier-than-thou youngsters like Matthews who tried to tell them otherwise. A pamphleteer later reported that the workers at one Canal Street shop dubbed Robert "Jumping Jesus." When their taunts failed to stifle Matthews's sermons, the men had their boss fire him.[20]

Somehow, Matthews persevered for three years, saving a little money, passing into young manhood as a pious working-class oddity. Finally he snapped and lashed out—not at his fellow workers, but at a woman. Details of the incident are sketchy, as no one, including the most relentless reporters of the Matthias story, ever said anything about it. All that remains is a set of formulaic indictment papers, which disclose that on the fifth of June, 1811, one Hester Matthews, the wife of James, a grocer—and quite possibly Robert's sister-in-law—swore out a complaint to the effect that the day before, Robert had assaulted and beaten her "without any justification." The case came before the Court of General Sessions and Robert was convicted; the papers do not say what sentence he served, if any.[21]

When news of the beating reached Coila, Robert's old townsmen stirred themselves to save him from the city. (There is no evidence to indicate any similar solicitude on behalf of his female accuser.) By the end of January 1812, he had returned to Coila and rejoined his old congregation. In February, the local wheelwright, Robert Thompson (a Matthews uncle, one source says) arranged to convey to Robert a house, a shop, and an acre of land adjoining the Coila meeting house, in exchange for a one dollar payment—all "in consideration of the love and affection" he held for the young man.[22] Plucked out of New York, Matthews became a country storekeeper in the bosom of his hometown, and his tempests temporarily ceased.

Although he lacked any practical experience, Matthews proved to be a capable businessman, and before long he was laying aside part of his profits and making plans to expand his store. He could not completely avoid reminders of his past troubles, for like other country dealers, he had to return to Manhattan regularly in order to inspect the Pearl Street wholesalers' stocks and place his orders. (We will never know if, while on his rounds, Matthews ever encountered the young Elijah Pierson. Their paths may well have crossed in the course of everyday business, but neither man recollected as much in later years.) Robert endured the trips by passing time with the Wrights, and the visits turned into a courtship of Margaret. In 1813, the two were married in the Nassau Street Seceder Church. A year later, they named their first-born son Robert, and baptized him at the yellow meeting house in Coila.[23]

Reprieved by his clan connections, Robert Matthews was suddenly, at age twenty-six, a respectable independent citizen, ranking above the average of his neighbors and pleased at how his life was tending. Many rural men of Robert's years lived and worked in their fathers' households, dutifully waiting to inherit the family farm. Others—younger sons and the sons of poor men—scrambled to find enough land or a cash-paying job to support a family of their own. But Matthews, an orphan who had known a string of stand-in fathers, was now himself a propertied patriarch. (Over the next fourteen years, Margaret would bear him no fewer than six more children, a traditional country brood.) A stalwart of Coila society, an esteemed member of the Anti-

Burgher congregation, Robert had apparently weathered his tribulations well.[24]

Success suited him, so the story goes. A kind and affectionate husband, attentive to his growing family, Matthews lost his excessive boyish severity and befriended everyone in town. He did have some strange seizures of intense peevishness; his wife, disturbed, asked one of the store clerks about them and learned that they happened quite regularly. Still, the bad moments passed. Matthews allowed himself pieces of extravagant clothing; on this point alone he was vain.[25] Otherwise, although no mortal could be certain, there was every outward sign that John Calvin's God had spared Robert Matthews's soul.

3

Matthews the storekeeper was one of Cambridge's few men of long-distance commerce. His neighbors, almost all of them simple subsistence farmers, had only limited contacts with the wider world of getting and spending; Matthews brought part of that world to Coila in the form of drygoods, tools, and petty luxury items shipped up from New York. The market revolution advanced by the Pearl Street merchants had, by now, begun to engulf the northeastern countryside, tying even the remote rural settlements of Washington County to cash-crop agriculture and new forms of credit. More than he may have realized, Matthews was the new market's chief agent in Coila.

In the euphoric aftermath of the War of 1812, this country commerce was bursting with promises of material riches for anyone with the initiative and the funds to participate. (Within a generation, rural entrepreneurs in and around Cambridge would make the area an important center for garden-seed cultivation and the raising of Merino sheep.) Matthews had obtained his initial stake through a lucky intervention; his business energy seemed to come to him naturally. But the new market also had its perils, as Matthews discovered in 1816. Having done all-too-well early on, he badly stretched his resources in trying to enlarge his store. Within months, a contraction of credit by his New York wholesalers bankrupted him and a business associate, damaging his reputation among his once-forgiving neighbors. God was testing him again. But now his misfortunes had cost him money and most of his friends.[26]

Matthews had no choice but to take his family back to Manhattan and to start all over again, as a carpenter. Gradually, he recouped his losses, and after three years of working as a journeyman, he set up a business of his own, as a master builder and house joiner. But the Matthewses knew no end of misery, of a kind that was increasingly common among families in New York's poorer, crowded working-class neighborhoods. In the autumn of 1816, their eldest boy, two-year-old Robert, died of an undisclosed illness. Two years later, their second son died. Then, shortly after he opened his carpentry business, Matthews himself fell ill for several months, leaving his family without a steady income. While he convalesced, a financial panic devastated the city's economy and suspended building projects throughout Manhattan.[27]

His prospects ruined, Matthews moved what was left of his family (himself, his wife, their toddler daughter, Isabella, and three small sons) to even cheaper quarters. Like thousands of other American men, he had experienced the market revolution not as a liberating triumph but as a fitful, agonizing descent into wage labor. Never again would he regain his economic independence.

Just at this time, Matthews began making strange religious professions. As he struggled to regain fully his physical strength (Margaret Matthews later wrote), his bad moods returned, more frequently now, and in the form of headaches, violent fits, and sudden rages. "He would complain that his mind was very confused; that it seemed as if he should lose his senses," Margaret recalled; when afflicted, "he would talk very harshly to me, and punish his children for the least thing, and beat them very severely." It was only by chance that he found some relief, when on an evening stroll he stumbled upon the service of an African Methodist church near his home.[28]

The Methodists had been active in New York since the 1780s. Against long odds, they had made some progress among the city's mostly unchurched poor and middling classes—especially among black New Yorkers, slave and free, who were stirred by the Methodists' redemptive egalitarianism and anti-slavery principles. By the 1790s, when just over 700 persons belonged to the city's Methodist connection, one in five members was black. Yet while the Methodist leaders welcomed the blacks as children of God, they also placed restrictions on black worship, including a policy of strict segregation at their church on John Street. In 1796, after a series of polite complaints, a group of black worshippers won permission from Bishop Francis Asbury to start a separate congregation with their own black preachers. Five years later, construction began at the corner of Leonard and Church streets on a new church building, funded by those members who had risen to the top of New York's sizable free black community. Over the next two decades, their African Methodist Zion congregation expanded to include more than 700 members.[29]

Matthews's sympathies may have been instantly aroused by the sight of African Methodists at prayer. Along with the Quakers, the Methodists, and some smaller denominations, the Anti-Burghers had stood in the religious vanguard of American anti-slavery since the end of the eighteenth century. Although Matthews would never register any formal anti-slavery commitment, he would have learned as a boy to regard human bondage as a cruel blasphemy, a violation of Christ's Sermon on the

Mount. He also would have learned to reject the cruder forms of racialist dogma. Anti-Burgher churches, including Coila's, willingly admitted to full membership any blacks who were drawn to the faith.[30]

On this night, however, Matthews felt more than sympathy. At the Zion Church, he saw people redeemed in the tremors of the Holy Spirit, an ungodly display to any strict Calvinist. Here was the kind of service he had been warned against in Coila, promising salvation not to some unknowable elect but to all who received Jesus in their hearts. Yet instead of repelling him, the proceedings filled Matthews with fresh inspiration. Arriving home breathless, he announced to Margaret that he had just witnessed the true spirit of religion for the first time. The Methodists, he exclaimed, had the purest church. The time was near when blacks and whites would associate. Margaret had borne up for years under the stress of her husband's strange turns—but to see a lifelong Anti-Burgher Calvinist suddenly shout the Methodists' praises was to watch an abused and agitated mind slip its moorings.[31]

Weirder announcements soon followed. Even as he talked up the Zion Church, Matthews began putting it about that he was no Christian at all, and that his ancestors had not been Christians. He was, in actuality, a prophesying Hebrew, just as the Judea carpenter had been—and just like his new hero, the New York newspaper editor, Mordecai Manuel Noah.[32]

Noah, the self-proclaimed Judge of Israel and Messiah of the Jews, was an idiosyncratic combination of political party insider and Old Testament visionary. Born in Philadelphia in 1785 to prosperous German-Jewish immigrants with Sephardic connections, he, like Matthews, had been orphaned young and apprenticed to a craftsman (in Noah's case, a gilder). But unlike Matthews, Noah was a resounding success. After dabbling in play-writing, he cultivated local Jeffersonian politicians, and won, at age twenty-eight, a consular appointment to Tunis, making him one of the most prominent Jews in American public life. Upon his return to the United States in 1815, he settled in New York and assumed the editorship of the *National Advocate,* aligned with the fledgling Tammany Hall organization, and, in time, the statewide Bucktail faction, led by the young upstate legislator Martin Van Buren. A maverick by inclination, Noah became a stout defender of the democratic Bucktails in their battles with the entrenched Clinton family interest that controlled New York State government.[33]

Noah's greatest ambitions, however, lay outside politics. A leader of New York's Jewish laity, he dreamed of building a Jewish homeland (which he called, fittingly, Ararat) on Grand Island in the Niagara River—a spectacle to dwarf anything a mere politician could accomplish. Earlier seers had proposed schemes for Jewish colonization in the New World, but Noah was the first to take concrete steps toward completing the task. Led by their American Moses, the Jews of the world would converge on the promised land of upstate New York, where they would receive an uplifting, enlightened education, never more to wander persecuted among the gentiles. Noah talked about the idea to anyone who would listen and earned his share of print as far away as Germany (where the *Verein für Kultur und Wissenschaft der Juden,* a small band of young Jewish activists and intellectuals, endorsed the plan as a potential escape from European oppression). Late in 1819, Noah drew up a formal proposal to the New York State legislature, looking for approval to purchase his desired site.[34]

Noah's politics made no recorded impression on Matthews. Since his boyhood, Robert had apparently ignored party affairs. Like other Anti-Burghers, he distrusted secular governments as potential tyrants, a legacy of the Covenenter wars. Apart from marking Noah as a celebrity, a religious outsider who made good,

Noah's political schemes held little meaning for Robert Matthews. But Noah's religious plans touched him deeply. Matthews may never have met a Jew, but he had read the Old Testament and had heard plenty about Moses the law-giver at the Coila church. Now detached from the Anti-Burghers and impressed by the pugnacious Noah, he decided that he, too, was descended from the Israelites. He planned to apply his skills by building a model of Solomon's temple. He expected to join his fellow wanderers upstate. He proclaimed to his family that Noah could not possibly get along without him. Hearing all this, Margaret began to believe that her husband, quite apart from his physical ailments, was periodically insane.[35]

As soon as he was well enough to work, Matthews moved his family back to Washington County, to exploit what family connections remained—first to Argyle (where one of his sisters lived), then to Fort Miller, and finally, about 1824, to the town of Sandy Hill, home to one of his brothers. Country living restored Matthews's health, but work came his way infrequently, and his bad moods and talk of Noah continued. Margaret relied more and more on the Christian charity of her female neighbors, who somehow convinced her to stick by her children and her troubled marriage.[36]

If he ever visited Ararat, Matthews left no record of it, not that it would have mattered. In September 1825, Noah, having acquired a portion of Grand Island, finally launched his operation. Dressed in a Richard III costume and wearing a gold medallion on loan from New York's Park Theatre, he gathered his followers at St. Paul's Episcopal Church in Buffalo, and held a ceremony to dedicate the 300-pound cornerstone for his new asylum. Joined by the aged Seneca Indian Chief Red Jacket (Noah believed that the Indians were "in all probability descendants of the lost ten tribes of Israel"), a long procession filed into the church to find a communion table, inscribed with the words of the *Sh'ma* from the

Book of Deuteronomy and decked out with silver goblets filled with wine, corn, and oil. The assembled then listened to Noah read the Ruler's Proclamation that dictated Ararat's basic laws— including a provision that "all who . . . partake of the great covenant and obey and respect Mosaical laws" had to be admitted into the ranks of the Jews. By Noah's decree, Robert Matthews was as eligible as anybody to take sanctuary in the Jewish homeland.[37]

One month later, Governor De Witt Clinton staged a grand celebration to mark the opening of the Erie Canal, featuring a procession of vessels from the canal's starting point near Grand Island down to New York harbor. Not to be outdone, the Messiah of the Jews outfitted a steamboat—dubbed, naturally, Noah's Ark—and filled it, one newspaper reported, "with all manner of animals and creepy things." But the Ark never made it, as planned, to Manhattan, and Ararat attracted increasing public criticism and ridicule. Noah, caught in his sometimes competing loyalties to world Jewry and the Tammany pols, quietly let the project die.[38]

Matthews could have read about all these events in the newspapers, including the details of how Noah turned his private visions into arresting public shows. After Ararat's failure, however, he had to make new plans. Sometime in 1825 or 1826, finding no more work in Sandy Hill, he departed alone for Albany, and for three months he sent back no word to his family. When he finally mailed some of his earnings to Margaret, they came with orders that she join him. Margaret obediently gathered up the children (now numbering one daughter, Isabella, and three or possibly four sons) and the family's few belongings, although, she later claimed, she scarcely knew why.[39]

The previous ten years had been an agony for everyone. Two of the Matthews children had died. The family's fall into nomadic poverty was complete, making a mockery of Robert Matthews's earlier transient respectable independence. Robert's bad moods now came continually: his religious seeking had taken him from Scots Calvinism to Methodism (briefly) and then to Judaism, with no end in sight. He had found a new spiritual guide in Mordecai Noah, only to have Noah turn away from Ararat and back toward profane politics. There was always the possibility—so Margaret Matthews hoped—that a new situation in a new city might restore her husband to his former self and her family to tranquility. But they could not survive a further downward spiral. Albany would be their last chance.

4

Twenty years earlier, when Matthews had first traveled down-river from Coila, Albany was only beginning to shake off its ingrown Dutch colonial somnolence and had little to offer an ambitious young man. Since then, an invasion of New England merchants had loosened the hold of the established Dutch families and turned the place into a commercial center. In 1817, Albany was New York State's second largest city, and ranked seventh in the nation in population and trade. The completion of the Erie Canal in 1825 vastly accelerated this growth by linking Albany (and the river traffic to and from Manhattan) to the Great Lakes. Now an important entrepôt of the market revolution, Albany had developed both an enterprising civic leadership of Yankee improvers and a rough-and-tumble working class.

Simultaneously, Mordecai Noah's political friends, the Bucktail faction of Martin Van Buren, had overthrown the Clintonians and consolidated the state's first modern political machine, with Albany, the state capital, as their seat of power. Under Van Buren's guidance, this so-called Albany Regency became a national force, pulling together the opposition to the incumbent administration of President John Quincy Adams. (Two years after Matthews's arrival in Albany, the Regency, in concert with southern planters, would be the chief operatives behind Andrew Jackson's election to the White House.) Except during the summer, when the legislature was adjourned, the city crackled with the latest rumors and political intelligence, circulated by partisan editors and a swelling retinue of in-the-know gossips and hangers-on.[40]

Resettled in an Albany working-class neighborhood, Robert Matthews seemed to be on the mend. To Margaret's delight, he resolved to be a better husband and father. Work came steadily. He turned his religious zeal in respectable directions, by attending the North Dutch Church, joining a genteel temperance society, and enrolling the older children in the North Dutch Sunday school. For several months, he and Margaret lived in peace.[41]

In all of Albany County, there was no more dignified place of worship than the North Dutch Church—Albany's oldest congregation and the preferred religious home for the remnants of the city's Dutch elite. Situated on North Pearl Street among the homes of merchants and professionals, it was a far cry from the simple meeting house in Coila, or from any of the marginal assemblies that Matthews had recently attended.[42]

Like many of Albany's other nominally Calvinist churches, North Dutch had softened its doctrines about grace and damnation. Whereas, in colonial times the church had bound together an entire Dutch community under the command of the town's leading men, by the 1820s it had become a preserve for affluent, respectable women, Yankee and Dutch alike, as well as for the older Dutch mercantile families. Although still formally attached to the beliefs of their forefathers, the North Dutch congregants heard little fire-and-brimstone oratory at their Sunday services, and listened instead to more hopeful lessons about how to convert to the ways of Christ.[43] Matthews found the sermons appealing, especially when the resident minister, John Ludlow, was in the pulpit.

Ludlow was a young cleric who had quiet sympathies for the new-style, middle-class revivalism that, in upstate New York, was chiefly associated with the evangelical preachings of the Reverend Charles Finney. Ludlow aimed his sermons mainly at his wealthier congregants, to help goad them toward lifting the less fortunate sinners who lived all around them. God, he reminded his listeners, was no respecter of earthly riches or power. Too often, the worthy found themselves depressed while the worthless were exalted. A man could not be judged by his present external situation; neither could people claim to be true Christians unless they cared for their fellow creatures:

> It is also his [the Christian's] duty, when providence directs, to come to the heights of Zion shorn of all severity [to] proclaim glad tidings to those ready to perish—to encourage the weak & fainting—to confirm the wavering—to assist the tempted—by every kind word—by every precious promise to bind up the broken-hearted.

Ludlow's God was a God of love—not, he hastened to add, of carnal love, with its selfish worship of unholy objects, but of a higher Christian love, "unfeigned, sincere, honest," utterly opposed to malice, guile, and hypocrisy.[44]

Ludlow's sermons lifted the weight of the world off Matthews's shoulders, as the carpenter steadied himself and resolved to do his best for his family and the fallen unfortunates of Albany. He too would be a loving man; in his temperance work, he would lead others to righteousness. But Matthews's best efforts, his wife later recounted, were not nearly enough to hold himself together when disaster struck again. After the entire family contracted smallpox, the youngest child, a year-old boy, died in agony. At home following the funeral, Robert told Margaret that he would never forget her selfless care during the boy's last days—but soon after he lost control as never before, and Margaret bore the brunt of his anguish. "I well recollect the night he first brought home the raw hide," she later wrote. The usual penalty was five or six strokes, for any imagined slight. "I often told him he would kill me," she recalled, "but he said he didn't care, that the gallows had no terrors for him."[45]

Matthews bellowed that she didn't understand him, that she was faithless. All she wanted was a new stove, or some new clothes, or a better apartment, or some other worldly comfort. She stood in the way of all he was destined to accomplish, especially in his religious work. A bad spirit had entered the woman, he said, a spirit that traveled out from her to others and opposed him at every turn. The whippings, supposedly, drove the spirit out.

Margaret, ashamed and fearful, told no one of what happened. The women of the neighborhood may have overheard and spread the word, but no one interfered.[46]

One evening in 1829, while in the midst of a spell, Matthews heard some ladies and a minister—not John Ludlow—praying in the consistory room of the North Dutch Church.[47] The noise intrigued him, just as the Zion Church blacks and Mordecai Noah and Ludlow had intrigued him before. The minister was Edward Norris Kirk, late of Albany's Second Presbyterian Church, who had engineered an evangelical schism and was using North Dutch (with the kindly Ludlow's permission) as a temporary meeting place. The sounds that Matthews heard from inside were the first rumblings of Albany's Finneyite revival.

5

Beloved Bro. Finney,   Albany, April 14th, 1829

Our correspondence was closed too soon by my increasing cares. I have rejoiced to hear that the Lord is still permitting you to gather gems for the Redeemer's Crown. Oh brother Finney how this employment & these results will be estimated when the delusions of time have passed away & we are in the world of truth & holiness! I rejoice that to you it is still given not only to believe but also to suffer for his name. The Lord is scattering a few mercy-drops in this parched vineyard. Bro. Beman has assisted me. His head work was excellent, but his heart was too cold. Our meetings are crowded & solemn. The females in our church are in some measure awake. But upon the men the Lord has not poured that agonizing Spirit of prayer which precedes the outpouring of convicting and converting influences. . . . But I think the Lord is shewing us that he is ready to bless faithful efforts to tear down the throne of Satan here & crown Jesus Lord of all. Some few Christians here are beginning to see the utter inconsistency of praying for grace, any more than for crops of grain, where the requisite instrumentality is not employed. The responsibility of private Christians is not extensively felt. To creep to heaven & do no harm is about the amount of what the most of professors aim to attain. The idea of a determined, fierce attack upon the battlements of Satan is not in their creed & liturgy. . . .

Give me some analysis of the refuges of lies to which awakened sinners fly; and shew me how you beat them out.

Pray for us. Yours in Jesus.

E. N. Kirk[48]

Kirk had arrived in Albany in June 1828, at the invitation of the Reverend James Chester of the Second Presbyterian Church. Chester, an avuncular Old School Presbyterian, was always on the lookout for bright young ministerial talent to serve his church part-time. Now gravely ill, he needed to travel south in order to recover from the harsh Albany winter. (He would die the following year.) Kirk came with strong credentials from the com-

missioners of the American Board of Missions and from the impeccably conservative Princeton Seminary, where he had completed his studies two years earlier. As soon as he assumed
Chester's duties, however, he shocked the congregation to
distraction—for he turned out to be a convert to Charles Finney's
crusade.[49]

Second Presbyterian had its own claims to prestige, and was
an unlikely breeding ground for evangelical enthusiasm. It had
been formed as the main church for the city's relocated New
Englanders—a tie symbolized by the codfish and golden pumpkin
emblems on the weathervane atop its fine building. In time, the
church also attracted some of New York State's leading politicians, including men with scant devotion who attended services
as a way of keeping up appearances. Governor De Witt Clinton,
a pious Christian, was a member until his death in February 1828.
In a nearby pew sat Clinton's arch-rival, Martin Van Buren, along
with some of Van Buren's chief political cronies.[50]

To the Van Buren men in particular, Kirk's arrival was embar-
rassing. Finneyite evangelicals had been making trouble for them
for months in the western part of the state—chastising the self-
styled democratic pols for their compromised views on religion,
their tolerance of Sabbath-breaking, their measured distance from
Christ. (Over the ensuing decade, the political and cultural battle
lines would harden, dividing moralistic Finneyite Whigs from
anti-evangelical Jacksonian Democrats). Now one of these extremists was in Van Buren's own church, denouncing the "ecclesiastical formalism" that had overtaken the services and scolding
the congregation for valuing the prominence of their celebrated
fellow church-goers more than the living God. Chester had never
demanded too much from his listeners, but Kirk made them pay
attention, with booming sermons that caused some of the ladies
to sway and grab the pew in front of them. Immediately, the
church's lay leadership decided that Kirk needed some correction.

The assignment fell to Van Buren's law partner, Benjamin Butler—a Regency fixer, future attorney-general of the United States, and Second Presbyterian Church trustee.[51]

Butler had Kirk stop by his law office, where he and the other church trustees confronted the minister with the complaints about the services. Instead of replying, Kirk asked one of the men to lead the group in prayer, in a confused scene that Kirk later recounted with pleasure:

> The appearance of these gentlemen was literally comical. Their manner seemed to say, "What! Prayer in a lawyer's office in State Street, at nine o'clock in the morning?" The thing is right; but if anyone should come in it would seem very queer. To be sure, it [that is, lawyering] is the King's business, but it will not do to have Him take part in it.

After an uneasy silence, the men shuffled their chairs, rigged up a curtain to hide the proceedings from the office scriveners, then prayed.[52]

The meeting sealed the minister's fate and the next day he received his dismissal letter along with his back pay. Yet Kirk also had a small number of supporters. Some gentlemen members of Second Presbyterian paid a visit and congratulated him for his courage. When the dissenters failed in a petition drive to have Kirk reinstated, a number of them formally withdrew from the congregation and helped Kirk establish his own prayer circle. The group's initial prospects looked dim. The vast majority of the breakaway dissidents consisted of a band of about forty women, with neither the money nor the clout to sustain a fledgling congregation. And even among his original supporters, Kirk later recalled, there were those who suspected that the secession was "an unholy enterprise, unwise and uncalled for," that had emanated from Kirk's own "fanaticism and boyish indiscretion." But with the help of his good friend, the evangelical Reverend

Nathan S. S. Beman of Troy, and with the timely intervention of John Ludlow, Kirk was able to consolidate his secession at the North Dutch consistory. There he laid the institutional founda-tions for what would become Albany's Fourth Presbyterian Church.[53]

Kirk's initiative had all of the familiar theological and social makings of the Finneyite evangelical revivals. His sermons forth-rightly denounced the mainline Calvinist churches' "extravagant views of human depravity and inability"—views which had turned men into machines, with their "responsibility entirely de-nied" and their "sense of obligation paralyzed." All vestigial be-liefs in predestination fell away in Kirk's services, as did the idea that evil was the inevitable offspring of man's innate depravity. Salvation, Kirk thundered, was a matter of choice; sin and disor-der would abate only when men and women chose to live righ-teously, had a heart-felt conversion, and set to work getting other wrongdoers to heed His word. In place of the "half-day" worshipping of other churches, Kirk's Sunday services lasted from eight in the morning until long after dark; shorter prayer meetings gathered each morning at six (before business hours). At other times, Kirk's followers spread out across the city, greet-ing strangers and then asking them if they loved the Lord, and if they did, had they heard the Reverend Mr. Kirk preach?[54]

In its first year, Fourth Presbyterian gained 134 new mem-bers—a modest success by the standard of other revivals, but enough to encourage Kirk to stay the course. Most of the congre-gation's men came from the ranks of the city's middle-class mer-chants, professionals, and public officials, much as in the other evangelical churches in the rapidly developing northeastern cities. But the truly striking thing about Kirk's group (again, like the other evangelical churches) was the decisive role that women played in expanding its size. At the height of the Albany revival, two-thirds of the new members were females who entered on their own or with female relations. And behind this statistic lay Kirk's evangelical rejection of the Calvinist patriarchal order in favor of an image of womankind as the chief uplifting force within families and the community at large. "[T]he hope of human society and the hopes of the Church of God," he contended, "are to be found in the character, in the views, and in the conduct of mothers." After seceding from "the worldy men [who] had held the church in check too long," Kirk's most fervent followers created a community of revivalist women, backed by obliging husbands and fathers, themselves now converted to loving, evangelical restraint.[55]

The wife-beater Robert Matthews could hardly have realized where he was headed when, after overhearing the evangelicals' prayers, he approached Kirk and asked about joining the congregation. Kirk did not forget the encounter:

> In our first interview, his conversation was sensible, scriptural, and in the highest tone of the reforming spirit. But there was nothing very remarkable to make a favourable or unfavourable impression. He subscribed a small sum towards the erection of our church edifice. It was remarked at the time by some of whom had purchased lumber, "He is a lazy, thriftless, dishonest fellow, and will never pay it." Whether the declaration was true or not, the prophecy was.[56]

Matthews may have known little, if anything, about the rumors, and he was sure that he had come to Jesus just as Kirk told all the faithful they could. He attended Kirk's services regularly; at work, he again began hounding other carpenters about their swearing and drinking; their ridicule brought back his old moods (which, in turn, put Margaret on her guard to watch her tongue lest he reach for the raw hide). Finally, he stopped working completely and turned to full-time evangelizing, leaving his family without decent food and clothing. At the dinner table, he led strange prayers over the meager evening meals, extending his arms above his head, standing, not bowing, in the presence of the Lord (in this as in other respects he remained a Jew), sometimes weeping bitterly for the sins of the people (this more in keeping with Anti-Burgher devotions). Margaret, aghast, would leave the premises during family worship.[57]

As Margaret later recalled, her husband especially admired the evangelical preachers' moral bravery. "He was sensibly affected in view of the wickedness of the world," she wrote, "and the great need, as he said, of ministers speaking with boldness, and without fear of offending their hearers, or wounding their feelings." The challenges laid down by Kirk and his associate Beman far surpassed the gentle nudging of the Dutch Reform preacher John Ludlow. (A few of Kirk's own congregants actually complained about the sermons, especially Beman's, which commanded all those who would not be saved to depart and go to hell.) Above all, Kirk had stood up to some of Albany's—and the nation's—leading citizens, the kinds of men who had prospered while Matthews failed. Ludlow merely tugged at his congregants' consciences; Kirk had ripped into the rich and powerful men in their very own church, and then carried away forty of their wives and daughters. For Matthews, the displaced working-class patriarch, it must have been a powerful display of manly piety.[58]

Yet as any of Kirk's true followers could have told him, Matthews was laboring under profound misconceptions about the revival. Despite all of his protestations of faith, he was violating the most basic precepts of evangelical manhood, with his unsteady work habits, his self-glorification, and his domestic tyranny. The more he tried to impress Kirk and the others with his devotion, the more they found him wanting. When he finally applied formally for admission, he could not keep from lodging severe charges against two of Kirk's most reputable congregants—further proof, Kirk remembered, "that we should bring a firebrand into our society if he were admitted." After a few discreet inquiries, the membership rejected Matthews's application—and, in predictable evangelical fashion, turned their attentions instead to his long-suffering wife and children. Right away, Kirk presented Margaret with a cloak and bonnet, and with suits for the boys so that they should not be ashamed to be seen in church. The Christian ladies welcomed her as a victim of devilish masculine passions. Although Margaret apparently did not enroll in the church, she accepted the evangelicals' kindness and began attending their services.[59]

Matthews, humiliated, made a last-ditch effort to live as Kirk and the others approved. He stopped his bullying. He took a new job making sashes for the Albany City Hall. He attended meetings of the Young Men's Bible Society and applied for admission to a Methodist church. But the Methodists knew all about his reputation and turned him away. And when Matthews showed up again for one of Kirk's Sunday services, the minister halted the proceedings, shamed him for daring to show his face in God's house, and forced him to leave. Asked by his wife why he had returned home so early, Matthews told her of the scolding, then remarked that Kirk knew very well that he was a friend of God's, but that a poor man like himself, lacking the loaves and fishes, could expect to be mistreated.[60]

Margaret did her best to ignore her husband and continued to pray at the evangelical meeting house, where Charles Finney himself had come the previous July to stoke the Albany revival. Matthews retired to his Bible and to a commentary on the Book of Revelation by the theologian Alexander McLeod, reading furiously, working little. He claimed that he had visions of great events about to take place on the earth, and he stopped people on the street to tell them what he had seen. Having found no place in other men's churches, he began to invent a religion of his own.[61]

6

On a Monday in mid-June 1830, Matthews quit work early and returned home, mumbling about how his chisel had fallen from his hand and stuck in his work—God's sign that the time for earthly labor was done. (Learning about what had happened, Margaret could only think of the family's bare cupboard and the unpaid grocer's bill.) After some Bible reading, Robert decided to attend church; he began to wash up and make himself present-able. Suddenly, while lathering his face, he stopped, put away the razor, wiped off the soap, and declared to his wife that the scrip-tures were clear: God had intended that men should never shave. That evening after attending an installation service at a Presby-terian church, Matthews listened as Margaret pleaded for money to pay the exasperated grocer. Calmly he assured her that another way would soon be open whereby everyone would get plenty to eat.[62]

The next morning, after praying with his family over a break-fast of boiled beans, the stubble-faced carpenter headed for City Hall, where he entered the mayor's office and shouted at those present that they should take heed, for God was about to dissolve all the institutions of man. He walked back home to Margaret with a limp. (A cramp, he explained, had come upon him whenever he tried to climb the stoops of rich families who were unwilling to receive his blessing.) After slipping off to rest, he fell into a fitful trance, perspiring heavily: the spartan bedroom dis-solved into a vision of a destroying angel sweeping into Albany; beneath the angel a great flood crashed in from the north and west—a vision, Matthews knew, of the days to come. They could escape, he told Margaret after he awoke—but first he had to baptize her in the Holy Spirit.[63]

Margaret became alarmed as Robert locked the door and approached her carrying a bowl of water, telling her that she had no God, that the husband was the savior of the wife—that as man was not whole without woman, she must accompany him on his escape. But this time, for the first time, Margaret resisted effectively. First she threatened to jump out the window if he came nearer; then, collecting her thoughts, she related a dream she had had the night before in which Mr. Finney *came to her with a Bible in his hand, and after reading a verse to her, asked her if she believed it. She said yes. He then read to her again and again, asking her each time if she believed; to which she answered in the affirmative; and he then told her that she must read it for herself, for the time had come when she must no longer believe what other people said to her, but that she must read for herself.*[64]

The words stung Matthews and he put down the bowl of water and retreated back to bed. Several hours later, aroused by the distant mission bells that announced the start of the mission service (where, Margaret had told him, Mr. Finney was supposed to preach), he picked up his Bible and set off to confront his nemesis. He arrived just after the service ended, and asked permission to address the congregation. The trustees allowed him to say his piece, which turned out be be a discourse on the millennium. Eventually, the sexton lost his patience, doused the lights, and left Matthews to preach alone in the dark.[65]

Matthews now knew that the flood was imminent—as his enemies had blown out the light against the Spirit, he reflected, so their own lights would go out—and he rushed home to save his family. Margaret refused to leave and berated him once more for being such a poor provider, but he managed to persuade his three boys to slip out of the apartment and join him in his flight. Margaret raised the alarm, and when Robert and the boys failed to return after eighteen hours, her new evangelical friends swung into action. Newspaper notices announced the disappearance of an insane man with his three innocent children; ministers prefaced their sermons with descriptions of the missing boys and their father. On the Sunday following Matthews's departure, the mayor of Albany presided over a meeting at the state capitol, which dispatched search committees to the north, where Matthews and the boys had been spotted.[66]

Finally, on that same Sunday, father and sons turned up at his sister's in Argyle, where Matthews had been apprehended the previous day, after disrupting a local church sacrament lecture. (In later years, he would describe this episode in grandiose terms as the Declaration of Judgment that marked the beginning of his kingdom's history.) A few of Margaret's friends collected him and the boys, and Robert was confined as an insane pauper in the Albany almshouse. The children, to everyone's relief, were cold and tired but "comparatively well," one newspaper reported; their father's insanity, "instead of producing personal violence toward his offspring," had led him to act as their protector. The carpenters of Albany immediately circulated a subscription to aid Matthews's distressed family.[67]

At Robert's release two weeks later, Margaret received him back home kindly, struck with Christian compassion for the father of her children—but her forgiveness did not last long. A few days later, her own father, Andrew Wright, paid a visit, and Robert tried to explain to them both why he acted as he did. Their replies to what Margaret called "some of his hard sayings," sent him into a rage—"he said that he was determined to be obeyed by myself and the children"—and he ordered her to leave the house. Margaret did so, but, concerned for her children, she stopped by the mayor's office to find out what she could do—and learned that, in the eyes of the law, she could do very little. Divorce was out of the question: New York law barred full divorce except in cases of adultery. And although the Reverend Mr. Kirk might easily condemn Robert Matthews, being a bad husband was not, in itself, a criminal offense. (If it were, Albany's jails would be badly overcrowded.) Wife-beating was another matter; if he struck her, the men at the mayor's office advised, the police would confine him for sixty days. Margaret returned home and Robert allowed her back in; noïsy rows ensued over the next few days (though apparently without the raw hide), and the police finally did come and take Matthews away. But within several hours, he returned, released for lack of any credible charge.[68]

Too debilitated to look for work, Margaret begged for food from her friends and neighbors. (She eventually found the boys some paying jobs with a printer and a tobacco manufacturer.) As for Robert, his bearded appearance began to provide plenty of material for the neighborhood gossips. At the time, mass-printed, illustrated family Bibles were reaching the homes of humble believers. Those who saw Matthews were struck by how, whether accidentally or by design, he had come to resemble closely the engravings of Jesus Christ.[69]

In June 1831, Matthews packed up once more, destined this time for western New York State. He had thought long and hard since his first prophecy failed, poring over scripture, reflecting on everything that had happened since his childhood, mixing class resentment with a new-found hatred of preachy Christian women. Gradually, the pieces fell into place. Polished, well-educated, self-professed Christians like Edward Kirk were really devils, he now realized, come to spread disorder in the world. They achieved their objective by wresting women from their godly subordination to men and by telling them that they had special powers. Together, the genteel evangelicals and their female dupes would wreak havoc, until a messenger of the Lord appeared to undo their trickery. In the end, God would destroy the mock-men Christians and put women back in their proper place.

As he headed west, toward the center of the Finneyite revivals, the final bits at last made sense. His own name, he began to understand, had a special significance, although just how he figured this out remains unclear. In the Bible, Matthias had been the disciple chosen by God to replace Judas after the latter betrayed Christ. And in various church and secular histories, a man named Jan Mathys—rendered in English as "Matthias"—figured large in the chapters on the German Reformation.

Mathys, a Dutch baker and prophet, had traveled to Münster in the early 1530s along with his disciple, Jan Boockelszoon, later renowned in the English-speaking world as John of Leyden. Under Mathys's leadership, the city's Dutch immigrant population helped galvanize the resident plebeian radical Protestant party to elect a majority to Münster's city council. An alliance of Catholic and Lutheran princes, outraged at the insurgency, laid siege to the city in 1534–35, and Mathys was killed. John of Leyden, however, assumed the chief prophet's mantle and established an apostolic kingdom within the besieged city walls, governed by a strictly enforced community of goods and a subjugation of women to men.

For months, John of Leyden ruled over his New Jerusalem (which Mathys had renamed Mount Zion) wearing an elaborate royal wardrobe of silks and velvets ordered from local drapers and tailors. Finally, in the spring of 1535, the city fell to the princes' troops, and Leyden and his cronies were tortured and executed. Yet their exploits did not die with them. Three centuries later, the story of the Münster holy men and their beliefs was familiar to anyone versed in Protestant history. According to the best-known English account of the episode, Matthias (that is, Mathys) was the all-important protagonist, responsible for all the kingdom's proceedings—a man "who, in the style and with the authority of a prophet, uttered his commands, which it was instant death to disobey."[70]

Matthews may have read these lines. (Some later commentators strongly suspected he had.)[71] But no matter what his sources were, by 1831, the Coila carpenter at last knew who he really was, and he could not wait to reach the canal-city of Rochester, where he would proclaim himself to a weary world. He was not, he now knew, Robert Matthews at all. He was Matthias, Prophet of the God of the Jews. He had come, like John Ludlow, to bind up the broken-hearted, and to gather the faithful on the heights of Zion. But he did not bring the word of Ludlow's Christ, or of Edward Kirk's; not the word of the Zion Church blacks or of the Reverend Thomas Beveridge; not the unreliable word of his fellow Jew, Noah; but the Holy Word of the one true Lord, the Word of God the Father.

7

Rochester was roaring with the conversions of hundreds of women and their businessmen husbands. It was the Finneyites' grandest triumph thus far, the greatest revival of religion the nation had ever seen, in one of America's fastest growing cities. The Prophet Matthias was sure that he could capture the revival for himself and rout the phony Christians. But before he did that, he would look around Rochester for his long-lost older brother John, an imaginative man who had left Washington County years earlier. For one last time, on the eve of his great mission, the Prophet would make contact with his original family.[72]

J. L. D. Mathies, as John called himself professionally, was a free-thinking artist, and he did not care at all for the evangelicals. Since leaving Washington County sometime around 1815, he had taken his family's original Scots surname, entered into a series of brief business ventures in Canandaigua, and become an accomplished portraitist—far better than most of his fellow country limners who, on commission, would commit awkward likenesses of local farmers and merchants to posterity. Mathies looked elsewhere for beauty and the sublime, in the faces of gentle mystics and Indian warriors. In 1816, he sought out and painted the ex-Quaker Publick Universal Friend, Jemima Wilkinson, whose liberal preachings on love, sexual equality, unlimited salvation, and modified communism guided a community of believers in nearby Yates County. Four years later, Mathies executed a portrait of the Seneca chief Red Jacket.[73]

Unable to support himself either by his painting or his little businesses (a soda fountain then an oyster and porter house), Mathies relocated to Rochester in 1823, where he became the landlord of the Clinton House hotel and continued with his art work. Like other painters of the day, he was fascinated with the terrors of the natural world, which he captured in views of Niagara Falls and two canvases of the wreck of the steamboat *Walk-in-the-Water* on Lake Erie in 1821. But he was most interested in portraying the Senecas, still to be found in western New York. Such savagery had no place in Christian homes; still, Mathies had ways to get his work displayed. He saw to it that his portrait of Red Jacket, perhaps his finest picture, won pride of place on the wall in the entryway of the Clinton House parlor.[74]

As it happened, another creative Matthews brother, James Mathies, had also ended up in Rochester. James was a mechanical inventor, a poet, and something of a drinker. A firm anti-evangelical and supporter of Andrew Jackson, he, like J. L. D. had fallen away from the religion of his youth in favor of freethought. Yet also like J. L. D., he took pride in his Scots background (and in the Mathies name), and he couched his satiric verse in the brogue of Coila. Reminiscent of Robert Burns's "Holy Fair," the poems reflected what J. L. D. called his brother's overly sensitive mind, "most sensibly alive to insult and injury, even so much so that he was often rendered almost miserable by bare suspicion." By the sound of things, he had suffered most acutely from the insults of Rochester's middle-class Christians.[75]

James despised the evangelicals and their political supporters (on their way to becoming Whigs) who were "not satisfied wi' fu' command / On fair conditions." Religion, he allowed, was perfectly fine when rightly understood, for it improved people's morals—but too often, religious zealotry had ventured beyond improvement and *"caus'd many quarrels."* The effrontery of Rochester's evangelical zealots, in particular, knew no bounds. "It seems to be their prayer sincere, / To have our Congress interfere, / To gar us *whip our keg o' Beer,"* Mathies wrote. The Christians, having "gied rules for us to think," were "forging fetters link by link"; and, said Mathies, "what is mair provoking, / They now are on the very brink, / To stop our *Smoking."*

When he moved off religion and politics, James ridiculed other Rochesterians, reserving special scorn for the city's urbane young women, so different from the dutiful rustic mothers and daughters he remembered from his youth:

> But now-a-days their only study,
> Is t' fix themsel's both vain and gaudy,
> Wi' heads and t***s without a body
> To trap the men,
> But who, except a dandy noddy,
> Wad tak them then.
>
> Unnat'ral and outlandish trash,
> Na ane in ten can bake or wash,
> Nor even cook a plate o' hash,
> That's fit to eat,
> Their only drift is to cut a dash,
> And rin the street

Although James and Robert had long since parted ways—and although they resolved their hurts and grudges very differently—the two brothers would have found they had a lot in common, especially on the subject of women. But James died suddenly before they could meet, quite possibly of alcohol abuse. J. L. D.

collected his brother's manuscripts, arranged for their publication, and wrote an affectionate introduction. By the time Robert turned up in Rochester, James had been dead for nearly a year.[76]

Still, even without the poet James it must have been a fascinating reunion, of the Prophet Matthias and the painter J. L. D. Mathies. Both men had forsaken their fathers' faith. Both despised Finneyism and its new moral order. It would be interesting to know what J. L. D. made of his brother, what memories the two might have shared, and what Matthias may have learned about James's poetry and early death. All that survives is a report that the two men quarreled and that the Prophet left Rochester two weeks later, his mission a total failure.[77]

The surrounding countryside suited Matthias better, especially the little towns simmering from the Freemason controversy. Five years earlier, William Morgan, a disgruntled ex-Mason, had vanished near his home in Batavia, New York, which raised suspicions of foul play by a Masonic conspiracy. Popular distrust of the Freemasons, as a closed society with sinister business and political aims, had long been latent. Now provoked by the Morgan scandal, and helped along by the political enemies of Martin Van Buren (himself a prominent Mason), Anti-Masonry became a potent political force, uniting a coalition of farmers, Finneyite evangelicals, and wealthy Clintonians. James Mathies, in some of his sharpest poetic polemics, denounced the Anti-Masons as liars, dupes, and nincompoops, "who'd make the whore o' Babylon sware/If in Communion"—the standard Jacksonian view.[78]

Normally indifferent to politics—and a fierce anti-evangelical—Matthias nevertheless took an interest in Anti-Masonry, as an attack on the hidden interlocking power of the rich and well-born. For weeks, he traveled the back roads of New York State, declaring that the Masonic lodges and all other secret institutions were henceforth abolished. By November, he had worked his way back to Albany, full of preposterous stories about the thousands whom he had converted, and carrying what he claimed were the bits of William Morgan's clothing. A troubled reunion with his family ended after three days, when Margaret told him to leave if he did not intend to work. Matthias traveled west again, then south and east to Washington, D.C., and finally up the coast to New York City.[79]

New York had changed nearly as much as he had. Manhattan was now a major international port, its population three times what it had been in 1808, when Robert Matthews had first arrived. Fortunes beyond the wildest hopes of earlier generations had piled up in the Pearl Street countinghouses. And with metropolitan wealth had come metropolitan poverty, Old World poverty. The little house on Henry Street where Matthews had started out now abutted the wretched Five Points slum.[80]

The Prophet, too, was a frightening sight, even to hard-boiled New Yorkers who were used to seeing the down-and-out strewn about city sidewalks. His beard had grown luxuriant, out of keeping with the prevailing clean-shaven style of the day. (Urban dandies had begun wearing mustaches, but in city and countryside alike, Americans recoiled at the sight of full beards as unsightly and offensive.) His eyes widened in fury at the least hint of an insult. Taking his missionary turns while sitting straight-backed on an old, half-starved horse, he was an obvious mark for street urchins, who pointed and snickered and tried to pull at his whiskers until he chased them off with a menacing scowl.[81]

Matthias spent most of his days on his sacred rounds, preaching to whomever he could get to listen. He thought to look up his brother-in-law, Andrew Wright, but when Andrew asked him why he had abandoned Margaret and the children, Matthias broke into curses and declared that he had entered the devil's house. Thereafter, when he was not preaching, he mainly kept to himself, retreating in the evenings to a rooming house near the Battery.[82]

Years later, an anonymous informant supplied the journalist William Leete Stone with a memorandum, which contained the most detailed account we have of the Prophet's countenance and religious dogma as of the spring of 1832: ". . . I was acquainted with a lodger in the same house with Matthias. . . . My friend was desirous that I should have a conversation with the prophet, as they called him, and managed that an interview should take place at the tea-table. I treated him with great respect, and used no small degree of delicacy in my own questions; this deference seemed to win his confidence, and he gave me something of his creed. I followed up my inquiries in a second interview, but found that he had in some measure changed his ground; but taking all that he said together, as far as such incongruities could be put together, it was this: —That from time to time God had sent his messenger on earth to enlighten mankind, from Moses to Jesus Christ, and from him to Matthias himself. Of his own nature he spoke freely: he acknowledged that he belonged to the human race, but had been set apart as a chosen vessel to be filled with inspiration of a lesser or greater degree, as the Father directed his services; and that sometimes he was ordered to speak in the first person. He did not appear to have a very extensive knowledge of the Bible in general; his recollection of the prophecies was good. He was particularly fond of quoting from Isaiah, and more than insinuated that the prophecies concerning the Messiah, which he quoted, were said of him and his mission. He seemed vain of his person, and quite charmed with his beard. On my pushing a few questions a little closer on my next visit, he became quite cautious of committing himself, and I found it would be useless for me to spend any more time on him and his creed. I thought him to be more of a knave than a fool; but still, I believe, at that time, he was a dupe to his own fraud, as the actor made himself crazy by so often repeating the character of the madman."[83]

Another lodger learned rudely one morning that one did not

trifle with the Prophet. Accosting the man (with whom he had not yet spoken), Matthias asked him to guess his age. The bemused stranger said he had no idea; Matthias told him that he had been on the earth more than eighteen hundred years.

"The devil you have," the stranger replied, "then all I have to say is, that you are a remarkably good looking fellow for your age!"

With that, the Prophet cracked a sardonic smile, became indignant, said the stranger was a devil, and walked away.[84]

Fully expecting that he would impress the masses, Matthias dropped in at the tiny newspaper office of the anti-evangelical free-thinker Gilbert Vale. Despite their theological differences, the Prophet hoped that Vale might lend him a hand against their common Finneyite foes and do some printing for him free of charge. Vale recognized his visitor at once as a man he had seen lecturing to street crowds. The preacher's doctrines—about the evils of clerics who visited women and who tried to convert them in the absence of their husbands—had struck Vale as odd. But otherwise, the editor sized up Matthias as only the latest in a series of deluded unfortunates who wandered the streets of lower Manhattan, predicting the end of the world or the coming of Christ, or some other humbug. Vale turned down the Prophet's request—but the two would meet again.[85]

No one knows exactly how Matthias came to hear about the strange doings that had taken place on Bowery Hill, or about the man who called himself the Tishbite. The only certain thing is that on May 5, 1832, the Prophet rode into Fourth Street and found the right house, where the black-skinned mystic servant, Isabella Van Wagenen, answered his knock at the door and received him warmly.

Pearl Street, New York City, c. 1831. *"Pierson and his fellow Pearl Street merchants were a new breed of urban businessman"* (p. 18).

The Five Points, New York City, 1827. *"Passing through crowds of dirty children and idle men, stepping over passed-out drunks and heaps of garbage and excrement, Sarah and Elijah confronted fallen women on their own territory"* (p. 34).

Sing Sing, New York, c. 1840. "In April 1832 . . . Benjamin and Ann Folger and their three children had moved into a country place near Sing Sing, a thriving village on the Hudson some thirty miles north of Manhattan" (p. 103).

THE PROPHET!

A

FULL AND ACCURATE REPORT

OF THE

JUDICIAL PROCEEDINGS

IN THE

EXTRAORDINARY AND HIGHLY INTERESTING CASE

OF

MATTHEWS, *alias* MATTHIAS,

CHARGED WITH HAVING

Swindled Mr. B. H. Folger,

OF THE CITY OF NEW-YORK,

OUT OF CONSIDERABLE PROPERTY:

WITH THE

Speeches of Counsel, and Opinion of the Court on the motion of the District
Attorney, that a *Nolle Prosequi* be entered in the Case.

ALSO,

A Sketch of the Impostor's Character,

And a detailed History of his Career as a "Prophet," together with many other Particulars, which
have not hitherto been published.

BY W. E. DRAKE, CONGRESSIONAL AND LAW REPORTER.

NEW-YORK: PRINTED AND PUBLISHED BY W. MITCHELL, 265 BOWERY,
And may be had of him, and all the Booksellers.

1834.

Price Six Cents.

Cover of W. E. Drake's Pamphlet
The Prophet!, 1834. *"Newspapers
around the country picked up their a
counts; pamphleteers began composir
exposés confirming rumors about the
Kingdom's sexual practices"* (p. 146

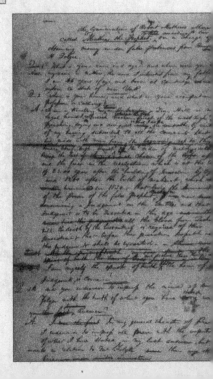

Transcript of the Police Examination of Matthias the Prophet,
1834. *"A bewildered Manhattan
police scribe did his best to take
down what the Prophet was saying"* (p. 145).

THREE

❦

The Kingdom

I

POVERTY AND OLD CLOTHES would have made most visitors
uncomfortable in Elijah Pierson's house, but Matthias was no
ordinary man. He was taller than most, and a second-hand coat
could not disguise his sinewy frame and the stateliness with
which he moved. His hair and beard were the color of ashes; his
stare projected power and danger.

Matthias was a carpenter as well as a prophet, and he surveyed Pierson's parlor with the eyes of both. Most of the usual
gentleman's adornments—the carpets, the drapes, the brass
fixtures, the mirrors—were gone. But where the carpets had
once been there were the matched grains and careful dowelling of
a rich man's floor. The undraped windows revealed graceful
moldings and clear, heavy glass. Everywhere there were straight
lines, perfect woods, an air of spaciousness and peace. Pierson
had stripped the room to make it fit for preaching and prayer,

but the prophet from the Battery would have known better. For all its pretense to humility, the place breathed understated money.

Isabella brought Elijah Pierson into the parlor.[1] He was the kind of man Matthias would convert or destroy, a merchandiser who made money through what the Prophet deemed effeminate mock-work that impoverished better men. Pierson never grew angry and seldom raised his voice. He spent long hours praying on his knees, and he preached errors to women when their men were not around. He had shared his God-given power as a husband and father with a Christian wife who prayed and talked out of turn. Then, when that woman died, he had spent months sobbing and mourning like a little girl. Pierson's companion Sylvester Mills (whom Matthias met either this day or soon thereafter) was no better—another Christian merchandiser in mourning, another of the frightened men who walked the earth in these, the last days of the gentiles.

Matthias told Pierson that it was a big mistake to pray for the Son's Kingdom, when it was the reign of the Father that was at hand. Matthias's mission was to establish that reign of Truth and redeem the world from devils, prophesying women, and beaten men.

The Father's Kingdom had begun, Matthias said, with the Declaration of Judgment at Argyle on June 20, 1830. At that Pierson looked up, puzzled and excited, for it was on that same day that God had spoken to him on the omnibus. Matthias listened carefully and thought quickly. Yes, he said, he had commissioned Pierson as Elijah the Tishbite on June 20. And while Elijah preached and prayed, Matthias had suffered ridicule, poverty, and imprisonment at the hands of the gentiles, until he came to Fourth Street and found the first Jew fit to enter his Kingdom. Elijah Pierson, Matthias explained, had ceased to be Elijah Pierson when the spirit of Elijah the Tishbite had entered his body on the omnibus. Now that spirit was joined by the spirit of John the Baptist, and John the Baptist was finally in the presence and under the protection of the living Spirit of Truth. It all made sense to Elijah, and at the end of the interview he and Matthias rose, went into another room, and washed each other's feet. Elijah preached in his parlor chapel the following Sunday. He finished, turned his pulpit over to Matthias, and never preached again.

In mid-May, Matthias, dissatisfied with the accommodations on Fourth Street, moved into the house of Sylvester Mills.[2] He took over the best rooms for himself, set aside the downstairs for feasting and preaching, and taught Truth to a dying world. His lectures regularly drew fifty to sixty hearers, among them the worried Christian friends of Elijah Pierson. It is from them that we obtain reports of what took place.

All that summer, Sylvester Mills's neighbors complained about the noise. At his evening meetings Matthias preached in a rage, his arms waving, his great voice screaming that the gentiles and their womanish world would burn: "Ours is the mustard-seed kingdom which is to spread all over the earth . . . ," recorded a speed-writing Christian auditor. "All real men will be saved; all mock men will be damned. When a person has the Holy Ghost, then he is a man, and not till then. They who teach women are of the wicked. . . . All who admit members into their churches and suffer them to hold their lands and houses—their sentence is, 'Depart ye wicked, I know you not.' All females who lecture their husbands, the sentence is the same. The sons of truth are to enjoy all the good things of this world, and must use their means to bring it about. Every thing that has the smell of woman will be destroyed. Woman is the capsheaf of the abomination of desolation—full of all deviltry. In a short time the world will take fire and dissolve—it is combustible already. All women, not obe-dient, had better become so as soon as possible, and let the wicked spirit depart, and become vessels of truth. . . ."

Along with the sermons came lists of those upon whom Matthias would cast judgment:

All who say that the Jews crucified Jesus

All who say that the first day of the week is the Sabbath

All who say that immersion with clothes on is baptism

All who say that sprinkling is baptism

All who drink wine in bowls

All who eat passover in a lower room

All women who do not keep at home

All who preach to women without their husbands

All merchant tailors who hire women at 4s. per week

All merchandisers, particularly those who buy and sell land

All clergymen, doctors, and lawyers

All men who wear spectacles

All who offend John the Baptist (Elijah Pierson)

In short, Matthias would damn the enemies of the Jews—above all, the meek Christian devils and their disobedient women.

At quieter times and before smaller audiences, Matthias provided details about his own past and the world's future.[3] Matthias was the Spirit of Truth—the male governing spirit, or God. He could enter any body or take on any shape, and had been doing so for thousands of years. His spirit had given life to all the plants and animals, and it remained in them. He had created Adam, and had endowed him with the male governing spirit; during his earthly lifetime Adam was God. (Eve's feminine deviltry prevailed only because Adam left his Spirit in another part of the Garden of Eden.) The Spirit of Truth had entered Abraham, who used it well: "He ruled his household, educated his son himself, and was to be found in his tent-door, through which nothing could pass without his inspection to disquiet the family." The

Spirit then entered each of the prophets and apostles in their turn, and was strengthened each time by the knowledge and faith acquired in a righteous man's life. The Spirit had been Jesus Christ. After the Crucifixion he entered Matthias, the Apostle chosen by God to replace Judas. At the end of New Testament times, the Spirit of Truth made a bargain with death (the devil, the female spirit): Truth would abandon the world, and Christians would reign until Truth returned. Some people (those governed by the male spirit) would remain obedient to Truth; most (female spirits, regardless of their sex) would participate in Christian chaos and disobedience.

The state of things in 1832 was the result of eighteen hundred years of Christian misrule. At the center of Christian deviltry was a system of preaching and teaching that destroyed Truth. The Spirit of Truth, Matthias explained, was the spirit of male government. God wanted women to have none of it. In the proper order of things the governing spirit passed from father to son in a fixed system of spirit genealogy. When a righteous man died, his spirit joined his father's spirit in the body of a newborn child. The child then carried those spirits through life, adding acquired knowledge along the way. And at his death the child's spirit rejoined the spirit of the father who was his teacher in the body of yet another child. Thus God demanded that fathers teach their families, for that was the one way that Truth accumulated and stayed in patriarchal hands. Other teachers weakened Truth and polluted its divine lineage.

Patriarchs had taught their families until Matthias made his pact with the devil (death, the gentiles, the female spirit) and the world passed into the hands of Christians. The Christians proceeded systematically to steal women and children from fathers. Their preachers lured young and female spirits out of their houses and into churches and prayer meetings. Their teachers put the older children into various schools; they even concocted devilish infant schools for the little ones. In all these places fathers lost their children to other teachers. Weak spirits learned to disregard Truth and to pray, read, and think for themselves. The spirits of the young and female were filled with error and, at death, had no place to go. Truth was hopelessly scattered, and death was really death.

Mercifully, the reign of devils was nearly over. Matthias would preach until 1836; all who had not entered the Kingdom by that date would be damned. Christian confusion would continue for fifteen years after Matthias shut the door. Then, in 1851, the gentile world would burn.

On the day of the conflagration the spirits of Hebrew patriarchs would waken in the men gathered under Matthias. They would walk out of the ruined cities and into a countryside that had been made new. The earth would be pure and green, and it would stretch out forever, for the fire would dry up the sea and turn it into fertile land. The living spirit of an Old Testament hero would govern every father. Each of them would inhabit a rural palace and live in luxury, and each would be surrounded by worshipful children and a happy and dutiful wife. Fathers would give their women and children just enough of the governing spirit to suit their stations. Boys would work with their fathers, then join their sisters at night to learn Truth at the father's feet. Wives would cheerfully assist the patriarchs, bearing their children, preparing their food, keeping their houses spotlessly clean, and obeying husbands who were their only source of knowledge and material support.

The return to Truth would provide each household with far more than it needed, but the surplus would never go to market. In the Kingdom of Matthias there would be no market, no money, no buying or selling, no wage system with its insidious domination of one father over another, no economic oppression of any kind. Independent father-producers would keep what their households needed, then take the rest to the temple in the New Jerusalem—the golden city that Matthias would build in western New York. The ground floor of the temple would be a great warehouse where Levite priests received the surpluses created by farmers and artisans, allowing them to trade for the surpluses of others. Thus the Levite priesthood replaced the market, and every household would live in comfort and independence.

Matthias possessed detailed plans for the temple. It would be much larger than the one that Solomon had built, and the walls, like all the vessels, tools, and much of the furniture in the New Jerusalem, would be fashioned of silver and gold. In the great upstairs hall Matthias would sit, dressed as the king of the world should dress, high on a golden throne. In front of Matthias and beneath him (not above and behind him in the Christian way) would stand a golden altar with a massive gold candlestick with seven branches. To the right and left of the golden candlestick would stand smaller candlesticks of iron, behind each of which would stand lesser thrones. On those thrones, busy with their varied and important duties, would sit Sylvester Mills and Elijah Pierson.

Matthias spent the summer of 1832 teaching Pierson and Mills the ways of Truth—but much of what he said actually had to do with money.[4] Matthias insisted that the earth and everything on it belonged to God. Matthias had worn rags and lived hand-to mouth during the reign of devils. Now the earth would be rid of gentiles and transformed into paradise, and it was time to start furnishing the New Jerusalem and its prophet. Within weeks of his arrival at Elijah Pierson's door, Matthias lived as a wealthy man.

It began, as did so much else in the Kingdom, at the supper table. Matthias ended his religious meetings with meals, and he transformed Pierson's simple suppers into extravagant celebrations of Truth. First he ordered the plain plates and bowls off the table. Then he and Sylvester Mills went to an elegant Broadway shop to inspect its silverware. None of it would do, and Matthias instead ordered custom silver decorated with the Lion of Judah— the beast that would open the book revealing the names of the righteous. (Matthias advised the proprietor to begin manufacturing these exclusively, for soon there would be need for no other.) A few days later Sylvester Mills returned to the shop with a tea service and his family silver, insisting that silversmiths engrave it with the Lion of Judah and fix a silver lion's head around the spout of the teapot. He also asked them to inscribe all his family plate with "The Kingdom is at hand" and other pronouncements, and ordered an engraved silver chalice for the Prophet's personal use.

For his appearances in public, Matthias demanded furnishings and clothing befitting the incarnate Spirit of Truth. Pierson and Mills dutifully provided him with an elegant landau drawn by matched horses, and accompanied him on a tour of New York's finest drapers and tailors. With his followers' money, Matthias built one of the most extravagant wardrobes the city had ever seen. That summer, when he joined the crowds on Broadway and in Battery Park, he descended from his carriage in a black cap of japanned leather shaped like an inverted cone; a military frock coat of the best green cloth lined with pink or white silk and decorated with gold braid, frogs, and fancy buttons; ruffles at his wrists and a black cravat; a fine silk vest and a crimson sash that he also wore around the house; green or black pantaloons; and (depending on the weather) sandals or Wellington boots, highly polished and worn outside the pants. He wore the fine two-edged sword that came from Him who was first and last, and he carried the iron rod with which he would rule the world. Sometimes he appeared with the plumb line that would straighten the people of Israel. He was seldom without the great iron chain and key with which he would lock up Satan in the bottomless pit.

As he paraded down Broadway, Matthias entered various stores, where with eyes burning, chains clanking, and the green coat flashing pink he shouted warnings at the merchants and their astonished customers. On the street and in the park at the Battery he muttered Truth while walking at the edges of crowds. Sometimes he descended from his carriage and walked with great dignity through the park, leading Sylvester Mills's confused children by the hand—a serenely demented vision of what fatherhood can be.

Christians who saw Matthias on the street or who attended his sermons were appalled.[5] The Prophet's vulgar wardrobe and blasphemous pretensions were bad enough, but even more unsettling was the state of their old friend Elijah Pierson. Pierson had always been a bit overzealous, and as he had spiralled out through retrenchment, perfect holiness, and attempts to raise the dead, all but a few of his evangelical associates had turned away. But their love and concern for an old laborer in the field remained, and what had happened since May was horrifying. Some had seen Matthias on promenade, with poor Pierson shuffling alongside him "in constant and reverential attendance." One went to the house of Sylvester Mills and spotted a bent man "sitting in one corner of the room, in the most humble, meek, and docile attitude that can be imagined." The man had long fingernails, mock-prophetic black hair parted in the middle, and a scruffy inch-long beard. It was a long moment before the stunned Christian recognized his old friend Elijah Pierson.

By late summer the black beard covered Elijah's face, and attendance at the Prophet's love-feasts had given him a belly. Charles Sommers, Pierson's old Baptist minister, recorded Elijah's attempts at manly ferocity, his eyes fired with "uncommon lustre, a piercing and almost startling fierceness of expression" twisting his once-gentle face. But Sommers also noted that Elijah was terrified of Matthias, and that when the Prophet showed anger Pierson shrank into himself and "trembled like an aspen-leaf."

Elijah dismissed the queries of his old Christian friends. He was happy that Matthias was teaching him to be a real man. He was happier still with the messages that God gave him at night. He had come to understand that his earlier prayers and conversations with Jesus about Sarah's return had been devilish delusions. God now told him that Sarah would come back from the dead, and that this time she would be a proper vessel of Truth. God also insisted that she would arrive at the time appointed by Him, not earlier. God let Pierson know that the matter was settled, and that He was tired of talking about it.

These conversations took place in June 1832, on the second anniversary of Sarah's death and failed resurrection. At about this time, Sarah paid her last visit to Elijah. It seemed as though she too had been talking with Matthias. "The union God has established between man and wife was brought to view as being one flesh," Elijah recorded in his diary. "Sarah's spirit was with me. It appeared as if we were remarried. She called me Lord."

Elijah wanted to hear it again: "Suppose I felt as a husband ought, in point of office," he asked. "She said, I have peace, my Lord."

2

Matthias knew that gentiles would attack him. He spent the warm months of 1832, like Abraham of old, protecting his door. Within his first few weeks at Sylvester Mills's, he put all of Mills's female relatives out of the house. He also fought off invaders from the outside. When a Methodist girl knocked at the door and announced that she had been sent by Jesus, Matthias whipped her, told her that God did not talk to girls, and sent her home to her father. Pierson's old Christian friends fared little better. Matthias allowed them to stay while they listened, but when they questioned him he roared that in his house there was no teacher but himself, and they all left. The most dangerous of these was Mrs. Bolton, the reformed prostitute who had managed the Asylum House for Sarah and Elijah, and who had been a leading member of Pierson's Fourth Street church. She argued with Pierson's woman-hating Prophet, only to be branded "a devil, and a lewd woman." Bolton fled the house and never came back.[6]

Matthias's victories could not go on forever. In September, Sylvester's brother, Levi Andrew Mills, procured legal papers claiming that Matthias "practiced a system of pretension & hypocrisy for the purpose of defrauding, & that the said Matthews has for several months procured his subsistence thereby." He came to the house with his business associates Thomas M. Hooker and Alexis L. Dias. Behind them stood a larger group of Christian businessmen, and behind *them* stood the police, armed with a warrant claiming that Robert Matthews and Sylvester Mills were "so far disordered in their senses as to endanger their persons, or the persons or property of others, if permitted to go at large." Mills's servant, a man named Galloway, tried to block their path; a few of the intruders rushed past him, snatched Mills, and carried him off. The others, fighting an infuriated Isabella Van Wagenen, pounced on Matthias and wrestled him to the floor. While the Christians lectured Isabella and held her out of the fray, policemen stripped Matthias, took his money, gave his pocketwatch to Levi Mills, and "tormented him in every way." Finally, with Matthias screaming that he was God Almighty and that the gentiles must leave God's house, the police cut off the prophet's beard.[7]

They threw Matthias into the ward for the insane poor at Bellevue.[8] Elijah Pierson and the Prophet's brother, George Matthews, got a bill of habeas corpus and obtained his release. Almost immediately, the police arrested him again, stating that in calling himself God during the first arrest he had violated the New York blasphemy statutes. However, the officials did not want to attempt legal proof that Matthias was not who he said he was, and they agreed to his release.

The Kingdom now lived in fear of the gentiles, and some followers lost their faith and fell away. Sylvester Mills might have stayed, but on his brother's warrant he was confined at the lunatic asylum at Bloomingdale. (Sylvester admired the architecture and concluded that the asylum was a branch of the New Jerusalem, suffering an unfortunate but doubtless temporary occupation by devils.) Isabella Van Wagenen remained true, though her friend Katy, with Pierson's blessings, had returned to her native Virginia. Catherine Galloway, the wife of Mills's servant, joined the Kingdom at this time; she stayed even after Matthias, furious that her husband had allowed the police into his house, cursed him—and then watched him die a slow and agonizing death. (Galloway's sudden demise may, indeed, have proven to his widow that Matthias truly possessed god-like powers.) Pierson's old friend Mrs. Dratch began visiting. Elijah Pierson, of course, stuck by Matthias. Fighting back his fears of mob attack, he let the Prophet move back into his house. Then, in October 1832, Pierson rented a house on Clarkson Street for the Prophet's sole use. Matthias moved in with Van Wagenen as his servant, and stayed through April 1833, preaching at his old haunts on Broadway and along the Battery, and haranguing curious crowds from his doorstep. Whenever necessary, he took time off to lecture his servant on housework.

Over the winter, Matthias and Isabella were joined by the Prophet's brother George Matthews and his family. George was a heavy drinker. The Prophet and his brother argued, and George disappeared one day with much of the furniture. This incident, along with a temporary weakening of his own faith, led Elijah Pierson to cut the Prophet's allowance. Matthias closed the house on Clarkson Street and moved into a hotel. Isabella Van Wagenen went into service with a gentile family, but continued to do the Prophet's laundry. Elijah Pierson tentatively resumed private prayer. The Prophet, his beard regrown, stalked the Battery, alone and in year-old clothes.

3

In April 1832, a few weeks before Matthias arrived at Elijah Pierson's, Benjamin and Ann Folger and their three children had moved into a country place near Sing Sing, a thriving village on the Hudson some thirty miles north of Manhattan. Heartt Place, as the Folgers' new property was named, was a pleasant estate— a mansion house and twenty-nine acres facing the river where it widened into the tranquil and beautiful Tappan Zee. Benjamin bought commercial properties in Sing Sing and transferred some of his business interests up the Hudson. The Folgers joined the neighborhood Baptist church, organized male and female Sunday schools, and settled into a life of rural domesticity and Christian service. Benjamin kept his hardware store on Pearl Street, and when he made the trip to the city he often spoke with Elijah Pierson, in whose house he occasionally boarded. But for the most part the Folgers stayed at Sing Sing and saw little of their old spiritual guide. It came as a shock when, in August 1832, they read newspaper accounts of Elijah, the Prophet Matthias, and their troubles with the police.[9]

In New York the Folgers found Pierson with a black beard, outlandishly long hair and fingernails, and a whole new set of beliefs.[10] Elijah told them that Christianity was the work of devils and that God the Father had returned to set things right. Matthias had taught him Truth, Pierson explained; now Pierson would teach Benjamin and Ann. Their spirits were deformed by Christian teachings and they would at first understand only parts of what he had to say. They must begin by quitting their church, staying away from prayer meetings, and disbanding their ungodly Sunday schools. Ann must not preach or teach; Benjamin must get control of his house.

Sometimes Matthias himself appeared at Benjamin's office on Pearl Street, and by the end of the year, the Folgers were inching toward belief. Pierson declared their marriage by a Christian preacher invalid, and he remarried them in Truth on the last day of 1832. Benjamin Folger helped support Matthias on Clarkson Street (at least until Pierson temporarily lost faith and cut the allowance), and in July 1833, the Folgers left the Baptist church and closed their Sunday schools. Through it all they resided at Sing Sing, and kept largely to themselves. Benjamin's business affairs took him into the interior for long periods of time; Ann spent most days alone in the big house beside the Hudson.

In late August, Ann later testified, "on our return from a short visit to New York we found Matthias at our residence. He had been there about two days."[11] Elijah Pierson had foretold that something like this would happen. He had also warned the Folgers against provoking the angel sent by God. Ann and Benjamin invited Matthias to stay the weekend.

A short time later Isabella Van Wagenen answered her door in New York. It was Ann Folger, accompanied by Elijah Pierson's young daughter Elizabeth. Ann explained that Matthias now lived at Heartt Place, and that she had come to fetch Father's clothes. Two weeks later Matthias himself appeared at Isabella's. Elijah Pierson had also moved to Heartt Place, he said, but he was sick and throwing fits, and Ann Folger needed help in caring for him. Isabella agreed to visit Sing Sing to talk with Pierson and survey the situation. She returned, asked Benjamin Folger to have her furniture sent up the Hudson, and joined Father's new house. The Kingdom of Matthias had moved to the countryside.

Matthias named his new house Mount Zion, and settled into a

life as Prophet and country gentleman. Safe from the police, complaining neighbors, meddling Christians, his followers' kinsmen, and the other persecutors of New York City, Matthias used prophecy and terror—not to mention his disciples' money—to make Mount Zion the first perfectly reformed rural household in the coming Kingdom.

The neighbors later recalled that Mount Zion had looked like any other well-ordered house: the men and boys labored in the fields, and the women and girls worked in the house, all under the command of an authoritative father. In fact, of course, Mount Zion was unique. Work assignments and domestic roles derived not from gentile custom but from Truth: Matthias discerned the spirit inhabiting each follower, then arranged those spirits into a proper and harmonious family. Matthias was not just father but *the* Father, occupied with government and prophecy. He put the men and boys to work on the farm: the stronger men handled the heavy work, the boys helped the men, and Elijah Pierson dithered aimlessly and happily in the garden. From time to time new members entered the Kingdom, and Matthias discerned their spirits and assigned them suitable tasks: an English tailor named Henry Plunkett ("a little bit of a fellow," Isabella Van Wagenen later called him) worked in the garden and made clothes for the children; the German Lewis Basel, another new recruit, became the group's coachman. (Another new member, a Dutchman named Anthony, had an unspecified job.) As for women, Matthias kept them in the house. Isabella performed heavy household work and did most of the cooking; the widowed servant Catherine Galloway assisted Isabella. Pierson's daughter Elizabeth became a chamber maid; the other female children performed chores around the house, while the boys helped out in the garden. Matthias discerned a peculiarly gentle spirit in Ann Folger. He appointed her to wash and groom the children, help with light housework, and direct the kitchen as Father's delegate.[12]

Yet if Mount Zion was based on unique forms of prophecy and terror, the neighbors were not completely mistaken when they saw Matthias's household as a traditional farm family arrangement. Repeatedly, Matthias revived the rural ways he had known in his youth and endowed them with new prophetic meanings. At the heart of his cosmology was a strenuous effort to elevate, in sometimes twisted and exaggerated forms, the ideals of manhood he had learned to respect back in Coila.

Take, for example, Matthias's wardrobe. The prophet dressed at Mount Zion much as he had in New York. His hallmark, as ever, was a perfectly tailored green frock coat with a straight, military collar. He now had several of these coats: some with brass buttons, some with gold braid, some with elaborate frog fastenings, and at least one with a silver sun embroidered on the left breast, a shower of silver stars on the right, and a lining of pink silk. (The green fabric, by one estimate, cost a stupendous $14 per yard.) Matthias wore the coat open to display a waistcoat of buff cassimere or richly figured silk; he never appeared in public without a red sash with twelve tassels around his waist (each tassel representing one of the Israelite tribes). At his wrists and throat were lace ruffles of cambric (a fine, thin material that held starch very well). His pantaloons were always of the best fabric, and he had many pairs; surviving descriptions have him variously in brown, black, green, and white. He wore Wellington boots outside the pantaloons. (Sometimes he wore sandals, and on one occasion gray stockings and pumps.) He kept a collection of strange hats, but seems to have worn his huge green three-cornered hat or his black leather Merlin-the-Magician hat only on special occasions. Matthias seems to have carried his chain and key, his iron rod, and his two-edged sword less often in the country than in Manhattan. New additions were more befitting a country gentleman: he often carried an umbrella and he displayed a gold watch and fob purchased by Benjamin Folger for $115—a replacement for the much cheaper watch stolen at the Prophet's arrest the previous year.[13]

Whatever influence the stories of the garishly dressed Reformation prophet, John of Leyden, may have had on his thinking, the Prophet's custom-tailored wardrobe explicitly recalled the heroic masculinity of the Age of the Democratic Revolution—an age that expected men to possess physical courage and military skills, and that encouraged male elegance and swashbuckling display. His green frock coat was a "Wellington," a close-fit military style with standing collar that was named for the hero of Waterloo. These had appeared in London in 1818 and had enjoyed a brief vogue among the fops of British and American cities before passing out of fashion in the late-1820s. Matthias's cravats and rich waistcoats were in up-to-date dandified style, as were his tight pantaloons. But while gentlemen accompanied their pantaloons with patent leather Hessian boots, Matthias favored the more substantial and imposing Wellington boots. The effect was military, and Matthias finished it off with martial touches: the sword and the red sash that reporters described as "regimental," and *"à la militaire."* The wardrobe contrasted sharply with the garb of fashionable and consciously anti-heroic men of business, who wore modest footwear and who rejected the military frock coat in favor of the morning coat or the more relaxed frock with turned-down lapels and minimal decoration. The Prophet's vaguely out-of-fashion clothing proclaimed in part that God the Father had come to reassert a swaggering, authoritarian, and resolutely anti-bourgeois way of being a man.

At the same time, Matthias attached holy properties to these styles. His full beard and long hair, for example, clashed severely with the clean-cut, military masculinity tied to his heroic wardrobe. (If Matthias was a soldier, he served in the forces of the Old Testament Jehovah.) Moreover, the exquisite tailoring, the silk linings, the showers of stars—the sheer splendor and variety of the wardrobe—spoke a prophetic vocabulary that belonged only to the Prophet. Indoors, where the neighbors did not intrude, Matthias wore intricately stitched linen nightcaps—one with twelve points named for the tribes of Israel, another with twenty-four points named alternately for the Hebrew tribes and the Apostles. He also had a black velvet nightcap with gold stitching that proclaimed him "Jesus Matthias." While testimony from Mount Zion did not mention the magnificent robe that he wore at Sylvester Mills's house in New York, it is almost unthinkable that Matthias would have left it behind.

When queried, Matthias explained his clothes and tools: The white linen nightcaps were "pale mitres"; the green three-cornered hat with gold trim was the rainbow surrounding the head of Him that sits upon the throne; the silk coat linings of pink or white signified Joseph's coat; he wore a crimson sash because Matthias was the one in Isaiah who treads the wine press alone; and the rich green of his coat told the world that the Dove (the Holy Spirit) had at last found a resting place. It was a confused and outlandish pile-up of Biblical references, but to Mount Zion's believers it made perfect sense.[14]

The Prophet's combination of familiar forms with singular religious meanings reappeared at the supper table. Matthias was a prophet of abundance, and every night Isabella and Catherine Galloway piled the table with food. There were flesh meats (excepting pork), along with plenty of poultry and fish. All of these were boiled, for Matthias forbade roasting. Beside the meats sat steaming bowls of rice, beans, and potatoes, along with a wide variety of green vegetables. Matthias loved fresh fruit, procured it in quantity, and encouraged his followers to eat all they wanted. There was of course no alcohol in Father's house. (The family took coffee and tea at different times throughout the day, but the principal mealtime beverage seems to have been water.) Matthias allowed only "plain cakes" on his table; he resolutely banned puddings and pies; witnesses' accounts never mentioned any of the fancy pastries, sauces, spices, jellies, and compotes that were appearing on the tables of the well-to-do. The Folgers testified that even when Matthias replaced retrenchment with abundance "we continued to live plainly in our family." A journalist described the meals as "good plain food," adding that Matthias "banished *pies,* and other superfluities, but *lived well.*"[15]

Within this display of rural plenty, Matthias enforced rules about food and its preparation. Some reflected Jewish law as he understood it. Above all, pork was strictly forbidden. In New York, Matthias had preached hard on the subject: "All who eat swine's flesh are of the devil; and just as certain as he eats it, he will tell a lie in less than half an hour. If you eat a piece of pork, it will grow crooked through you, and the Holy Ghost will not stay in you, but one or the other must leave the house pretty soon. The pork will be as crooked in you as rams' horns, and as great a nuisance as the hogs in the street." Matthias also insisted that fowl destined for his table have their heads cut off; anyone who wrung the neck of a fowl, he explained, "has not got the Holy Ghost."[16]

Parts of the Prophet's food code, however, had nothing to do with even the most wildly imagined Judaism. The ban on puddings and pies and the insistence that meat be boiled and never roasted stemmed not from Matthias's kinship with the ancient Hebrews but from his hatred of new-fangled, middle-class ways introduced by the market revolution. In the early nineteenth century a few grand houses had brick ovens built into the kitchen hearth, but most American housewives knew nothing of baking or oven roasting. They either spitted meat and cooked it in the hearth or—particularly in Coila and other Scots communities—boiled it in a pot; similarly, the hoecakes, pancakes, and johnny cakes that passed for bread in rural America were cooked in the hearth, never baked. That had begun to change in the 1820s. The market revolution brought Caribbean sugar, local eggs, Rochester white flour, and—most important—cast-iron stoves into the more prosperous households; by 1830 oven-roasted meat and fancy baked foods were emblems of a family's economic standing and of its readiness to embrace domestic improvements. The boiled meats and plain cakes of Mount Zion, by contrast, echoed the rustic abundance of the Prophet's half-remembered, half-idealized Coila. They also anticipated the old-style country food to which real men would return when mock men, their preachy women, and their roast beef, white bread, and effeminate pastries had gone up in flames.[17]

Matthias reaffirmed Mount Zion's traditional, rural character when he insisted that the evening meal be called "supper." The urban merchant classes were beginning to eat "dinner" (a word that Matthias and most others reserved for the noon meal) and to practice "dining" as a civilized art. Plain "supper" remained standard in the countryside. Noah Webster's 1828 *Dictionary of the American Language* put it this way: "The dinner of fashionable people would be the *supper* of rustics." Mount Zion was a rural household, in which God's people supped in plain abundance; in New York City, wealthy devils ate dinner.[18]

Supper at Mount Zion dramatized material plenty and familial informality at the same time that it dramatized the absolute dominion of Matthias. Matthias sat at the head of the table, but there seem to have been no formal seating arrangements for the others; the one surviving description has family members simply taking seats that were available. Nor was there the ordered sequence of served courses that typified urban dining. The women prepared the food, put it on the table, and took their seats. Members of the household then served themselves. It was what Americans called the Old English style—standard in all but the highest circles until the 1830s, standard in most country households long after that.

The informality stopped, however, with Matthias. The Old

English style placed the father at the head of the table, from where he led prayers, carved and served the meat, and exercised a quiet authority over the meal. At Mount Zion the Father's dominion was more distant and far less quiet. The women served Matthias separately, bringing plates of food for his sole use; Ann Folger recalled that "all were branded as 'Judases' who dipped their hands in the same dish with him." In New York (there is no evidence that this changed on the farm) Matthias washed his food down with water from his engraved silver chalice; the others drank from ordinary glass tumblers.[19]

At bottom, supper at Mount Zion recalled the family worship meals with John Maxwell, Edward Cook, and the other patriarchs of Coila, along with the great Lord's Supper of the Anti-Burgher Church. Matthias's repeated references to the original Last Supper (his proscription against dipping one's hand in his dish, his denunciation of those who take Passover in a lower room) seem to have been taken seriously; in New York, Sylvester Mills had promised a guest that "he should positively sup with the twelve Apostles." At Mount Zion, Matthias made supper a nightly sacrament that restored God's own balance of domestic intimacy and patriarchal control: a table laden with simple country food; a serving style that reinforced both communality and individual dignity (the family neither ate from common bowls nor waited to be served, but filled individual plates from common vessels); seating arrangements that made for informality within a gendered hierarchy (Matthias served separately at the head of the table, women sitting only after cooking the food and bringing it to the family). Most of all, supper at Mount Zion recalled supper at Coila through its exquisite, father-dominated counterpoint of guilt and redemption. For it was at the supper table that Matthias spun out a fine-tuned spiritual economy that inflicted terror and conviction of sin, then resolved them through obedience to the Father.[20]

From his seat at the head of the table, Matthias disciplined his house and delivered the meandering, often angry sermons that became the one source of Truth at Mount Zion.[21] In New York, Matthias had banished preaching and prayer. Prayer, the means by which Elijah Pierson had gained spiritual power, perfect love, and an ever-deepening fund of apostolic gifts, was "all nonsense." So was Christian preaching: "God don't speak through preachers," raged Matthias, "He speaks through me, his Prophet." For a time at Mount Zion he allowed the Folgers and some of the others to read their Bibles and pray; while they knelt in the Christian manner, he sat upright, closed his eyes, and kept his silence. Within weeks he banned those practices. All that remained were Father's mealtime lectures. He preached for hours, delivering Truth, ordering the details of his house, and dealing out punishments when they were deserved.

In designing the Kingdom's work assignments, Matthias ordered family members to work only at their prescribed tasks, then left them to labor without supervision. He warned, however, that he had granted each of them a part of his own spirit; he would know precisely what they did. When the farm and house ran smoothly, Father congratulated his children, reminding them that they were strong and happy only because through obedience they shared the Father's spirit. When things went wrong, Matthias flew into a rage and threatened his household with terrible judgments. Then he went looking for the disobedient follower who had let the devil into Father's house. These searches involved real terror. Sylvester Mills's manservant Galloway had, after all, suffered a long and painful death under the Prophet's curse. The Prophet's followers, including Galloway's widow, knew that an angry Matthias could do the same to them.

Matthias vented his most awful rages on those who got sick, for sickness was a sure sign of disobedience.[22] Matthias, repeating occult knowledge that had been outlawed by the Reformation but that survived as folk belief well into the nineteenth century, insisted that sick people harbored detached spirits, or devils; blind men had blind devils, cripples had limping devils, and so on. Matthias could cast out these devils, and sometimes did so. But his usual response to sickness in his house was rage. Ann Folger recalled that "the least complaint would bring forth, in the utmost fury, the charge that we were bringing the devil into the house of God, and he would threaten with many curses, such as, shutting up in the bottomless pit,—annihilation—or, if we would thus encourage the devil, we should be subject of disease or leprosy." On one occasion, Matthias whipped Isabella Van Wagenen severely for getting sick; Father's children learned to keep their illnesses to themselves.

The regime seemed to work. Elijah Pierson, for instance, came to Mount Zion beset by "fitty devils," proof that he had not cast off all the delusions of his Christian days. Matthias refused him treatment and left him on his own; within weeks the devils were gone. For her part, Ann Folger enjoyed the best of health. In her Christian days she had often been sick, and she had gone to doctors who gave her pills; like other wealthy Christian women she wasted her days in bed, treating devils with other devils. Matthias took away her pills and demanded that she get well; and Ann got well.

4

The critical turning point in the Kingdom's history—and in the scandal that followed—was Ann Folger's seduction of Matthias. Our witness to that event was Isabella Van Wagenen, the black mystic who worked in the kitchen, shared the household's religious life, and became a loyal yet unsettled witness to its excesses.

Van Wagenen had grown up a slave in the Hudson Valley, and her relation to Mount Zion's Old Testament patriarchy—a truly strange alternative to her own twisted history of family relations—must have been charged and problematic. She was born about 1797 (no one recorded the birth), the youngest but one of her mother's ten or twelve children (again, no one knew the number). Until she was nine she belonged, along with her parents and her younger brother Peter to a wealthy Dutch family named Ardinburgh. When her master died, Isabella was sold alone to a John Nealy, then to an innkeeper named Shriver, and finally to John J. Dumont, a farmer of New Paltz. Isabella was Dumont's slave for eighteen years. She remembered him as a kind master, though she also hinted that terrible events occurred in his house, events she could not reveal "from motives of delicacy and to protect the innocent."[23]

When still in her teens Isabella attracted a young slave named Robert, but the bondage that had robbed her of her mother, father, and brother took her suitor as well. Robert's master did not like the match, and beat him nearly to death in front of Isabella. Dumont then gave her over to a much older slave named Thomas. She bore Thomas four daughters and a son.[24]

Isabella retreated into religion. As a little girl she had learned from her mother that there was a God in the sky, and young Isabella prayed in a voice loud enough to reach beyond the clouds. The illiterate slave girl also heard people talk about Jesus, and assumed that He was like Lafayette, Washington, and other eminent men. She grew certain that one day she would meet Jesus.[25]

Isabella talked to God and waited for Jesus until 1827, when she was about thirty years of age. The State of New York was set to free the last of its slaves by law on July 4, 1827, and Dumont had promised to liberate Isabella a year early. When Dumont reneged, she walked off, leaving behind her husband and all but the youngest of her children. She then went to work for Isaac Van Wagenen, a kindly farmer who bought her remaining slave time from Dumont, and then gave her to herself. (It was from him—and not from any of her owners—that she took the surname she kept for the next sixteen years.)

Isabella was working on the Van Wagenen farm when, at the approach of the Negro festival of Pinkster (Whitsuntide), she began to miss her family and friends and, as she put it, "looked back into Egypt." She predicted that Dumont would come for her the next day. He arrived on schedule. But as she walked toward Dumont, God stopped her in her tracks. In an instant she knew that He was everywhere, not just in the sky. He knew her private thoughts, and He heard her even when she did not shout. Isabella realized that she had accepted God's protection without keeping her own promises, and that she owed Him fearsome debts. Shaking with fear and guilt, her spirit returned to Van Wagenen's barnyard to find that Dumont had gone. "Oh God," she cried, "I did not know you were so big." Clearly, God had plans for Isabella—plans that included neither slavery to John Dumont nor reunion with her husband and children.

That same year Isabella (now Isabella Van Wagenen) joined the Methodist church in nearby Kingston. The simplicity and power of Methodism—its rejection of worldly divisions, its respect for dreams and visions and other forms of lay experience, and its clear emphasis on the loving Jesus over the wrathful Jehovah—attracted her as it attracted thousands of others among the poor and unprivileged. She had experienced Jesus soon after the vision on Isaac Van Wagenen's farm; Jesus was "transcendently lovely," and he stood between her and an angry God. When a Christian friend told her that Jesus and Jehovah—the God of love and the God of wrath—were one, she was overjoyed.

Isabella's experiences and understandings were close enough to what the Kingston Methodists demanded, and they welcomed her and used her spiritual gifts.

In 1828 friends accompanied Van Wagenen to New York City and introduced her to the perfectionist James Latourette. She joined Latourette's household as a servant, and stayed with him even when she worked for other families. She also joined the colored class at the John Street Methodist Church, then switched to the African Methodist congregation on Church Street—the same congregation that had startled and briefly inspired Robert Matthews years earlier. All the while she attended Latourette's perfectionist meetings and lived in his house. By this time she was a formidable presence: angular and nearly six feet tall, with a voice that commanded attention, and with eyes that had seen things denied to others.[26]

The move to New York City opened spiritual possibilities for Van Wagenen. It also introduced her to her older sister Sophia and her brother Michael, siblings she had never met, but who had found their own ways to New York and into the congregation on Church Street. At the same time, Isabella's own slave family moved further and further into the distance. Her aging husband Thomas survived emancipation for a few years, then died in the poorhouse. Isabella paid periodic visits to her children in Ulster County, but does not seem to have become close to them until very late in her life. As late as 1850, a friend hinted that while she was aging and in danger of becoming destitute, her children could have helped but had thus far failed to do so.[27]

Only her son Peter remained. Peter was a special child, probably named for Isabella's lost little brother. Just before Isabella left the Dumont household, John Dumont had sold Peter to a Dr. Gedney, who then gave the boy to a brother-in-law who, in violation of the New York manumission statute, carried him to Alabama and a lifetime of bondage. Resolutely chanting "I'll have my child again," Isabella confronted Mrs. Dumont and Mrs. Gedney, receiving satisfaction from neither of them. She then went to Quakers who had heard of her son's illegal sale, and who helped her to file a complaint with the Grand Jury in Kingston. There she secured a writ to be served by the constable at New Paltz on Mr. Gedney. Gedney's lawyer informed the Alabama in-laws that they risked fourteen years in jail for stealing Peter, and Peter was returned. It was not the last time that Isabella would successfully confront the high and mighty.

Peter accompanied Isabella to New York. But while she joined the households of Latourette, Pierson, and Matthias, Peter fell into bad company and began lying to her, stealing from his employers, and getting into trouble with the police. In 1839, years after the Matthias scandal broke, Peter shipped out on a Nantucket whaler, apparently to avoid further trouble. Isabella received a few letters; then the letters stopped, and Peter was gone. Isabella Van Wagenen never remarried, and never tried to make another family.[28]

Isabella met Elijah Pierson at the Magdalen House on Bowery Hill, befriended his servant Katy, and joined Pierson's household on Fourth Street in the autumn of 1831. It was she who opened the door to Matthias the following spring, and she recognized him right away as the Jesus that she had always expected to meet. But she was puzzled, for Latourette, Pierson, and the Methodists had told her to expect a loving God—not the angry Father who stood before her. When Matthias explained that in this incarnation he was the Father and not the Son, Van Wagenen suspended judgment. She became a believer only when her pious, learned friend Pierson came to believe.[29]

At Mount Zion, Isabella retained the position that she had occupied with James Latourette and Elijah Pierson: she was both housekeeper and a full participant in the household's religious life. Yet Mount Zion's domestic order and the Prophet's rantings on fatherhood and obedience may have touched her differently than they did Elijah Pierson and other damaged white men. It was, after all, slavery, the most perfect patriarchy, that had given her a misshapen, half-intended family and then destroyed it. Later, when Matthias and Ann Folger began to talk not only about male government and female perfidy but about match spirits and holy children, Isabella developed a detached sense of hurt and dread. She believed in Matthias devoutly, and almost surely desired her own match spirit. But with Ann's ascendance in Matthias's affections, she coupled her faith with her own notions of what was going on, notions that had to do less with divine patriarchy than with devilish lust.[30]

From her station in the kitchen Van Wagenen kept a curious watch over Father's new Kingdom. They all seemed to enjoy their new lives. But Isabella noticed that Ann Folger lived out her subjection to Truth more cheerfully than any of the others. Ann had discarded the plain dress of her Christian days soon after Matthias moved in. And as the Kingdom settled into its routine, Ann descended the stairs early each morning, "dressed with much taste, highly scented," and took it upon herself to prepare Father's breakfast seat and to air his clothes and linen. She began sewing and embroidering fancy night caps for Matthias. She presented him with a gold ring. During the days she hovered in the kitchen and asked Isabella (who by now had been with Matthias for a long time) to explain the Prophet's views on every subject. At the nightly feasts she used what she had learned to speak Father's thoughts before he spoke himself. Matthias smiled with pleasure, and pronounced Ann Folger a true possessor of his spirit. Ann claimed the same discovery: she and Matthias were match spirits.[31]

Under Isabella's watchful eye, Ann's attentions to Matthias continued for three months. The two walked in the garden and took long rides in the carriage, sometimes with Ann's children, sometimes alone. Ann kept a pianoforte in her room, and she and Matthias amused themselves at it for hours on end. In their lengthy conversations Ann always deferred to Matthias, but she continued to please him by anticipating his thoughts.

In time, the Prophet's and Ann's religious conversations turned to talk about women and men. Matthias had always maintained that the gentile way of romantic love and free choice of marital partners led to unhappiness, particularly for women. In the Kingdom, marriage would unite compatible spirits, just as harmony at Mount Zion rested on a proper constellation of spirits. Fathers would arrange mates for their children at an early age, then educate young spirits in ways that matched them with their fated husbands and wives.

Ann listened intently. As a result of her earlier immersion in perfectionism, her own attachments to the ideals of middle-class marriage had apparently weakened, and she had already toyed with alternatives. Two years earlier she had dreamt that Frances Folger—a married woman—and the bereaved Elijah Pierson were match spirits and should marry. And in the early days of her conversion by Matthias, she had consented to the end of her own Christian marriage to Benjamin Folger, and had allowed Pierson to remarry them in the Spirit of Truth.[32]

After weeks of such conversation, Matthias looked into Ann's eyes and whispered a great secret: long before he had met her, he had envisioned Ann as Mother of the Kingdom.[33]

Isabella Van Wagenen, who could see what was happening, had her own ideas about Ann Folger. The servant believed without question (as any member of the Prophet's household had to believe) that devil spirits could enter the bodies of human beings. Back in New York, the devil had entered Mrs. Bolton and sent her against Matthias, and Matthias had turned back the assault. The Spirit of Truth could withstand any straightforward feminine assault. But now, Isabella concluded, the perfidious female spirit had turned to other means, by entering the more graceful form of Ann Folger, and by attacking Matthias with perfume, flattery, and all the other tools of feminine seduction. The Ann Folger that Isabella observed was no longer the chaste and humble housewife of her Christian days. She was now a sexually charged temptress who threatened Matthias with a peculiarly feminine chaos.[34]

As Isabella went about her domestic duties, she began bumping into Ann and Matthias. Late one night, about three months after the move to Mount Zion, Isabella entered the parlor to get hot coals for the morning. She found Ann and Matthias sitting by the fire, deep in conversation. Sensing that she had intruded, Isabella retreated to the room that she shared with Ann. In a few minutes Ann followed her and went to bed. The same thing happened the next night. Isabella stepped into the parlor and discovered the couple talking intently. She was struck—almost thrown back—by Ann's amber eyes. (They "flashed fire," she recalled.) Again Isabella retired silently to her room. Again Ann followed.

Two days later Ann told Elijah Pierson a secret. The spirit had informed her that Matthias was her match spirit, and that she was to have him for a husband, and that they would have a son who would be the Messiah.[35]

Not long after that, Ann gave Matthias a bath. Regular baths were as yet unknown to most Americans, but Mount Zion's believers washed their hands daily and took a purifying bath each week. The men bathed the men and the women bathed the women, though most of the time they were nude and in the same room. Matthias explained that shame was sin, and those who truly participated in his spirit could be naked without shame. On the night in question, Isabella prepared the bath, expecting one of the men to assist the Prophet—but when Matthias was in the tub Ann Folger brushed past her, opened the door, and asked, "Father, shall I wash you?" Ann went in and shut the door behind her. The whole household watched in silence. Isabella stood just outside the door, which remained shut for a very long time. At last Pierson's ten-year-old daughter Elizabeth broke the quiet, asserting that "Father would be clean enough this time."[36]

5

Benjamin Folger spent most of the autumn of 1833 in Manhattan, shuttling between his Pearl Street office and his room at No. 8 Third Street, a house Elijah Pierson had rented and made available to members of the Kingdom. Rumors were spreading about Folger's financial ties to the Prophet Matthias, and he had returned to the city to protect his reputation and his fortune. The problems were severe. Over the previous year he and Elijah Pierson had invested heavily in business ventures that would support the Kingdom. Pierson communed with the Spirit of Truth (he no longer talked with Jesus) and proposed the deals, and Benjamin signed the papers. The Spirit told Elijah to buy stocks, and Benjamin bought stocks. The Spirit told Elijah to invest in real estate; Benjamin bought land, then sold it when his associates balked (and when Matthias had second thoughts about buying and selling the earth, which was his mother and rightfully his in the first place). Once the Spirit told Elijah simply to give a man one thousand dollars. Finally, there was Pierson's new interest in patented inventions. He and Benjamin bought interests in a planing machine and a self-loading cart, and they invested very heavily in a patented globe heating stove. Pierson had a lot of faith in the stove enterprise: he named the product the Ne Plus Ultra Kingdom Stove, and pledged the profits from it to the temple he would build for Matthias. Few of these ventures made money, and none of them helped Benjamin's reputation among the businessmen of New York. In November, when word spread that Benjamin had transferred all of his property to Matthias, Folger found himself on the edge of ruin. (This was untrue, though Folger *would* transfer Heartt Place to Elijah Pierson the following March, perhaps to protect it from his own creditors; Pierson then immediately leased the property to Matthias for ninety-nine years, at a rent of one dollar a year.) While Ann theorized about marriage and scrubbed the Prophet's back, the unsuspecting Benjamin stayed at the house on Third Street, trying to reassure his worried business friends and creditors.[37]

Late in November at the Third Street house, Catherine Galloway greeted Ann Folger and Elijah Pierson, who had come down from Mount Zion to have a talk with Benjamin. God, they said, had revealed that Matthias and Ann were match spirits, and that she was to present the Prophet with a holy son. Benjamin was to give up Ann in marriage to the Prophet. Catherine watched as Benjamin, fighting rage and disbelief, heard them out. There is no record of what was said, but Catherine remembered that "there was a terrible to-do nearly all night." By morning, perhaps with the promise of a match spirit of his own, Benjamin consented. The party returned to Mount Zion and, on the following Saturday, Benjamin Folger gave his Christian wife Ann (under her maiden name Disbrow) in holy matrimony to Matthias the Prophet.[38]

The night of the wedding Benjamin watched as Ann and Matthias prepared to retire to the bedroom that had been his, and he began to have second thoughts. He stopped his lost Ann in the hallway, yearning for some token of affection. He followed her all over the house, plaintively calling her name. When he reached out to touch her, Ann caught his hand and scolded him as a child: "Benjamin, behave yourself." Benjamin retired to Matthias's old room.

From that time onward, the Kingdom recognized Ann Folger

as "Mother," while Benjamin sulked about the house and snuck off to his crumbling business career in New York. Isabella Van Wagenen remembered that he looked "like a dog with its tail singed, or one drawn through a gutter."[39]

6

In January, Benjamin agreed to run an errand for Matthias: he would travel to Albany, locate a Mrs. Matthews, and bring Father's children to Mount Zion. Benjamin Folger's evident prosperity and his pleasant manners impressed Margaret Matthews, but his stories about her holy erstwhile husband and the abundant order in Sing Sing surprised her; she had given Robert up for dead. After she asked around about Benjamin Folger and learned that he was a respectable man, she agreed to send her children to Sing Sing on the assumption that her daughter Isabella (who was now about twenty years old, and who worked with her binding shoes for a local manufactory) would return to Albany after a short visit.

Although she would miss her children, Margaret had grown weary of supporting them, and was pleased that, at long last, Robert would assume his fatherly duties. She was no doubt all the more pleased when, on the day of their departure, Benjamin Folger handed her thirty-two dollars (saying that it was her husband's money) and assured her that a check for the same amount would henceforth arrive at the post office on the tenth day of each month. She saw nothing wrong with allowing her eleven-year-old son Johnny and Isabella to accompany Mr. Folger in his coach. Nor did Margaret raise any objection when Mr. Folger presented Isabella with a riding habit and a gold watch, kissed her, and remarked that she looked much like his former wife. ("My heart was full," Margaret later recalled of the farewell scene.) It remains uncertain whether she mentioned to Folger that her daughter had been married one month earlier to a beery English immigrant combmaker named Charles Laisdell.

By sundown, when the coach made an overnight rest stop, Isabella Laisdell had spoken with Benjamin about her marriage. The information had no impact on Benjamin: late that night he crept into Isabella's room and, with her little brother asleep in the room, slipped into her bed and had sex with her.[40]

At Mount Zion, Isabella Laisdell was shocked at the sight of her kingly father, whom she had not seen in five years. She refused to submit to his authority, or to call Ann Folger "Mother." As the Prophet's anger rose, Benjamin stepped forward and confessed his sins of the previous night. Matthias stared at his daughter and Benjamin Folger, thinking hard. That night Matthias whipped Isabella for disobedience. (Ann Folger, a witness to the beating, uttered at the end of it, "Now I love Father more than ever. . . .") Matthias whipped his daughter again the next morning, but he was still thinking.[41]

On the morning after the arrival of Benjamin and Isabella Laisdell, Ann Folger entered the kitchen and asked Isabella Van Wagenen and Catherine Galloway if they would like to attend a wedding. Van Wagenen followed Mother into the parlor and stayed near the door. Elijah Pierson sat across the room. Catherine Galloway and Ann Folger stood near the fire. In front, in a neat and happy row, sat Benjamin Folger, Isabella Laisdell, and the Prophet Matthias.

Matthias rose and began the ceremony. He told the Kingdom that "an act on the road" had voided the marriage between his daughter and the man named Laisdell. Benjamin Folger and young Isabella were clearly fond of each other, and the situation might best be resolved by marriage in the Kingdom. He asked the couple if they agreed, and they smiled and said yes. Then he asked the others. They agreed one by one, though Catherine

Galloway seemed strangely tentative and sad. Matthias placed one hand on the head of his daughter Isabella, the other on his wife Ann Folger. "You will be blessed in obedience," he said, "and in disobedience you will be cursed." Benjamin turned, kissed his bride, kissed Matthias, then kissed each member of the Kingdom in turn. The wedding completed, he looked to his new wife and gestured toward the upstairs rooms.

Matthias, however, was not finished. The happy couple—the man Matthias had cuckolded and the daughter he had beaten that morning—returned to their chairs while Father laid down moral rules and spiritual advice, speaking for what seemed a very long time. Benjamin listened in a state of "ridiculous uneasiness," standing whenever Matthias paused, hoping against hope that he was done. From her station at the door, Isabella Van Wagenen stifled giggles throughout the sermon. At long last the Prophet said Amen. Benjamin and his bride, humiliated once more by the Father, retired to their room. They had been truly wed in the Kingdom of Matthias.[42]

FOUR

❧❦

The Downfall

I

AFTER BENJAMIN AND ISABELLA'S WEDDING, when everyone else had gone to bed, Isabella Van Wagenen and Catherine Galloway were cleaning up in the kitchen and they began to talk. The black woman had detected Catherine's gloominess during the ceremony, and she wondered whether Catherine, as she later put it, thought "any thing of Benjamin Folger." It was a queer idea, that homely, uneducated Catherine, fit only for servant's work, should take a serious interest in a polished gentleman. Isabella inquired anyway and Catherine confessed.[1]

Shortly after Matthias and Ann Folger had wed, Catherine recounted, Ann had visited her at the Third Street house, to tell her about some dreams she had had about match spirits. A few nights after Mother's visit, the Lord came to Catherine as well in the form of strange feelings and voices, saying that she and Benjamin were matched. (The Spirit was strong enough to send

127

❧❦

Catherine rolling on the floor.) Apprised of Catherine's fits, Matthias confirmed that the Lord had indeed spoken and that she and Benjamin were match spirits who should be united.[2]

Catherine did not say how Benjamin came to hear about God's instructions, only that she had slept with him while he was in the city on business—and then did so again, several times, until Isabella's sudden arrival at Sing Sing ended their match. Surely, Catherine insisted, she had a greater right to Benjamin Folger than did Mrs. Laisdell. Maybe, she wondered aloud, someone would go to Benjamin and ask him whom he liked better in the dark, Catherine or his new mate. Isabella Van Wagenen ignored the implied request and told no one of what she had heard.[3]

Over the next few days, Ann Folger all but ceased performing her regular household duties. Practically the only thing on her mind (or so the others thought) was her new-found bliss. She said the same things to different people, on several occasions, about how all former connections were nothing, about how she had never known a man but Matthias. He alone, she claimed, could "enter the most Holy of Holy;" he alone could "penetrate to the Sanctum Sanctorum." Matthias called Ann by romantic pet names and let her hang about his neck, whispering and cuddling. When something went wrong in the kitchen, he listened to Mother's complaints, then scolded the servant Isabella.[4]

The bulk of the Kingdom's household drudge work now fell on Isabella Van Wagenen, who was especially peeved that Mother and Father rose late in the day, which threw her back in her chores. One morning she spoke up while lighting the fireplace in the front parlor, where Matthias and Ann now slept. From under the covers, Matthias told her that she would be furnished with his and Ann's spirit—that if he and Ann were in bed, their spirits would be with Isabella, enabling her to do twice the work in half the time. It sounded less than spiritual to the former slave.

Benjamin Folger and Isabella Laisdell did not indulge in a

honeymoon. Each morning, Benjamin awoke early, well before his match spirit, hoping for breakfast but knowing that none could be served until Mother and Father came to the table. Hungry and curious, he would pace the hallway, just outside the room where his ex-wife lay with Matthias.

It took Folger three weeks from the time he left Albany before he got around to writing Margaret Matthews a curt note, advising her that her children were fine but that on orders from the Father he would send no more money. The message persuaded the combmaker Charles Laisdell, Isabella Laisdell's first husband, to go to Sing Sing to investigate. By the time he arrived, the entire Kingdom save Isabella Van Wagenen had removed to Third Street; the servant turned Laisdell away from Mount Zion without answering any of his questions. But Laisdell persisted, taking a room up in the village and returning every day to the Folger estate. Hearing of what had happened, an exasperated Matthias returned to Sing Sing with Elijah and berated the black woman for not treating the outsider more severely—but he allowed Laisdell to be admitted to the house. The Prophet behaved imperiously, as if Laisdell should submit to God's doings without grumbling. Elijah Pierson took a different tack and offered Laisdell enough money to return to Albany, purchase the tools and raw materials of his trade, and set up a business in Sing Sing. Laisdell assented, hung around for two or three days (bearing up under Matthias's lectures), and finally received his cash. As soon as he left Mount Zion he stopped off in Sing Sing village to tell everyone what he had seen and heard.[5]

Laisdell's stories spread quickly and crowds of people gathered daily on the road leading up to the estate, knocking down fences and gabbing about different versions of what was going on inside Benjamin Folger's house. Laisdell, meanwhile, traveled to Albany, then to Manhattan (where he vainly tried to get inside the Third Street house), and then back to Sing Sing, where he at last delivered a writ of habeas corpus signed by an Albany judge, commanding the release of his wife. Once again, the Kingdom would have to submit to civil authority.[6]

On the morning of the tribunal, a crowd showed up early at Mount Zion to hoot and holler, while Matthias and his followers boarded their carriage and drove off to meet the magistrates, who had assembled at Crosby's Tavern. At the hearing, Isabella Laisdell stated that she preferred to remain with the Kingdom, but Charles produced a marriage certificate and the magistrates ordered her to depart with her lawful husband. Matthias, full of imprecations at the start of the proceedings, grew quiet as he noticed the tumult outside the tavern, where there was talk of tarring and feathering. When the hearing concluded, only the forcible intervention of some cooler heads in the crowd prevented the administration of vigilante justice.[7]

The Kingdom, minus Isabella Laisdell, returned to Mount Zion unmolested, and within days Matthias formally united Benjamin Folger and Catherine Galloway as match spirits. Ann Folger encouraged the marriage (Isabella Van Wagenen later revealed) by giving Catherine some new dresses and "adorn[ing] her naturally rather plain person in the best manner." Up in Albany, Isabella Laisdell told her mother about Robert Matthews's new living arrangements, and about how he had whipped her, but she said nothing of the roadside seductions or her brief and irregular marriage to Benjamin Folger. Returned to the house of Charles Laisdell, she would not see either her father or Folger again for over a year.[8]

The Sing Sing villagers, unmoved by the magistrates' verdict, continued to harass Mount Zion. (Unable to travel to and from New York by steamboat without attracting attention, Matthias took to traveling strictly by carriage). One morning, a delegation of two local gentlemen, a lawyer and a teacher, arrived at the estate they knew as Heartt Place to persuade Benjamin Folger to rid himself of his outrageous house guests. Benjamin and Ann, awakened in their separate bedrooms, greeted the intruders and politely asked them to leave. Advice from outside the Kingdom was the advice of devils, they told the astonished men.[9]

2

By mid-March 1834, Ann was certain that she was pregnant with the holy child, and in her joy, she occasionally visited New York (sometimes alone, sometimes with the others), staying at No. 8 Third Street. Matthias, his prophecies confirmed, preached with renewed power and feeling. It was during one of these sermons, with the entire Kingdom present, that Catherine Galloway suddenly shrieked and fell to the floor, bleeding from beneath her skirt—an early miscarriage. Because she had not been pregnant long, Catherine recovered swiftly. Within a few days, the Prophet had her back at work.[10]

In the spring, a family of four, the Thompsons, joined the cult in Sing Sing. Mr. Thompson (the sources do not disclose his given name) was another Albany combmaker, who had seen something of Robert Matthews years before and learned of Matthias through Margaret Matthews, the mother-in-law of his workmate Charles Laisdell. Thompson seriously doubted that the Prophet was the supernatural character he claimed to be, but he was willing to sit through the sermons so long as he could live in a large communal family, where men could be as comfortable as possible. Matthias studied him, discerned the spirit of an ancient Levite, and made him the Kingdom's butcher. Thompson's wife Elizabeth was put to needlework.[11]

It took Thompson several days to figure out the Kingdom's sleeping arrangements. Once he did, he flattered himself that Elizabeth did not see what was really going on. But Elizabeth had her suspicions, which Ann Folger confirmed in a private chat.

Only one thing perplexed Mrs. Thompson: when Mother went alone to New York and Benjamin was also there, on business, did she not sleep with Benjamin? The question startled Ann. She admitted that she did, indeed, sleep with Benjamin, but claimed he was like a child, and that sleeping with him was like a mother sleeping with her son. "The Spirit worked with Matthias," Ann said, "but it did not work with *Benjamin.*"[12]

A singular incident three weeks later finally convinced Thompson to leave.[13] Matthias, one of the Matthews boys, Ann, and Benjamin had been returning to Mount Zion from a stay in New York when their carriage (with Benjamin at the reins) broke down, and they were forced to spend the night at a Yonkers tavern. The tavern keeper, recognizing Benjamin and Ann as man and wife, prepared them a double bed, and made up single beds for the others on the same floor. Normally when the presence of outsiders forced Benjamin and Ann to play-act as partners, Matthias would pull Benjamin aside and lay down a heavy curse or injunction, lest his disciple attempt to take any liberties with Mother. This time, however, the Prophet did not get the chance to see Benjamin alone.

Matthias awoke early, crossed the hall, opened Ann and Benjamim's door, and asked if all was well. Ann lay still, unable to rise until Matthias assisted her. Later, Matthias, in a foul temper, refused to ride with the others and set out for Mount Zion on foot. When Ann and Benjamin told the Kingdom what had happened, Thompson made up his mind. "There is too much changing of wives here," he remarked to Isabella Van Wagenen as he hastily packed his bags. "I have a nice little woman, and I should not much like to lose her."

Lacking the time to fetch his wife's things before the Prophet returned, Thompson fled with his children, expecting to come back for Elizabeth later, certain that she was still innocent of what was going on at night. When, several days later, he did retrieve her, she had a frightening story of her own. Shortly after the Prophet's return from the Yonkers tavern, Benjamin had voiced displeasure at his connection with Catherine Galloway. Although Catherine was extremely fond of the genteel Mr. Folger, he had never considered her as anything more than a temporary substitute—"a hack," in Isabella Van Wagenen's blunt phrase. Now Folger began musing aloud about how Benjamin and Elizabeth were both scriptural names, which indicated a likeness. Matthias had locks and bolts placed on all the doors, explaining that he had a tender lamb and saw a wolf coming to take her. Although no one interfered with Thompson when he came back to reclaim his wife and her belongings, Mrs. Thompson was certain that the Prophet wanted to match her with Folger, or possibly with Elijah Pierson.[14]

On Sunday, the first of June, the miserable Benjamin Folger appeared out of nowhere sitting in his mother-in-law's pew at the Dutch Reform Church on Franklin Street in Manhattan. After the service, he attended another church service on Allen Street. Elizabeth Thompson had just left Sing Sing; Matthias and Ann had reaffirmed their connection in a new ceremony; Benjamin was alone once more, and confused. Later in the day, he looked up his business partner Walter Hunt. Hunt had visited Mount Zion some days earlier at the Prophet's invitation, to talk over money matters—in particular (or so Hunt expected) the Ne Plus Ultra Kingdom Stove, which had proven a financial disaster. But the Prophet and Elijah Pierson had refused to discuss their failures, and had instead greeted Hunt with news of their temple scheme, a project to build twelve enormous structures to exceed the splender of Solomon. They asked Hunt if he wanted to join in; Hunt, disappointed, demurred and left Mount Zion. Judging from the size of the estate, he had noted that the residents must still have considerable funds.[15]

For four hours on the Sunday afternoon, Hunt walked the

streets of Greenwich Village with Benjamin Folger, trying to confirm his friend's growing suspicion that the Prophet was a fraud and that Ann was in terrible danger. ("If Matthias is not true, I am a ruined man," Folger exclaimed to his old associate.) Before departing for Sing Sing, Folger looked in on another friend, Isabella Van Wagenen's former employer, Perez Whiting, who gave him the same advice Hunt had. That night in Sing Sing village, Folger drank heavily in the company of several villagers before stumbling off to a nearby bed. The villagers assured him that they would help him in any way that they could.[16]

Isabella Van Wagenen's account of what happened the next morning had all the trappings of a stilted Bowery Theatre melodrama.[17] After storming back to Mount Zion, Folger accosted Ann in the entryway, grabbed her, and announced that he was taking her and the children away.

ANN (*scolding*): Benjamin, behave yourself.

Enter Matthias, his hand outstretched in friendship.

MATTHIAS: Behave yourself.

BENJAMIN: You're a d——d imposter!—I will have you out of this house—put you where you will not be heard or seen.

ANN: I am not your wife!—Behave yourself!

Benjamin grows furious; Ann hides behind Matthias.

MATTHIAS: I never courted her favor, nor ever *asked you* for her; but *you came* and gave her up to me, in the name of Disbrow; and you actually told me, she was not *your* wife, but that she was *mine*.

Enter the Folgers' ten-year-old son, Edward, and Elijah Pierson from the garden, where they had been cutting weeds.

BENJAMIN (*catching at the weeding knife in his son's hand*): D——n you, I'll stab you!

> *The boy tosses the knife away; the group has, by now, moved into the parlor. Benjamin rushes to the fireplace and picks up the poker.*

BENJAMIN: I'll split your brains out!

> *A melee, as Benjamin and Matthias struggle until Matthias, alarmed, wrests free and rushes toward the front door; Isabella seizes Benjamin, who is staring wildly and trembling.*

BENJAMIN: Isabella, Isabella go down in the kitchen!

ISABELLA: I have never done you any mischief.

MATTHIAS (*grabbing his sword and swinging it slowly*): Let that spirit be destroyed!

PIERSON: Now, Benjamin, let me have a private interview with you.

BENJAMIN: Pierson, when you told me that the Lord told you, not to let Matthias get any more money, that was a true spirit. Why don't you stick to that. (*To Ann*) Fix yourself to go with me.

ANN: Benjamin, I will not.

> *Folger, still insistent, leaves the house, then returns at lunchtime with a wagon; he re-enters Mount Zion, markedly calmer, to find Ann and Matthias sitting on the parlor sofa.*

BENJAMIN: Now, Ann, I want you to go. Come, fix yourself.

ANN: Now, Benjamin, eat something, and I will tell you what I will do.

BENJAMIN: Won't you come with me at all?

ANN: Stop a bit, and I will tell you.

After lunch, Ann led Benjamin off to the north wing of the house for a private talk; when they rejoined the others, Benjamin was completely subdued ("like a tamed elephant," Isabella's narrative recalled) and he agreed to quiet the feelings he had raised against Matthias in Sing Sing. Right away, Benjamin departed for the village, but he failed to placate the villagers, several of whom followed him back to Mount Zion, their mood growing surlier, until Folger at last convinced them to retire. That night, as usual, Ann and Matthias slept together in the parlor. But in the morning, Ann, dressed in her bed clothes, visited Benjamin in his chamber.[18]

By midday, villagers clogged the road to Mount Zion; children hung from trees to get a better look. One Elephant Taylor, a local wag, had bet his tavern friends that he could cut off Matthias's beard and bring it back as a trophy. Dressed as a constable, he approached Mount Zion with a counterfeit writ, demanded that the Prophet surrender, and suggested that he shave, lest he be recognized by the mob outside. Only the Sing Sing topers fully knew what had happened when they spotted Elephant Taylor in his old wagon, winking to the crowd and gesticulating to the tall beardless man in front of him. When the coach reached the village inn, Elephant feigned surprise and told Matthias that there had been some mistake, that the writ was defective and that he was free to go.[19]

Elephant Taylor had worked his plan well, but he had forgotten to collect the Prophet's beard. By the time he returned to Mount Zion for it, Matthias had fled for Manhattan, and the rest of the Kingdom had realized they had been duped. Rebuffed by Ann and Elijah, Taylor returned to the village having lost his wager, but with the satisfaction that he had rid Sing Sing of the man who said he was God. (He would gain additional satisfaction the following autumn, when he ran for sheriff of neighboring Putnam County—appropriately on the Jacksonian Democratic ticket—and won by a wide margin.) The day belonged to the drinkers.[20]

Ann grieved all evening for her departed match spirit, and Isabella heard little talking until Benjamin approached Mother and led her off to his room. "Come Ann, let's go to bed," he said. "I've had a great deal of trouble to get you."[21]

3

Matthias's departure provided an opportunity for Elijah Pierson.

Pierson was a pathetic sight by now, a seedy ex-businessman grown prematurely old. His eyesight was failing and his teeth were crumbling in his head. The previous autumn, an attack of paralysis had temporarily felled him; the following spring, his "fitty devils" began to appear about once a week, which prompted the Kingdom to have the Folgers' son accompany him whenever he was out puttering in the garden. Every one of Elijah's schemes was ruined: Walter Hunt had gone to court and in time collected hundreds of dollars owed him in connection with the Ne Plus Ultra Kingdom Stove; the twelve-temple plan would get nowhere. And with all of the shuffling of sleeping partners, Eiljah Pierson had yet to meet his match spirit.[22]

The day after Matthias fled Mount Zion, Pierson assumed the Father's seat at the head of the dinner table, spoke of the recent events as God's will, and announced in a voice that mimicked Matthias's that *he* now possessed the governing spirit. Offended, Ann, Benjamin, and Isabella fled to New York, leaving the deranged Elijah and the children of the Kingdom to the care of Catherine Galloway. When Ann returned to Mount Zion alone several days later, she managed to calm Elijah down by telling him that he did have a match spirit after all, and that the spirit was his old friend Frances Folger. Excited, Pierson set off for Oyster

Bay, Long Island, where Frances and her husband Reuben had resettled. After hearing why Pierson had come, the Folgers unceremoniously told him to leave. Elijah, dejected, retreated to the Third Street house, where Matthias reassured him that the time had not yet arrived.[23]

In mid-July, the entire Kingdom except for Benjamin Folger (who was away on a business trip) reassembled at Mount Zion. Elijah now suffered horribly from his fits, as without warning, his head would droop to one side and he would start to utter gibberish. Dimly aware of the seizures, Elijah instructed Isabella to restrain him whenever the devils appeared, and to keep detailed accounts of what ensued. The black woman could not help noticing that special things happened whenever Ann was present during the seizures. Elijah would stare at Mother intensely, stretching out a hand as if to draw her closer, exclaiming over and over, "Ann, Ann," repeating the name with greater rapidity, getting wilder as the fit advanced, moaning at the end, "My wife, my wife." The first time Elijah reached for Mother in this manner, Isabella saw in horror and disgust that his other hand was fumbling beneath his trousers. Matthias, trying to bring Pierson to his senses, would ask him what he was saying, what he was about, while the others held Elijah down and removed his hand.[24]

On July 28, Matthias, Elijah Pierson, Ann Folger, and Catherine Galloway sat down to supper. At the end of the meal the Prophet spooned out plates of blackberries that he and Pierson had picked that day. Ann Folger ate only two berries. Catherine finished her plate, and Elijah wolfed his down and had another. Matthias had none at all. He explained that while there was a plate within easy reach it had not been placed directly in front of him. For that reason, he "had lost his blessing in the enjoyment of eating blackberries," and in response to the mishandled situation he screamed that "the Father was not honored in the house but the sons were honored in the house." He ate nothing but dry toast and coffee.[25]

About four o'clock the next afternoon, Elijah was salting hay and munching berries from the bushes, when he suddenly collapsed. The Kingdom supposed it was the fitty devils again. This time, though, Elijah was sicker than usual. By the time the others got him back into the house, his beard was smeared with blackberry vomit and the smell of him was nauseating. Only Isabella had a strong enough stomach to assist. During the night, he lost control of his bowels.[26]

Matthias forbade any doctors or medicine to aid Elijah, and Elijah agreed: prayer and prayer alone could relieve his affliction. The Prophet took over Elijah's haying job, and Ann sent Isabella into the fields to assist him, leaving Pierson to lie alone for most of the day, in his own vomit and excrement. On August 5, the widow Rosetta Dratch, Matthias's old follower from New York, turned up, wishing to see Elijah Pierson. Told he was sick, the widow retired upstairs to bed. Through the night, she heard the sound of gurgling, as Pierson attempted to drink water through the mucus that had collected in his throat.[27]

In the morning, Ann Folger told the waking disciples that Pierson was dead. Elijah lacked faith, Matthias solemnly intoned; for that reason his body had perished. But the good part of his spirit remained at Mount Zion.[28]

Sing Sing learned of Pierson's death from Widow Dratch on her way back to New York, and a hastily assembled coroner's jury went to Mount Zion to confront an unhelpful band of witnesses. The coroner was especially interested in the circumstances within the house, and he elicited strange testimony about spirits. Ann, who at first refused to say anything, eventually divulged the details of Pierson's illness, and confirmed that Elijah had received no medicine. The devil (death) had robbed Elijah of his body, she explained; to have sent for doctors and medicine would have been worse than useless, it would have been sinful. The coroner's jury, finding no physical evidence of foul play, saw no reason for an autopsy and rendered its verdict that Pierson had died of natural causes.[29]

Soon there arose further complications. Matthias wanted to bury Pierson at Sing Sing as quickly as possible, and arranged for the ceremony with a neighbor, only to have Benjamin Folger arrive at the last minute. Folger had heard of Elijah's death from Mrs. Dratch, and at the Pierson family's request he had arranged to have the body sent on for burial at Morristown. The Prophet gave way and the Kingdom removed to Manhattan. Immediately, the Westchester County treasurer seized the Sing Sing estate (which Folger had deeded over to Pierson the previous March), in trust for Pierson's heirs. When, some days later, two lawyers arrived at the Third Street house to obtain the deeds, Matthias refused to hand them over. The property at Mount Zion belonged to the Kingdom, he insisted, and he was willing to test the strength of gentile laws in order to keep it that way. But when the lawyers returned, having initiated a suit in the Chancery court, Matthias surrendered the papers and reconveyed his lease on Mount Zion to Pierson's daughter, Elizabeth.[30]

Privately (the Folgers later claimed), the Prophet used Pierson's death as an example to the others. When Benjamin expressed surprise that Elijah had died so suddenly, Matthias snapped that all his enemies would get the same treatment, hinting that somehow he, Matthias, had been responsible for everything. All who opposed him could expect the same thing; he had the power to do it. Ann and Benjamin later testified that they believed him.[31] Matthias could not, however, stifle the persistent charges outside the Kingdom that something criminal had happened to Elijah Pierson. To settle the matter, the coroner ordered that Elijah's body be disinterred and inspected at Morristown by the Drs. Lewis and Nathan Condict, a father-and-son team who belonged to the Pierson family.

On August 18, the Condicts, assisted by two other doctors, cut open what was left of Elijah. The corpse's surface had turned a dark chocolate color and the face was nearly black, but the stomach, the key organ to the investigation, was noticeably better preserved than any of the surrounding tissue. The doctors removed the stomach for closer examination and discovered several things: a teaspoonful of dark brown mucus near the pylorus; a dingy white substance, resembling white chalk or calomel, on the stomach's forefront; an inner lining that was pulpy; and beneath the lining an effusion of dark blood. After writing up their confidential report, the Condicts placed the stomach in a jar and sent it to Dr. John Torrey, a professor of chemistry in Manhattan, for a second opinion. As far as they could tell, however, the bodily evidence conclusively showed that Elijah Pierson had been poisoned.[32]

4

The Kingdom's final month, spent at No. 8 Third Street, brought a flurry of renunciations and reconciliations.

According to Isabella, Ann and Benjamin slept together on numerous occasions after the Elephant Taylor episode, even as Ann slept with and declared her eternal love for Matthias. Following Elijah's death, Isabella recalled, Ann was increasingly open in her signs of affection for her first husband, indulging Benjamin in gracious smiles. She even agreed (after getting Father's permission) to accompany Folger on one of his business trips to Albany, where they stayed at a hotel as man and wife. Benjamin, thinking he had regained Ann, began telling the Prophet to leave and seek out some better site for the Kingdom in the west. One evening, Matthias agreed and set off, but as soon as he was out the door, Ann began to grieve; when Matthias came back, unexpectedly, the next day, she welcomed the Prophet with open arms. As far as Isabella could see, Ann was still enthralled with Matthias—and Matthias, unnerved by her sweetness to Benjamin, was taking every opportunity to test her loyalty.[33]

After the Prophet's abortive western journey, Benjamin called the Kingdom together and declared in a firm voice that he was giving up Ann forever, and that Catherine Galloway was his true match spirit. The Kingdom appeared to have regained some balance; over the next few days, Ann gave Isabella detailed descriptions of how Matthias kissed and embraced her. Yet Ann, now six months' pregnant, was living in a heightened state of confusion and divided loyalties. Isabella, our best witness, could only speculate in retrospect that Matthias's obvious jealousy of Ann's little smiles at Benjamin had lowered the Prophet in the Mother's eyes, just as Benjamin's flashes of resolution made him appear less childlike. Ann's artful professions of love for the Prophet seemed, to Isabella, to carry less and less conviction.[34]

On an afternoon in mid-September, Catherine discovered Benjamin and Ann alone in Isabella's bedroom. ("What a devilish shame it is," Catherine complained, "that a woman wants two or three men.") Matthias also found the couple. When Ann claimed that Benjamin had forced himself upon her, the Prophet denounced her as a harlot. The Kingdom was on the brink of dissolution.[35]

A series of noisy rows broke out over the next four days, in which Matthias turned on Ann Folger and blamed her for destroying the Kingdom. Benjamin Folger angrily ordered Matthias not to preach to his family. During one incident that would later prove of some importance, the Folgers gagged on some morning coffee brought to them by Isabella, who still evinced loyalty to the Prophet. Finally, Ann came downstairs for breakfast one morning and quietly addressed Benjamin as "husband." In the afternoon, Benjamin began needling Matthias about who was really the better man; when the Prophet turned to Ann to affirm the truth, Mother reneged. She had once had a complaint, she said, a falling of the womb. Matthias had corrected that problem by replacing the defective part. *That* is what she meant by his penetrating to the Sanctum Sanctorum. As for everything else, she found far greater pleasure with Benjamin.[36]

Folger leaped at the situation and offered to pay any sum of money to make Matthias leave. On the pretext that he would go west to buy the Kingdom a farm, Matthias accepted one hundred dollars in bills of the Bank of the United States and five hundred and thirty dollars in gold coins. Isabella, paid twenty-five for her services, also agreed to go, as did Lewis Basel and Henry Plunkett. (Whatever became of Anthony the Dutchman is unknown.) Folger in turn agreed to send Matthias's sons back to their mother. When they stepped outside, Matthias told Isabella that she could get word of him at the merchant tailor Paul Durando's at the corner of Chatham and Chambers streets.[37]

Benjamin Folger may have planned his next move or may simply have been improvising. Clearly, though, he aimed to remove Matthias from his life once and for all. With Matthias gone, Benjamin went to the police with a complaint that the Prophet had defrauded him and absconded with $630; he also placed a notice in the newspapers offering a one hundred-dollar reward for Matthias's capture. The police sent out a patrol to track down the alleged thief.[38]

After learning at Durando's that Matthias had left Manhattan, Isabella picked up her belongings at the Third Street house (where Ann and Catherine kissed her and bade her a safe trip) and journeyed to Albany to make sure that the Prophet's children, traveling on their own, arrived safely at their mother's. She was amazed to find Matthias at Margaret Matthews's house. Claiming that he and the Kingdom had to retire into the wilderness, the Prophet gave what was left of the $630 to Margaret for temporary safekeeping and returned to his boarding house on Washington Street, leaving Isabella to wait for his sons. Matthias returned to Margaret's when the boys showed up, only to learn from his son Johnny that Benjamin Folger has asked a Manhattan police officer to arrest Father for stealing and robbing things. The Prophet left once more to pack; the next day (after Isabella had left Albany to visit one of her children), he retrieved his money from his irate wife, gave her fifty dollars of it, and got her to agree to keep their sons until he returned for them.[39]

Before Matthias could escape Albany, two policemen from New York arrested him at his boarding house without a struggle. Inside his bags, they found some of the money they were looking for. They also discovered a great deal more: linen shirts from the finest clothiers, silk stockings and handkerchiefs, a gold watch, frock coats embroidered in gold and silver. One of the officers pulled out the "Jesus Matthias" nightcap embroidered with the names of the twelve Apostles, then he pulled out another cap, nearly identical to the first, but with the names of the twelve tribes. The Prophet himself held what he called the sword of Gideon, miraculously preserved for thousands of years, as well as his ancient carpenter's rule, to be used (the Prophet said) to measure lots in the New Jerusalem.[40]

The policemen gathered up all the stuff in preparation for the trip down the Hudson. The sword, they noticed, was inscribed with the words "E Pluribus Unum," and appeared to have been made for an army officer. The carpenter's rule bore the words: "Kutz, maker, no. 164 Water-street, New York."

The next day, the officers arrived in New York on the steamboat *Champion* and delivered Matthias to the prison ward at Bellevue Hospital, where he was formally charged with embezzlement and fraud. All the while, in Westchester County, court officials, having received the results of the Condicts' autopsy, had

prepared a warrant for Matthias's arrest for the murder of Elijah
Pierson.

5

A bewildered Manhattan police scribe did his best to take down
what the Prophet was saying. Although the prisoner was subdued, it was difficult to follow the substance of his remarks,
particularly his opening statement. He described himself vari-
ously as "a traveller," "the Spirit of Truth," and "a Priest of the
most high," who had come to pronounce judgment on the
gentiles—the "chief high Priest of the Jews after the order of
Melchizedek" (the poor scribe stumbled over *that* name) "being
the last chosen of the 12 apostles and the first of the resurrection
which is at the end of 2300 years after the rebuilding of Jerusalem
by Cyrus." (Had the police known more about marginal religious
movements, they might have caught the reference to Melchizedek, and begun to suspect that the prisoner had plagiarized at
least some of his theology from the Mormon Joseph Smith.) Fed
up with the sermon, the chief officer moved on to more pointed
questions about the alleged defrauding of Benjamin Folger. Matthias denied everything and insisted that whatever money he had
ever received from Folger or Elijah Pierson had been freely given
by men who acknowledged him as the Father.[41]

The Matthias affair instantly became a scandal of unprecedented proportions. The police placed Matthias's caps on public
display, and attracted a great number of viewers. But it was New
York's newspapers which did the most to publicize the case. It
was not, to be sure, the first time that American readers had been
treated to accounts of such bizarre, sensational stories. The partisan press of the 1790s and after had gleefully reported on the
alleged sexual indiscretions of various political leaders; through
the 1820s, pamphleteers recounted the careers of dozens of mur-

derers, thieves and other outlaws. But the Matthias story hit the police blotter just as a new genre of daily newspapers, the so-called penny press, was making its debut, and these papers would cover the story relentlessly. Pioneered by the ex-radical Benjamin Day of New York's *The Sun,* the penny papers based their success on gaining a mass circulation among the urban working classes, crowding out the political news and mercantile reports that were the staple of New York journalism in favor of more fanciful, at times lurid accounts of life and death in the emerging metropolis. The Matthias story, with its themes of religious delusion, sexual depravity, and (in time) alleged murder, was perfect fare for the penny press editors.[42]

With papers like *The Sun* leading the way, other dailies and weeklies, from the established party and mercantile newspapers to the city's radical trade union press, began reporting the latest disclosures. Newspapers around the country picked up their accounts; pamphleteers began composing exposés confirming rumors about the Kingdom's sexual practices; even staid periodicals like the *North American Review* eventually ran lengthy meditations on the Prophet and his cult. Historians of Jacksonian America normally focus on great political and social issues when interpreting the events of 1834 and 1835: the rise of the Whig party, the growing rifts over slavery and abolitionism. But to judge from the New York newspapers, the Kingdom of Matthias was among the lead stories.[43]

For the Prophet, the most pressing matter was obtaining a good lawyer, and, for once, he had good luck. At Isabella Van Wagenen's urging, Margaret Matthews had packed up her best attire and, in Isabella's company, come to Manhattan to assist her husband; there, the women made contact with Henry B. Western and N. Nye Hall, leading lights of the New York bar and men of impeccable social credentials. One of Margaret's friends also sought out a different attorney, named Wilson, and visited him with Isabella. But when Wilson referred to Matthias as a beast, and said that he was going to "act like a Christian" (ominous words to Isabella), the black woman insisted on hiring Western, who would work with Hall as his co-counsel.[44]

Western and Hall's decision to take the case spoke well of their liberality and their devotion to equal justice for all—for whatever their fees, defending Matthias the Prophet was bound to cost them something in public esteem. Margaret's motives were probably less pure, and certainly had nothing to do with any rekindled love for her husband. In fact, Margaret had decided to divorce him—now possible, in view of the rumors about Matthias's liaison with Ann Folger. One source claims that Margaret wanted to save her husband's neck only in order to obtain, in some future settlement, part of the money and property he had supposedly obtained from his followers.[45] But whatever her aim, Matthias was the beneficiary. His able lawyers could see from the start the flimsiness of the charges against their client.

Western's first move was to try and neutralize Benjamin Folger, who had problems of his own. By placing matters in the hands of the police, the courts, and the penny-press reporters, Folger risked ruining his already stained reputation as a Christian gentleman. Retrieving his house, his property, and his wife would mean little if the public believed Matthias and the loyal disciple Isabella Van Wagenen, and if the details of the Kingdom's sexual disorder were ever confirmed in a court of law. And so Folger took to the offensive. On the afternoon that the newspapers published the transcript of Matthias's interrogation, Folger drafted a public notice refuting the Prophet's story and advising all interested parties that he could prove that he had acted correctly at all times. Privately, he instigated a rumor that Isabella had tried to poison him and his family on the morning when she served up the undrinkable coffee. Matthias's attorneys, powerless to prevent Folger from buying up space in the papers, needed to preserve Isabella's integrity as a potential witness for the defense. On Western's advice, she initiated proceedings against Folger for slander, and gathered up signed testimonials attesting to her trustworthiness from several of her former masters and employers.[46]

By the time Matthias's fraud case came to trial in early November, even the Manhattan district attorney, Ogden Hoffman, realized the charges would not stick, for the same reason that the case against Matthias for blasphemy had failed two years earlier: the prosecution was powerless to prove that the accused was not in fact a prophet of the Lord. As the trial opened, in a courtroom overflowing with spectators, the prosecutor explained his doubts and produced a letter from Benjamin Folger, expressing a desire that the proceedings end. (Ever protective of his reputation, Folger took out another newspaper notice the next day, asserting that his letter in no way meant that he had relapsed into the Kingdom, only that he wanted to rid himself of the demon Matthias "with as little trouble as possible.") In any event, the district attorney continued, the fraud trial had become a trivial affair: Matthias was wanted in Westchester County for the alleged murder of Elijah Pierson.[47]

Matthias sat at the defense table, resplendent in his beard (which after his run-in with Elephant Taylor he had regrown yet again) and dressed in a claret-colored frock coat covered with silver stars, a yellow vest, and green pantaloons cinched with his crimson sash. (A reporter said the Prophet looked like a cross between a drawing-room dandy and a Spanish or Italian brigand as he chatted with those around him, more invigorated than awed by the courtroom crowd largely composed of curious females.) His lawyers challenged the prosecution's motion for a *nolle prosequi,* as it would leave the impression that the defendant had been cleared on a mere technicality. Only a full jury trial, Western argued, would bring out the facts of the case and put a stop to the false rumors about Matthias. But the court, in what one newspaper called "an elaborate opinion," consented to the prosecution's motion, and remanded the prisoner to Westchester authorities.[48]

Henry Western, left with only two weeks to prepare for the murder trial, faced daunting odds. Apart from his less-than-reliable client, the only informed witness friendly to his case was a black woman with a long history of religious extremism—one who, thanks to Folger's rumor-mongering, had herself fallen under public suspicion. Against him stood the Folgers and the family of Elijah Pierson; and behind *them* stood the mass of prejudice that would value the testimony of articulate white ladies and gentlemen far more than that of a broken-down carpenter-turned-prophet and his ex-slave devotée. The story making the rounds was that Matthias, abetted by Isabella, had poisoned Pierson with tainted blackberries at supper the day before Pierson fell fatally ill. There was every reason to believe that the story would convince a jury.

Yet Western could again see flaws in the prosecution's case. Benjamin Folger, for example, was an excitable and vulnerable man. Once Isabella began her slander suit against him, Folger went to his friends with an entirely new story, about how Isabella was actually a steady and upstanding servant.[49] Given his tendency to vacillate, how would Folger hold up under cross-examination? And what of the irregularities surrounding the original coroner's report about the deceased Elijah Pierson, and the subsequent autopsy? Was there really a legal reason to conclude that Pierson had died of anything other than natural causes?

Western was ready to proceed on the appointed date, November 25, but various developments wound up delaying the trial for months. The judge came down with influenza; meanwhile, in late October or early November, Ann Folger, attended by her husband's ex-lover Catherine Galloway, had given birth; mother and child contracted smallpox and slowly recovered with Catherine's help. Trial was rescheduled for April.

Ann's child was not the promised Holy Son, but a girl.[50]

6

With no trial news to report, New York's penny-press editors printed whatever scraps of information they could find about the Kingdom. All of the papers were hostile to the accused—"Matthews the Imposter," as they branded him—but they differed greatly in their appraisals of the causes and nature of his crimes. These differences, in turn, reflected deeper intellectual and political divisions. Democrats, Whigs, and radical working-men; deists, Finneyites, and high-church conservatives; all picked over the available evidence about Matthias and his cult during the winter and spring, looking for clues to some grander meaning, hoping to support their conflicting views respecting humankind, God, and the United States of America.

Much of the journalistic speculation focused on Matthias himself. Some writers rehashed Folger's version of the events and described the Prophet as a moral failure, a depraved, if shrewd, proletarian swindler—"a miserable strolling driveller," as one reviewer put it.[51] Yet many of these accounts, in keeping with more materialist explanations of insanity that were emerging in the 1830s, also sought some additional psychological understanding of the prisoner. Matthias, they suggested, appeared to believe his own professions; his failings were mental as much as they were moral, betraying what one journalist called a triplicate quality, part rogue, part fool, and part lunatic. Above all, Matthias seemed to exemplify a species of disorder that Jacksonian Americans had begun to label "fanaticism" (or what some called "ultraism")—an overheating of the emotions that led otherwise normal people to entertain strange and enthusiastic doctrines, which in turn led them to "overmuch righteousness."[52]

In shifting the discussion from moral to quasi-scientific grounds, the newspapers could not help undermining the assertion that Matthias was simply a common conniver, or that he was fully responsible for his deeds. (Given the accused's obvious insanity, one reporter predicted, he would probably never be convicted.) The editors of *The Sun,* the most energetic purveyors of Matthias news, added to this discussion by printing on their front page the phrenological findings of one "Vesta," who claimed that he had examined and interviewed Matthias during the New York trial. "Amativeness, large . . . Philoprogenitiveness, moderately large . . . Reflective and Perceptive Faculties, small," "Vesta" noted, before concluding that Matthias was a unique case of a committed and ignorant mind invested with unusual powers of imagination, self-esteem, and "marvellousness."[53]

"Vesta" sought to calm any fears that Matthias in some way exemplified some wider social disorder; other writers were not so sure. The radical Jacksonian editor George Henry Evans—a devout hard money advocate, free-thinking anti-evangelical, and trade-union sympathizer—saw Matthias as only one member of a new genus of frauds and confidence men that had arisen in "this age of imposture." It was, furthermore, "not at all surprising" to the radical Evans that, amid all the chicanery, "such a barefaced imposter met with dupes."[54]

At the other end of the ideological spectrum, an anonymous essayist in the Whiggish *North American Review* discerned no signs of grand social delusions in the Matthias story. He did nervously allude to the Folgers and Elijah Pierson as examples of how easily the barrier between sanity and insanity broke down:

If men who keep about their business, maintain their characters, make bargains, make money, and give no other proof of an impaired intellect, can fall into the belief of so revolting, so amazing a fraud and lie, who is safe?

Fortunately, the writer continued, the Kingdom did not spread beyond "the narrow circle of [the Prophet's] first dupes," and the cult fell apart, a victim of its leader's merciless character and lack of intellect—all signs that the common sense of the wider community was still intact. Far from portentous, the essay concluded, the swift downfall of Matthias affirmed that all was basically well in commercial America.[55]

Other conservatives, however, drew different conclusions. To "L. R.," writing in the stiff-necked, high-church *Evangelical Magazine* of Hartford, Connecticut, Matthias embodied the destructive forces of egalitarian individualism that had come to dominate American life:

> Upon every subject of interest at the present day, and among all classes of people, there is a strong tendency to fanatical excess . . . All action, whether moral, political, or religious, in a greater or lesser degree, is tinged with the color of the times. In the theory of government, the fanatical abuse of certain popular principles, is fast destroying everything which gives security to reputation, to property, or to life. Assuming the fundamentally wrong position that LAW is a creature of their own—a subject and not a ruler—the people have dared, in numerous instances, to destroy its authority, and anticipate its action. . . . Assuming certain principles to be self-evidently true, which have no self-evidence at all, save that of their own absurdity, we draw conclusions from them which are equally at war with the commands of the Bible and the dictates of humanity.

With his Christian authoritarianism, "L. R." appears to have been blind to the paradox that, in his own way, Matthias too was a deeply conservative man, seeking to restore the rule of God's patriarchal law. Instead, hidebound Christian conservatives were more likely to describe the Prophet as an example of the godless disorder proclaimed by Thomas Jefferson in the Declaration of Independence—a disorder which, in "L. R.'"'s view, also linked the Kingdom to the Finneyite new measure clergy, Jacksonian politicians, abolitionists, and others who endangered the nation with their "favorite doctrine regarding individual liberty, and equal rights."[56]

Mainstream Democratic editors, who venerated the Jeffersonian legacy, professed still another kind of horror at the Matthias cult, which they tied not to egalitarianism but to the activities of their Finneyite foes. Ironically, it was Mordecai Manuel Noah, now the editor of a new turncoat Whig paper, the *Evening Star* (and seemingly unaware of his early influence on Robert Matthews), who best summarized this view. It was bad enough, Noah argued, that "an ignorant and ferocious imposter" had managed to win the allegiance of a band of respectable persons. Worse, the fires of fanaticism had "lighted up from one end of our country to the other." Of course, he observed, the freedoms of religious toleration had to be respected. (The Jewish Noah remained sensitive on this point.) But the republic needed some means of halting the abominable practices of *all* religious frauds, lest the frame and substance of the social compact be destroyed.[57]

Noah's interpretation also suggested that the Prophet's perfectionist accusers were as much at fault as the imposter himself. Although clearly exploited by Matthias, Elijah Pierson and the Folgers had indulged in their own forms of fanatic flummery long before Matthias arrived on the scene. And all the available evidence showed that Matthias's followers had willingly participated in "the voluntary debasement of the family, chiefly females, subjecting themselves by a system of object menial obedience." Pierson and the Folgers, were not unfortunate innocents; they had surrendered to Matthias's command "for equally unworthy motives."[58]

Another editor, William Leete Stone of the *Commercial Advertiser,* challenged such views and cautiously defended the Folgers. Stone was not a radical evangelical, let alone a perfectionist. Years earlier, it had been Frances Folger's attack on Stone's wife, Susannah, that had divided the Brick Presbyterian Church over the work of the female missionaries; and his newspaper editorials attacked the city's pious moral reformers and abolitionists as "ultraists," who would tear apart the social order if given the chance. Still, Stone sympathized with the Prophet's supposed dupes, especially Ann and Benjamin Folger. Stone, having grown up with Benjamin in Hudson, New York, still held his boyhood friend in high regard. Moreover, Stone was a journalistic mouthpiece for many of the high-minded, Christian, Whig-leaning men of business with whom Benjamin Folger and Elijah Pierson had once been connected.

Obviously, Stone claimed, Matthias's followers had succumbed to a baleful spirit of fanaticism, of the kind that had turned the evangelized parts of northern and western New York into a moral and spiritual wasteland. Benjamin and Ann Folger, in his view, stood as living reminders to all good Christians to avoid the "ultraism" that had become "the great error of the times in which we all live." Yet Stone also insisted that ultraism was not a problem peculiar to evangelical Christianity or any specific religion, but a broader affliction, a kind of monomania or mental hallucination. The Folgers were victims who deserved charity, as people who had wandered into error and madness and who now sought spiritual restoration. Frances Folger was more worthy of blame, the malevolent woman who had first lured the Folgers into perfectionism. And the real culprits were the unrepentant fraud Matthias and his accomplice Isabella, the black servant who had poisoned the food, one of "the most wicked of the wicked." A disreputable ex-carpenter and an addled ex-slave: in the end, to a Christian gentleman like Stone, the affair turned on the evil in-tents of people with little claim to respectability, the kinds of people who were ever prepared to traduce their social betters.[59]

In December, while the newspaper wars raged on, Benjamin and Ann, seeing in Stone a potentially important ally, agreed to help him write a lengthy book giving their side of the story. The other important parties in the case likewise prepared for the com-ing trial. The attorney Henry Western, having already taken down a detailed narrative from Isabella, pored over the rest of the evidence and drew up a list of friendly witnesses, including Dr. John Torrey, the New York chemistry expert to whom the Doc-tors Condict had sent Elijah Pierson's stomach. Isabella, now armed with testimonials from her ex-employers, brought Western an additional source of information, Catherine Galloway. Cather-ine had had a falling out with the Folgers, who remained uncom-fortable in the presence of Benjamin's onetime match spirit. She agreed to tell Matthias's lawyer all that she knew. Meanwhile, Matthias preached from his Westchester cell, counting on the newspaper reporters to carry Truth to their readers. On the eve of the trial, he released a special decree, instructing all farmers to lay down their ploughs since there would be no spring thaw until he was freed. He also prophesied that, if he were ever found guilty, an earthquake would destroy White Plains, the site of the trial, and leave not a soul to tell of the town's annihilation.[60]

The busiest participant in the weeks and days before the trial was the Westchester district attorney, William Nelson, who was determined to win his case at all costs. After all the newspaper publicity about Matthias, an acquittal would deeply embarrass the prosecutor's office. Not wanting to risk relying on the Condicts' original autopsy, Nelson ordered that they conduct a new one. He carefully scrutinized every recoverable detail about Pierson's final days, from the serving of the fatal blackberries to the awful sounds of Elijah's gurgling. As a final precaution, he gathered evidence to try Matthias on yet another charge based on what he heard about the Kingdom—a charge of assault in connection with the Prophet's alleged beatings of his daughter Isabella Laisdell while she was at Mount Zion. By the time the murder trial began, Nelson had quietly obtained the necessary assault indictment from a grand jury. No matter what, he would see Matthias convicted of *something*.

7

Matthias's trials lasted four days and might have been shorter if the Prophet had held his tongue. As soon as the case was called, the defense asked for a brief postponement, to allow time for the arrival of various witnesses, including several who would vouch for Isabella Van Wagenen's character. (In his search for supportive testimony, Western had run notices in the newspapers, one of which reached the Kingdom's old coachman, Lewis Basel, who had joined the army and was stationed in Virginia.) Matthias was wearing a green frock coat with plaid tartan lining, a ruffled shirt, and green pantaloons, with his crimson sash as always tied around his waist. Led back to his cell, he met in mid-afternoon with a New York reporter who, impressed by the Prophet's bearing, asked him how he was. The ensuing interview was the longest Matthias would ever give to the press.[61]

MATTHIAS: I feel that the Spirit of the Omnipotent is my stay, as he will be my exceeding great reward, and I know that I shall come out of this fiery furnace of affliction, like the gold that is seven times purified! But my mind is debilitated, because by going into court I lost half my dinner. (*Here the jailor made his appearance.*) By the bye I should like to have a luncheon.

JAILOR: Yes, sir, you shall.

REPORTER: Matthias, they have obtained the witness they advertised for in the Courier.

MATTHIAS: Good God! Can that be possible? What Lewis—Lewis—Lewis! I forget the surname, but he is a most important witness. He knows that Pierson was not—but no matter; the end cometh which no man knoweth. Mr. Western has persevered so as to get Lewis, has he? Well, that's better than two dinners.

(Here a man came up to the cell door and cried out "Let's have a peep at the old devil!"*)*

MATTHIAS: Young man, it's a wonder that your tongue does not cleave to the roof of your mouth, thus to profane a discourse directed by the prophet of the Lord. Know ye not that in the days of Jesus of Nazareth they said "He hath a devil?" Even so is it unto this day. Depart ye, evil one, for ye know me not. *(He then turned round and continued to our reporter)*—But whence come ye, what is your mission?

REPORTER: I belong to the New York Press.

MATTHIAS: Aye! aye! a mighty engine—a blessing and a curse. Speak of me as I am—set down nought in malice—nothing extentuate—write the truth about me.

(Here we were reminded by the jailor that it was time to break off, and hearing that the prophet refused to press the palm of anyone, we tendered our hand at parting, with this remark, "Good bye Matthias.")

MATTHIAS: I never shake hands with mere mortals. Know ye 'tis written "touch not the prophet of the lord"?

Early in the next day's jury selection, Matthias politely addressed the court with a complaint about the use of secret witnesses before the grand jury that had indicted him. The presiding judge, New York State Justice Charles Ruggles, had a slight acquaintance with a member of the Kingdom; seven years earlier, it had been Ruggles who issued the writ that helped Isabella Van Wagenen retrieve her enslaved son from Alabama. Now faced with a very different case, he advised the defendant to leave all the arguing to his counsel. Matthias kept on talking and ignored the judge's call to order, screaming above the rapping of Ruggles's gavel about the unholiness of the grand jury proceedings and any such proceedings: "All secret institutions are *cursed of God!—cursed of God!*"[62]

After the sheriff restrained Matthias, the judge held the defendant in contempt, ordered him removed from the courtroom, and opened a hearing to establish his mental fitness to stand trial. Western did not formally object, although he noted that he had made no preparations for such an inquiry. Given sufficient time, he might have been able to contact dozens of persons in and around Albany and New York who would have confirmed that his client was insane.[63]

With Matthias returned to the room, the court heard eight witnesses (four of them medical doctors), who delivered conflicting reports. Only two could speak with any long familiarity of Matthias's life, but one of them, the Reverend Nathaniel Prine, had known the prisoner as Robert Matthews back in 1813 and 1814. Prine was "most decidedly" of the opinion that the man that he knew was sane. Margaret Matthews's brother, Andrew White, disagreed, but only partially: his brother-in-law was mad, he said, but strictly with respect to religious matters. In his charge to the jury, Judge Ruggles picked up on White's distinction, and asserted that only if Matthias was insane "on all subjects" could they declare him unfit for trial. The jury decided that the trial should proceed.[64]

Had the courtroom spectators been in charge of Matthias's fate, the outcome would have been uncomplicated: "almost every body here," one newspaper reported, "is in favor of hanging the prophet."[65] But the district attorney, whose evidence that a murder had taken place was fragmentary at best, had to persuade the jury with circumstantial and emotional testimony. First, he called the Morristown doctors who examined Pierson's body and had them recount all the gruesome forensic evidence supporting their conclusion that Elijah had been poisoned. Then he put Ann Folger on the stand, with the hope that her forlorn revelations would convince the all-male jury that, at the very least, Matthias was guilty of manslaughter for having left Pierson unattended as he lay dying. Western was well prepared for all the witnesses— so much so that, the evening before they testified, he hinted to reporters that he would not have to elicit any lurid stories from Isabella Van Wagenen.[66]

By the time Western and his co-counsel had finished cross-examining the Condicts and those who assisted them, the prosecution's case was in tatters. At the trial's outset, Western had placed in evidence an affidavit from John Torrey, stating that the stomach sent to him from Morristown did *not* show any signs of poisoning. All that was left for the defense was the simple task of showing that the Condicts and their helpers were bumblers. The keeper of the burial ground from which the body had twice been disinterred could not state positively that the corpse was actually Pierson's. The sexton of the adjoining church could do so with respect to the original autopsy, but not the second, because of the corpse's advanced state of decay. Dr. Lewis Condict, after testifying about the suspicious white powder he had found in the stomach, admitted that he had not performed any chemical analysis but had based his conclusion on conjecture—to him, "irresistible"—that the stomach's preserved state proved the deceased had been poisoned, probably with arsenic. His son conceded under cross-examination that the white powder found on the corpse's stomach could not have been the poison, and that the lower intestine (normally inflamed in cases of poisoning) had been left unexamined. It took no training in forensic pathology to see that the prosecution's advertised "conclusive autopsy" had been botched.[67]

Ann Folger took the stand at about three-thirty in the afternoon and stayed there (except for a ninety-minute recess) until close to nine that night. Her opening statement rehearsed the basic history of the Kingdom, without any mention of sexual improprieties. She slowed down when she got to the events of the previous August, leading her listeners step by step through Matthias's disenchantment with Pierson, the blackberries for dessert, and Pierson's last days of life. Without making the charge directly, she left little doubt that Matthias had poisoned Elijah and left him to die.[68]

Western bore down hard in his cross-examination, asking Ann if she was not considered to be the Mother of the Kingdom, and if so, if she did not therefore share responsibility for Elijah's death. Ann, unflappable, freely admitted her position as Mother, but insisted that she had no responsibilities other than those dictated by Matthias. Western then shifted his line of questioning to the state of Elijah's health before he met Matthias, seeking to show that Elijah's fits and delusions could not be blamed on the defendant. Ann held fast: whatever Elijah's beliefs may have been before Matthias showed up, she said, he was not an insane or weak-minded man; his occasional fits had been slight and infrequent until his last weeks at Mount Zion; she in no way considered Pierson's life endangered after he fell ill; indeed, she had believed that he would live forever. Without further questioning, Ann stepped down, her reputation as a gentlewoman unblemished, having been spared any questions about matched spirits and the Sanctum Sanctorum.[69]

The prosecution had one last witness, Catherine Galloway

(who, after giving information to Western, had reconciled once again with the Folgers). Catherine supported Ann Folger's testimony and added a few anecdotes of her own about Matthias's tyrannical rule. After some desultory questions from Western, she was excused, and the prosecution rested its case. It was nearly eleven p. m., and the court adjourned until morning.[70]

Western's job of acquitting Matthias of murder was nearly complete: without calling a single witness, he would ask for a dismissal on grounds of insufficient evidence. By now, however, he knew that the district attorney would not stop there, but would begin the trial on charges of assaulting Isabella Laisdell as soon as the murder case concluded. What Western also knew, as the district attorney did not, was that Mrs. Laisdell could be convinced to drop her accusations.

8

The fourth and final day began with Western's motion for dismissal. Judge Ruggles agreed that a murder conviction was out of the question and that if the jury found the defendant guilty, he would have to call a new trial. Matthias might, however, be convicted of manslaughter in the fourth degree, and Ruggles spelled out the reasons why: Pierson was known to be a sick man, he had died in a house nominally under Matthias's control, and Matthias had denied him medical assistance. One question remained: had Pierson truly died of neglect or of his severe and pre-existing fits? The distict attorney, rushing at the opportunity, tried to call the elder Dr. Condict to the stand, only to have Western object, on the technical grounds that Condict had not been present for Ann Folger's testimony describing Elijah's illness. Ruggles ruled in Western's favor, and ordered the jury to return a verdict of not guilty, "whatever you might think of the prisoner." The jury promptly did so.[71]

Before the shock of the outcome had settled on the spectators—before the relieved Matthias could even thank his lawyer for a job well done—the district attorney was on his feet, calling for the arraignment and immediate trial of Matthias for the assault and illegal imprisonment of Isabella Laisdell. The Prophet, who had alternated between defiance and stoicism during his murder trial, broke into tears at the mention of his daughter. Western, however, was ready and sprung his own surprise, in the form of a letter he had obtained from Mrs. Laisdell that very day, acknowledging that she had received "full and ample satisfaction for the assault and battery in this case" and requesting that the court drop all charges. (What the "satisfaction" was, the note did not say; nor did Western or anyone else ever reveal what it was.) The flustered prosecutor called Isabella Laisdell to the stand. A few minutes later she strode forward, accompanied by her husband, and swore that she had indeed signed the letter and had forgiven her father for everything.[72]

Now desperate, the district attorney called Charles Laisdell as his next witness. Laisdell testified that he could not concur with his wife's decision to let her father off the hook. It was left to the judges to decide whether to proceed; when Justice Ruggles announced that, in view of Mr. Laisdell's testimony, the charges stood, spontaneous applause broke out among the spectators.[73]

Matthias and his lawyers could have guessed, at the moment, that they were in trouble. Western's only hope for success would have been to open up the entire dark story of Mrs. Laisdell's involvement with Benjamin Folger, and then the rest of the Kingdom's secret history. But Western had not done so during the murder trial, possibly (as one writer later charged) because he had reached an agreement with the prosecution, possibly because it might only further inflame the jury against Matthias.[74] He worked just as gingerly in his examination of Mrs. Laisdell as he had with Ann Folger, getting her to testify that her father had beaten her for many reasons, among them her marriage to Charles Laisdell. Western focused on that point, and asked her why exactly Matthias had disapproved; she said only that he thought that she was too young to marry and that, in any case, all gentile marriages were unlawful in the eyes of God. Western did not press the issue and Mrs. Laisdell stepped down.[75]

The next witness, Charles Laisdell knew little about the Kingdom's inner workings, particularly its rumored sexual arrangements. All the same, Western tried to deflate Laisdell's testimony by asking him if he had taken money from Matthias after originally agreeing to leave Mount Zion without his wife. Laisdell, who saw nothing irregular in such bargaining, admitted to the transaction, and went on to say that he bore no ill will toward the Prophet. Nevertheless, he insisted, Matthias had violated his rights by beating Mrs. Laisdell, leaving behind welts and bruises that had still not disappeared. With husbandly assurance, Charles stated that *every* man should have his rights.

In his charge to the jury Justice Ruggles stated emphatically that the case against Matthias had been proved. The whipping the prisoner had administered might have been acceptable in the case of a parent correcting a child. But here, as Ruggles put it, Isabella Matthews's prior marriage to Charles Laisdell had "excepted her from the control of her father." In effect, the court sustained Laisdell: every man should have his rights, and the rights of a husband over the body of his wife superseded those of her father. On that basis, the jury found Matthias guilty.

Throughout the four-day drama, Matthias had muttered complaints about the testimony and about the entire character of the trials. He managed to restrain himself from repeating the outburst of the opening session; now, standing before the judges to hear his sentence, he at last received permission to speak. A newspaper reporter, expecting a harangue, leaned forward to catch the Prophet's final speech to the court.

"I have been confined for near seven months, and nothing has been made out against me, until this last case, and this has been a great affliction to me, though I have been sustained under it, knowing that I was innocent. The things which are apparent are so because they misrepresented my doctrines.

"Court: We don't want to hear any thing about them.

"Matthias: You don't—I was going to terminate by saying, that feeling that I was innocent I think this termination altogether extraordinary and unjust, and if it is in the power of the Court to make an offset in my favour in the latter case, I hope it will."

Justice Ruggles made it clear that he would be severe, and skirted close to relating all the facts that had thus far gone unmentioned at the trial. It was bad enough that Matthias had beat his daughter. Worse still, he had "endeavoured to inculcate in her the same immoralities that he had already inculcated upon the inmates of the house."

The sentence on the assault charge was three months in the county jail, with an additional thirty days for contempt of court. Turning to the prisoner, Ruggles ended with a classic piece of advice for clever idlers who had broken the law: Matthias should serve his sentence, shave off his beard, lay aside his peculiar doctrines, and go to work like an honest man.

"It is not true," was all that the Prophet said in reply, as the sheriff led him away.

Epilogue

I

MOST OF THE NEWSPAPERS expressed astonishment at the outcome of Matthias's trials. The testimony plainly showed, editorialists remarked, that at the very least the Prophet's neglect had accelerated Elijah Pierson's death; surely this called for a sterner verdict than the one the jury had handed out. Now Matthias would be out of jail before summer's end—free, one editor said, "to propagate his impious doctrine and prey upon the credulous and timid." An equally outraged pamphleteer, writing on behalf of *The Sun,* published a history of the cult "as a warning beacon to our fellow citizens against the impositions and delusions, arrayed as angels of light, by which others have been betrayed." The maverick Mordecai Manuel Noah, who was critical of the cult members as well as of their monstrous leader, took a more philosophical view. Although surprised at the verdict, he hoped that "the voluntary debasement" and "abject mental obedience" of the Prophet's followers would "forever form a theme for reflection, astounding and reprehensible as it is degrading and revolting to human nature."[1]

More ambitious literary efforts came from those closest to the affair. William Leete Stone led off with his lengthy book, complete with an explanatory appendix, some "exclusive" material selected from Pierson's diary (which was apparently in Benjamin Folger's possession) and a full-length narrative by Benjamin and Ann, prepared at Stone's request. Stone wanted to show the dangers of extreme religious enthusiasm—but also to cast Ann and Benjamin in the most favorable light. Readers who had been titillated by the salacious rumors about the Kingdom would find nothing of interest in Stone's book. Instead, Stone offered a catalogue of the Prophet's cruelties, while taking swipes at Frances Folger and Isabella Van Wagenen.

At the conclusion of the Folgers' long narrative section—the heart of Stone's volume—Stone briefly addressed the rumors about the Kingdom's "licentiousness and lust." Such talk was to be expected, he remarked, given the mystery that hung over Mount Zion and given the infatuated devotion of Matthias's followers. The stories would have surfaced, he wrote, "had every inmate of Mr. Folger's house been chaste and pure"—implying that at least some of the rumors had merit. But Stone would not dwell on who had been chaste and who had not. Switching course, he called upon the public to exercise caution regarding all insinuating reports about the Kingdom. The Folgers deserved charity, he insisted, as people "whose errors [were] founded on the mere perversion of reason." Then he dropped the matter for good and returned to the alleged perfidies of Matthias and Isabella Van Wagenen. It was a less than skillful whitewash.[2]

Other writers rebutted Stone's book and provided the public with some of the missing details. Margaret Matthews, suddenly thrust into public prominence, prepared a pamphlet (with the aid of the New York editor Origen Bacheler) that described Robert Matthews's early life, corrected some of Stone's factual errors, and defended the Albany evangelicals against Stone's charges that they were "ultraists." The chief villain, by her account, was not Matthias (who for all his terrible acts was clearly insane) but Benjmin Folger, whom she blasted as a clever seducer who had ensnared her daughter into the Kingdom.[3]

Of even greater interest was a rambling two-part work with a prolix title: *Fanaticism: Its Source and Influence, Illustrated by the Simple Narrative of Isabella, in the Case of Matthias, Mr. and Mrs. B. Folger, Mr. Pierson, Mr. Mills, Catherine, Isabella, &c. &c.*, researched, written, and published by the deist editor Gilbert Vale. Vale had kept a close watch for news about Matthias ever since the spring day in 1832 when the Prophet had wandered into his office looking for a favor. When Vale learned, shortly thereafter, that Sylvester Mills's family had arranged to have Matthias arrested for blasphemy, he wrote an angry piece for the *Sunday Reporter,* acknowledging that Matthias was either a fraud or a lunatic but condemning his detention as an outrageous act of violence by arrogant Christians—"disgraceful to the parties originating it, disgraceful to the police . . . and disgraceful to the country in which it could exist without a redress." As a deist, Vale detested all blasphemy laws on principle. Even worse, in Matthias's case, he saw those laws help a tiny group of well-connected men throw another man in jail for their own convenience.[4]

After the Kingdom's downfall, Vale became reacquainted with the Prophet, thanks to Isabella Van Wagenen. Passed over as a witness at Matthias's trials, Isabella had resumed her slander suit against Benjamin Folger. Before the case was settled, however, William Leete Stone published his book on the cult, claiming that she had been one of the most diabolical of Matthias's followers, and suggesting that she had helped poison Elijah Pierson and later tried to poison Ann and Benjamin Folger. Isabella had already taken the precaution of gathering letters of commendation from her previous employers. When first informed about the Folgers' collaboration with Stone, she had been defiant: "I have got the *truth* and I know it, and I will *crush* them with the *truth,*" she had exclaimed to Catherine Galloway. Now that Stone's book was widely available, Isabella decided that she needed to put her own story before the public as quickly as possible. An unidentified gentleman suggested that Vale was the man for the job.[5]

Gilbert Vale and Isabella Van Wagenen were unlikely allies. Vale, a radical British immigrant, was one of New York City's leading free-thinkers, a self-declared apostle of Thomas Paine, with close connections to George Henry Evans and the other rationalist allies of the city's early labor movement. Although he did not completely lack a sense of humor, he was a dry, discomfiting man, uncompromising in his religious views. (One of his friendlier journalist associates in the 1840s, the ambitious young editor Walt Whitman, would describe him decades later as "a valuable rare old man to know," but, withal, "a hard nut.") In a series of little newspapers, Vale had tried to shelter the tiny flame of radical deism amid the stormy rise of the Christian evangelicals. And although he directed much of his writing against Christianity, he aimed to expose the absurdities of *all* revealed religion. Matthias, to Vale, was no better from a philosophical viewpoint than his persecutors. The free-thinker was not predisposed to look kindly upon the requests of the mystic Isabella, who even now stubbornly professed her faith in most of Matthias's Biblical interpretations.[6]

Yet Vale and Van Wagenen also shared common ground. Like her—and like her prophet—Vale had run afoul of respectable Christian opinion. As his earlier remarks about Matthias's blasphemy arrest suggest, he was a ferocious anti-Finneyite. Further-more, Vale had come to suspect during Matthias's trials that a coverup was under way, whereby Christian gentlemen and ladies were conspiring with the courts, the district attorneys, and the Prophet's lawyer, Henry Western, to hide a sexual liaison be-tween Matthias and Ann Folger.[7] Finally, Vale, like most of his free-thinking comrades, was anti-slavery, and he was outraged at how Stone and the Folgers tried to shift so much of the blame for the Kingdom onto the shoulders of an ex-slave. In taking up Van Wagenen's cause, he offered no brief for her beliefs or the Prophet's. He would, however, strike a blow against the genteel Christians—and, he hoped (not incidentally), create a journalistic stir. Isabella confirmed all of his hunches about the Kingdom's sexual arrangements, and much more besides. With the obsession of a modern-day muckraker, Vale threw himself into the story, following up every lead and interviewing everyone he could track down who was even vaguely connected to the Kingdom, includ-ing Matthias himself. In the office of his newspaper, *The Citizen of the World,* he pored over Stone's book, Margaret Matthews's pamphlet, and the trial transcripts, locating inconsistencies and half-truths. He was well aware that the black servant Isabella's word, on its own, would not stand up against the Folgers', given public prejudices. And so whenever possible, he supplemented her narrative with "white evidence" from his interviews and from the public record.[8]

Vale was no stylist, and his two volumes suffer by comparison with Stone's book. Writing quickly, trying to nail every single lie, Vale let his narration spin out of control, often assuming that his readers knew as much as he did about the smallest details of the cult. Still, he accomplished what he set out to do by exposing what had been suppressed in the other accounts. With any luck, it would forever discredit the Folgers and William Leete Stone.

2

As it happened, Vale's hard work failed to prolong the scandal, and *Fanaticism* proved the final full-length treatment of the Matthias affair. The New York penny-press reporters and editors, having honed their skills in courtroom reporting, moved on to fresh copy: the prolonged trial following the brutal killing of the prostitute, Helen Jewett; the grotesque career of the impoverished carpenter and sadistic murderer, Peter Robinson; the baffling case of the missing cigar girl, Mary Rogers; and a profusion of other Manhattan crime stories that, in the late 1830s and 1840s, became a staple of American reading. Tiny follow-up items on Matthias did appear from time to time; and over the next century, a few crime buffs, academic specialists, and journalists with a taste for bizzare Americana stumbled across Stone's and Vale's accounts and retold them. The literary critic Gilbert Seldes picked up the story in the 1920s and included it in a book about nineteenth-century oddities; a watered-down account of the Kingdom, written by Christopher Ward, appeared in *The New Yorker* in 1934. But none of these efforts left any lasting literary impression.[9]

Yet if the story of Matthias went largely ignored by later generations, the penny-press journalism it helped to inspire had an impact on American life and literature that, according to one aficionado, Edgar Allan Poe, was "probably beyond all calculation." Appearing alongside the other penny-press dispatches—about shipwrecks, railroad accidents, freaks of nature, and more—the crime stories and the trial pamphlets that accompanied them prepared the public for all of the urban tales of delusion, amorality, imposture, and detection that would fascinate readers down to our own time. The more popular genres of paperbound thrillers and serialized fiction—too often dismissed by modern critics as merely cheap or sensational—would not be alone in spreading these tales. In the hands of writers like Poe, Whitman, Nathaniel Hawthorne, Herman Melville, as well as minor figures of the American Renaissance, metropolitan crime reporting furnished materials for more self-consciously artistic efforts. A Salem murder case went into the writing of Hawthorne's *The House of the Seven Gables;* Poe retold the Mary Rogers case (and claimed to have solved the mystery); bits and pieces of various penny-press sensations turned up in Melville's novels and Whitman's poems. By investing the crime stories with literary depth, these authors established their connections to the popular commercial culture of the day. But some of them, especially Poe, Hawthorne, and Melville, also found in the stories the means to explore, with devastating irony, the studied evil and deception that they discerned behind the masks of American ingenuity and innocence.[10]

None of these writers ever mentioned Matthias by name. One of them did, however, have a special reason to be aware of the cult. In 1830, the bankrupt Manhattan cloth importer Allan Melvill, on the run from his creditors, moved his family, including eleven-year-old Herman, up to Albany and entered the fur business. The Melvills settled on Market Street, not far from the North Dutch Church where Robert Matthews had first encountered Edward Kirk a few months before and begun the last stage of his transformation into the Prophet. Twenty-one years later, Herman Melville published *Moby-Dick or The Whale,* with a chapter devoted to a prophet named Elijah, who echoes the Biblical Tishbite by foretelling of Ahab's doom. In 1857 came *The Confidence-Man: His Masquerade,* Melville's dark comedy of manipulation and deceit on a Mississippi steamboat, peopled by an assortment of Broadway bucks and Santa Fe traders, squaws, spirit rappers, and green prophets from Utah: "an Anacharsis Cloots congress of all kinds of that multiform pilgrim species, man." Assuming many guises is a mysterious stranger who might be Christ and might be the Devil—the confidence-man, described at one point as "a liberalist in dress," sporting "a vesture barred with various hues." It all may have only been coincidental. But in back of Melville's writing lay his fascination with the penny press and its stories of sin and illusion. Among the first of those stories had been the history of Matthias and his Kingdom.[11]

The Kingdom holds a similar place in the history of American religion. To be sure, the group never became more than a marginal cult. Once the Folgers turned against Matthias, only Isabella Van Wagenen remained beside the Prophet—a dutiful and energetic disciple to the end. The blueprints for the New Jerusalem sketched out at Sylvester Mills's house, Mount Zion, and No. 8 Third Street wound up on the trash heap of American pseudo-theology. Yet the larger anti-Finneyite revival of which the Kingdom was a part did not disappear so suddenly. In the hands of more inspired and capable organizers—above all the Mormons Joseph Smith and Brigham Young—revelations not entirely unlike those of Matthias survived public hostility to carve out an important place among America's churches. Matthias's actions may have been more outlandish than most, even mad; his failure to codify and publish his revelations, coupled with his vengeful assaults on the Finneyites, doomed whatever small chance he had of enlarging his flock. But his prophecies were certainly congruent with those of the other traditionalist seers who, in the early nineteenth century, contributed greatly to one of the most extraordinary spells of sectarian invention that the nation, and the world, has ever seen.

Moreover, ever since the 1830s, various wild American holy men who resemble Matthias even more closely have formed their own communal cults, basing their prophecies on scripture and translating their personal disappointments into holy visions of restored fatherly power. To be sure, the social background to these movements has changed enormously over the past century and a half. Yet repeatedly, Americans caught in bewildering times have made sense of things primarily with reference to alterations in sexual and family norms, and a perceived widespread sexual disorder. Some Americans have appeared to welcome such disorder, as a sign that ancient hierarchies and discriminations are about to dissolve at last; others have seen it as threatening, even ungodly—the overthrow of all that is natural, a desecration of their parents' world, the root of all other forms of social turmoil. The more extreme of the traditionalist responses have included the manly cults, which have not only railed against the humiliations men suffer but have gone on to provide sacred, sexually charged, masculinist alternatives.[12]

Sometimes, the cults' leaders, like Matthias (or, more recently, like Jim Jones and David Koresh), burst into public notice, usually because of some confrontation with the law; immediately, they win notoriety, which in turn leads Americans to wonder about themselves and about what has become of their country to foster such lunacy. Just as suddenly, however, the prophets fail and then fade from public memory, until the next strange prophet comes along, and the questioning begins all over again. What gets lost is the fact that, for all their seeming eccentricity, these extremist prophets have a long and remarkably continuous history in the United States; they speak not to some quirk of the moment or some disguised criminal intention, but to persistent American hurts and rages wrapped in longings for a supposedly bygone holy patriarchy. It is easier to forget about these things than to understand them, for they do not match what we prefer to think of as the main currents of our uplifting, optimistic national creed. But while most of us (like Matthias's contemporaries) move on to other stories, the virile charismatic prophets of apocalypse are receiving their visions and gathering their followers at Zion, taking their place in an American spiritual history whose last chapter is not yet written.

None of this, of course, would have been apparent to the members of the Kingdom as they went their separate ways after Matthias's conviction. Yet even then, the full ramifications of the Prophet Matthias's rise and fall had yet to play themselves out for some of those who had been his most dedicated believers.

Sylvester Mills, having been wrenched out of the Kingdom by his family, regained his composure at the Bloomingdale Lunatic Asylum and rejoined the world of the respectable merchants. In 1835, he was reported as remarried and living in great style—"no longer a desponding Christian," Gilbert Vale wrote—the only one of Matthias's followers who had "decidedly benefited" from having joined the Kingdom.[13]

Mills's former servant, Catherine Galloway, left no recorded trace after her testimony at Matthias's murder trial. Lewis Basel, who had joined the army and was stationed in Virginia when called to testify, likewise disappeared after the trial. Henry Plunkett moved to Ohio with some friends. Nothing at all is known about Anthony the Dutchman.

One Orrin Thompson opened a comb manufactory in Albany in 1837; it may have been the same Thompson (the combmaker) who briefly enlisted with his family in the Kingdom. Charles Laisdell returned to Albany where in 1834–35, he was reported living a few doors down Fayette Street from where his mother-in-law Margaret Matthews (listed in the city directory as a tailoress) had lived the year before. Mrs. Matthews later claimed that soon after, he moved to the town of Schoharie expecting to prepare for his wife and mother-in-law to join him. Presumably, her daughter, Isabella Laisdell, returned to her married life with Charles.[14]

Margaret Matthews regularly visited her husband during his confinement in Bellevue in the autumn of 1834, passing messages from him to his lawyers and from his lawyers to him. By the time he finally came up for trial in November, the Hudson River had frozen over and she decided to remain in Manhattan for the winter. She wound up staying through at least the following summer in lodgings on Chapel Street. There she completed her memoir of her husband in reply to William Leete Stone. At the conclusion of her little book, she vowed that she would press on with divorce proceedings against Matthias, and thereby "throw off in some degree at last the reproach that rests on me and my children." But there is no record of any divorce being granted a Margaret Matthews in the City and County of New York in the 1830s and 1840s. After 1835, there is no listing for a Margaret Matthews in either the Manhattan or the Albany city directories.[15]

Benjamin and Ann Folger resumed their former existence with surprising ease. Pitied by the evangelicals and their more mainstream Christian friends, they received visits from the Methodist perfectionist James Latourette and the Baptist Charles Sommers, who exhorted them back to the Lord. (For his part, Latourette turned against his former servant and follower, Isabella Van Wagenen, and refused to give her a letter of commendation for her suit against Benjamin Folger.) Soon after Matthias's trial, Benjamin entered the land agency business with his old partner, Walter Hunt. And while Benjamin and Ann would take up a residence in Manhattan in the mid-1840s, they also lived in Sing Sing, where Benjamin continued making real estate deals through the end of the 1840s.[16]

The greatest difficulty the Folgers confronted had to do with the Kingdom's property. By his own estimate, Benjamin Folger had paid out a total of $4,500 during his association with Matthias, and (with all the bad business deals) he said he had gone bankrupt in March 1834. (No one could tell exactly how much Elijah Pierson had lost because at the time of his death his commercial papers were discovered in a state of impossible disarray—a cause of much consternation to Pierson's surviving relatives.) Among other things, the Folgers had to abandon Heartt

Place, which Benjamin had transferred to Pierson at the time he went bankrupt and was later conveyed, after Pierson's death, to Pierson's daughter and heir, Elizabeth. Pierson's estate, meanwhile, became the object of a protracted lawsuit between Elizabeth and Elijah's brother, Mahlon, who had been appointed administrator of the property. Elizabeth accused her uncle of bungling his tasks (or worse); the case wound its way through the Chancery courts, reaching as high as the Chancellor of the State of New York in the 1840s, but could not be decided for lack of reliable records.[17]

After 1850, the Folgers disappeared from the standard genealogical sources. We do not know what became of them after that date—or what became of the daughter that Ann had conceived while still Mother of the Kingdom. Heartt Place did win some notice, however, in later years. In 1836, the Reverend William Creighton bought the property and renamed it Beechwood; after considerable renovations and enlargements (and one more change in ownership) over the ensuing decades, Frank Vanderlip, the vice-president of the First National City Bank, bought the estate in 1905. Vanderlip added a library pavilion and new exterior decorations, and used the place as a salon for his celebrity friends. The rooms where Ann Folger had seduced Matthias became stages for informal performances by Sarah Bernhardt and Isadora Duncan (with the likes of Henry Ford in the audience). The lawn where Matthias made his getaway from Elephant Taylor became the site for a flying display by Orville and Wilbur Wright.[18]

As for Matthias, he served his four months and shaved his beard, but he did not follow the rest of Justice Ruggles's advice. Within a day or two of his release, he and Isabella Van Wagenen arrived in a carriage at Margaret Matthews's lodgings on Chapel Street. Isabella descended and delivered her good news to Margaret:

"Father Matthias is out here, prepare yourself to receive him and receive him joyfully."

Margaret let her visitors in, and she told her husband one last time that she should not be his friend because of the way he had acted toward her. He replied that she lacked patience, that he had been acting for her all the time, but that she lacked faith. "How long must I have patience," Margaret shot back, "have I not had it for sixteen years, and now, am I not worse off than ever?"

Upon hearing this Matthias went away with Isabella, and Margaret never saw him again.[19]

Three months later, Matthias turned up in Kirtland. Some stories say that after Joseph Smith dismissed him, Matthias wandered off to continue his preachings. One report in early 1839 placed the Prophet in Little Rock, Arkansas, where a group of townspeople supposedly seized him, shaved off his regrown beard, and threatened him with an even closer shave by "Dr. Lynch" if he did not depart immediately. Three years later, a St. Louis theology professor journeyed to inspect the Mormon settlement at Nauvoo, and he picked up a story about how Matthias was staying with non-Mormons west of the Mississippi River in Iowa Territory, and was preaching to the Indians. Other writers would state, with uncertain evidence, that the Prophet had died in Iowa in 1841.[20]

Isabella Van Wagenen, still the Prophet's disciple, did not accompany him out of New York, but returned to the service of her former employer, Perez Whiting. Her slander suit against Benjamin Folger turned out well, surprisingly, considering the social positions of the defendant and the plaintiff. Folger put up no real defense; Perez Whiting (among other deponents) confirmed that Folger had told him that Isabella had tried to poison him, then had changed his story. Isabella collected $125 from Benjamin and the matter was laid to rest.[21]

As of the summer of 1835, Isabella Van Wagenen still believed that Matthias's understandings of Scripture were the most rational she had ever heard. Having originally been persuaded by her employer Elijah Pierson that Matthias was holy, she now compared the Prophet with the Christian clergy and found in the Prophet's favor. Yet Ann Folger's seduction of Matthias had cast a shadow over her faith. She had seen holiness used as a pretext for the pursuit of carnal passions; she had lived in yet another deformed family, this one subject to a prophetic master. Now, having escaped what Gilbert Vale called the "peculiar pollution" of the Kingdom of Matthias, she continued her religious searching, always thinking over what had happened to her and the others at Mount Zion.

With her money from Folger in hand, along with the furniture she had brought into the Kingdom, Isabella became convinced that all of her labors in New York had been a failure. Her life, she thought, had been wrapped up in a great drama, which was itself but one great system of robbery and wrong, whereby the rich robbed the poor and the poor robbed each other. She must leave New York, she decided; she must find a way to give up all desire for money and power and truly live out the Golden Rule. For years, Isabella pondered these things until finally, in June 1843, the Spirit called her eastward, which is where she headed—first to the city of Brooklyn, then out into Long Island (where she lectured and prayed) and eventually up into New England. She made contact with a variety of sectarians and reformers, from Millerites to Shakers; in time, she would join the abolitionists, who would help her project an expertly crafted image as an indomitable, prayerful freed woman who had labored hard in the service of white men all her life. She had escaped the sexual contamination that had surrounded her (and stricken her fellow servant, Catherine Galloway), mainly, by her own account, because she was "near forty, not handsome, and coloured."²² But the Kingdom had marked her all the same.

A dozen years earlier, God had come to Robert Matthews and told him that he was the Prophet Matthias. After that, Matthias called himself a traveler, the Spirit of Truth. Isabella Van Wagenen, who had taken the surname of the man who had bought her freedom, and who had learned how to *crush* her enemies with *truth,* also became a traveler, and God renamed her too. About an hour before she left Manhattan, she told her mistress Mrs. Whiting that the Spirit had spoken to her and that she was not Isabella any longer, but Sojourner.[23] And so the world would come to know her as the ex-slave Sojourner Truth.

AFTERWORD TO THE
2012 EDITION

It is a delight and an honor to see this new edition of *The Kingdom of Matthias* appear nearly twenty years after the book's initial publication. Over that span, various readers have asked us how we came to write the book and how we divided up the research and the writing. This seems to be a good occasion to tell that story, as well as to reflect a little on the book's larger intellectual background.

We discovered the Prophet Matthias independently of each other. Johnson ran across him in the early 1970s, while researching a book about Protestant revivals in Rochester, New York. Years later, while browsing the stacks at Yale's Sterling Memorial Library, he found the little books that became the basis of this story, copied them, and read them for fun. Sometime in the future, he thought, he might want to write about Matthias. Wilentz, then a graduate student at Yale where Johnson was an assistant professor, had moved down to New York and begun research on his dissertation. While reading pro-labor newspapers from 1835, he found the material he was looking for—on trade unions and political movements—but it appeared on the latter pages of each issue. The front page was full of stories about the murder trial of one Matthias. It occurred to him that he might be writing the wrong dissertation, but for the time being he stuck to studying strikes and labor manifestos.

One day—we long ago forgot the exact circumstances—one of us mentioned Matthias to the other, and that is how our collaboration began. Both of us had it in mind to write this book, and it could have been awkward. But being friends, we joked and jockeyed about the project for a couple of years until deciding to write it together. We shared our notes, worked out a basic outline, and staked out what research remained to be done. As academics will do, we assumed that, by dividing the work in two, completing the book would occupy a summer. We finished it more than ten years later.

The great attraction, of Matthias and his demented Kingdom, was the opportunity it presented to write a story connected to a time and to places we had come to know well. As it happened, though, we were not the only historians attracted to interesting, little-known stories. When we started our work at the start of the 1980s, historians had already begun talking about a Return to Narrative, in which academic analysis would be woven into storytelling. In practice, this turned out to be a rejection of sociology and an embrace of anthropology, a part of the so-called Cultural Turn in historical study during those years. By the time we were completing the book in the early 1990s, "Microhistory" was the new buzzword. Here, historians picked at little stories to make them give up their bigger meanings.

The Return to Narrative produced some good cultural history, but only a few good stories. The microhistorians also wrote some valuable books, but like the Return to Narrative, Microhistory congealed into an academic discussion about storytelling. Some of the rediscovered narratives were not really all that interesting except to specialist scholars. Even specialists sometimes had difficulty understanding what, if anything, the tale being told had to say about larger historical issues. And when the professors were through with them, too many of the stories were dead on the ground.

Looking back, we can see that we breathed in the academic air in which these conversations were conducted; but, we never talked about either reviving narrative history or undertaking a "micro" study. We had had a good story all along, and we simply wanted to tell it as fully and as well as we could. There was nothing more to it than that.

We are, however, historians, and we were determined to make the Prophet Matthias and his followers a part of history. An occasional auditor at early presentations pointed out that the tale of Matthias was an archetype: a universal story of power and resentment, jealousy and lust, domestic order assaulted by passion—a D.H. Lawrence-style clash of Apollo and Dionysus that could have happened at any time or place. We might, as popularizers tend to do, have gotten around this by researching the story's material trappings (getting the clothing correct, say, right down to the buttons), and then encouraging today's readers to experience the Matthias cult as a period piece in which the characters are essentially like us.

But historians know that, in important ways, people in the past were *not* like us. Pride, jealousy, lust, and the other deadly sins (in the case of Matthias, we cannot neglect gluttony) may be Adam's universal bequest to humankind, but they always display themselves differently in specific times and places. Every sin (not to mention acts of love, bravery, and the rest) happens within a finite historical situation, Historians are not satisfied with merely dredging up the secrets of the dead. We reestablish our stories as a part of their time and place. Historical explanation is an explanation *in terms of* time and place.

We saw great possibilities for doing that with the Kingdom of Matthias, even though the story and its characters were eccentric in the extreme. Johnson had written a book about evangelical revivalism, and knew the academic literature on American religion in these years. Wilentz had finished a study of the New York City working class, and knew the social history in which the Matthias story takes place. We both saw that the Matthias cult was embedded in the 1820s and 1830s, and we found more and more links as the work went on. (Just one example of the historical character of the enterprise: The Prophet's resplendent wardrobe and his nightly sacramental feasts demanded historical explanation as well as description and evocation. We read anthropological studies of colors, textures, and the shapes of British breakfast biscuits, and remained confused. Then we went to the historical literature on American material culture and found clear and convincing answers to our questions, confirming the Prophet's relentless traditionalism and our own belief that the answers to historical questions are to be found in history.)

We are told that that the raw materials of history do not present themselves as stories. This time, they did. Better yet, it was a stage play. The setting is New York when that city was becoming America's great commercial metropolis. There is a small cast of characters, each of whom can stand for a *type* of New Yorker during these years. Elijah Pierson and Benjamin Folger were country boys who became successful wholesale merchants, intermediaries between Atlantic commerce and the explosion of consumer demand in the American countryside. They were also men who, like hundreds of thousands of newly prosperous businessmen, relinquished the domestic patriarchy under which they had grown up.

Their wives, the saintly Sarah Pierson and the more elegant but less substantial Ann Folger, were pious housewives who, in different ways, invented bourgeois ways of being religious and of organizing their marriages and families. Their homes were feminized, mother-centered refuges from the cold competitive world in which husbands made their money. Their households were also models of what the world could be, and they formed societies to convert the poor, democratize the churches, enforce the Sabbath, rescue prostitutes, spread revivals, and much more. They fasted, prayed, and simplified their lives, and some—particularly Elijah Pierson, who had long talks with Jesus, and who tried to raise his wife from the dead—made immediate and sustained contact with the supernatural. In different ways and with varying levels of intensity, each of them was in the perfectionist vanguard of cultural and religious innovations that would become dominant in the northern United States. At its religious core, their new life hinged on the effort to substitute Christian love for patriarchy and every other form of worldly power.

Enter Matthias, a bearded carpenter who could not support his family, who beat his wife and terrorized his household, and who claimed to be God on earth, declaring a restored patriarchy that would rid the world of capitalists, Christians, and their womanish ways. Matthias, in short, was the Bad Patriarch of evangelical nightmares, appearing at their doorstep as a prophet and avenger. He overpowered Elijah Pierson and a few others, then converted Ann and Benjamin Folger, and set up his fatherly Kingdom at his followers' houses in New York and at the Folgers' estate up the Hudson. Before long, he was riding about the city in an elegant coach and four, sporting a sanctified and expensive wardrobe, and giving nightly lectures featuring the male governing spirit and the perfidious female spirit. He declared death and damnation upon (these among many others) doctors, lawyers, merchants, men who did not govern their wives, those who ate pork (Matthias was the Prophet of the Jews), and men who wore spectacles.

At the Folgers' estate near Sing Sing, Matthias built a rural kingdom in which he was the Father, his followers labored at tasks that suited their individual spirits, and women were in their place—all put into their stations by the inspired dictates of Matthias. Shut up in a country house, the sexual tensions that had always simmered in the Kingdom boiled over, and Matthias and Ann Folger discovered that they were "match spirits." Then the Kingdom collapsed in a flurry of adultery and jealousy, riot and public outrage, suspicions of murder, and imprisonment and exile for the Prophet Matthias. The wife whom Matthias had abandoned took advantage of the situation and dictated a pamphlet about her errant and fanatical husband. A journalistic friend of Ann and Benjamin Folger, in an attempt to whitewash their soiled reputations, wrote a book that described the inner workings of the cult without mentioning the sexual arrangements that eventually blew it up.

That journalist made the mistake of implicating the ex-slave Isabella Van Wagenen in the Kingdom's worst excesses. The servant and coreligionist of Elijah Pierson, she came with him into the Matthias cult. She was a committed participant and wily observer from the beginning, and she became the teller of the most honest and complete account of the whole affair.

It was, in the larger scheme of American history, a minor story, and we avoided making more of it than it deserved. Yet we did not want to slight its importance either. All of those reports in the labor press were, we discovered, symptomatic: the story riveted newspaper editors just at the moment that the popular metropolitan penny press was coming into existence. Apparently, we were not the only ones who thought the story was interesting: a burgeoning newspaper readership at the time did as well. Writers as well as readers also tried to make sense of the Kingdom; and they talked and wrote about what they concluded. They, too, thought that Matthias's ravings and his (for a time) successful conversion of Pierson and the Folgers conveyed something deeply significant about the disjointed America of the 1830s. While trying to resist the exaggerations and heat that accompany any weird scandal, especially one that involves sexual play, we thought we would do the same from the vantage point of a century and a half later.

The trick was to try and do so without turning the protagonists into *mere* historical types. The forlorn Elijah Person, the unstable Folgers, and the demented Robert Matthews: none, obviously, lived his or her life in order to conform to what late twentieth-century historians thought of the America in which they lived. They suffered, raged, swooned, and betrayed without knowing anything about a "market revolution" or a Second Great Awakening, concepts that historians only imposed much later. They lived in their own histories, not ours, and we tried to respect their histories even as we tried to make it intelligible to our own sense of history. Once Matthias enters the scene, of course, the story jumps out of current historians' grooves, and the danger of stereotyping diminishes. But we were cautious, even here, about not forcing any of the characters into a mold.

We also had to deal with source problems. Right away, the two main sources we discovered first, the accounts of the story by William Leete Stone and Gilbert Vale, presented clashing versions of the facts. The difficulties deepened when we found the pamphlet written by Robert Matthews's wife. We decided to stick as far as possible to relating only what could be corroborated by independent sources, including archival materials. Where this was impossible, we found that certain claims, especially in Stone's book, were inconsistent with other verifiable facts. Without corroboration and whenever inconsistencies arose, we elected to omit the material in question.

Then came the matter of dividing the writing. As each of us admired the others' prose, we trusted that we could find a way to blend our voices. But our styles, at least then, were very different: Johnson favored compact, sentences with simple words in which less is more; Wilentz preferred more lyrical, even acrobatic prose in his own writing. We decided to break the writing in half, with each of us drafting two chapters, one of us writing the prologue and the other the epilogue, and then revising each other's drafts. Johnson's prose, we hoped, would expand and Wilentz would get sharper, and we would arrive at some sort of consistent combination.

It is not a practice we would necessarily urge on other writers contemplating a jointly written book. But in this case, it seems to have worked out pretty well. Nothing has pleased us more about the book's reception than hearing from readers that they cannot tell which of us drafted which chapter. We take it to mean that we managed to smooth out or at least hide the seams. In any event, this is the one part of what went into writing *The Kingdom of Matthias* that we prefer to keep a secret.

If we were writing this book today, the story would stay the same. Historical sources, after all, do not change their minds. Historians and the literature that they make do change, however, and we might well have emphasized different matters had we begun our research ten or fifteen years later. Continuing work on emancipation in the North, for example, might have led us to consider Isabella Van Wagenen's story a little differently, amid a more profound social transformation than we had imagined. The larger theme of the market revolution has come in for a great deal of criticism since 1994, and we might have presented a more nuanced view of the aspirations and hurts of our protagonists. Yet we do not think that these changes would deeply affect the book were we to take them into account now. Nor do we think that attending to the many academic fashions of the last decade or so would have made much difference to our rendering. Isabella's story could be rewritten in the jargon of subaltern studies, but we do not think it would have added much if anything of substance to what we wrote. Nor does the accumulation of work in whiteness studies, transnational history, or post-colonial history speak especially loudly or clearly to the conditions of our characters. For those reasons, and in line with the injunction to leave well enough alone, we decided to issue this updated edition without changing anything in the text.

The most powerful development since this book appeared in 1994 had to do not with theory or historical reinterpretation but with technology. The Library of Congress, Google Books, the Early American Newspapers project, and others have created a huge and expanding digitized archive. Type in "prophet" and "Matthias" ("impostor" and "Matthias" works almost as well) and click: research that would have been impossible when we were writing this book pops up on the screen. We recently made that search, and found nothing that would change our story about the Kingdom of Matthias and the legal troubles that followed its breakup. We did, however, find widely scattered sightings of Matthias after his release from jail in 1835. Together, they reconstruct the story that Americans read about the Prophet in exile.

Matthias got out of jail at Sing Sing in August 1835. He took the steamboat to New York City and looked up his lawyer, Henry Western. The prison officials had kept the prophet clean-shaven, but he retained his green frock coat and pantaloons. He told Western that he was destitute, having spent all his money on the trip to New York. Western, who doubtless wanted to get rid of Matthias, gave him three dollars and told him to "leave off all your nonsense and go to work." Matthias thanked him, shook hands (he used his left hand; the right was reserved for God), then collected Isabella and called on Margaret and the children at their lodgings on Chapel Street. (They arrived in a carriage, probably a rental secured by Western's money; in all subsequent sightings, Matthias traveled on foot.) After the unsuccessful visit to Chapel Street, New Yorkers spied Matthias on Broadway, still "full of his extravagances." The police scooped him up and put him onto an early morning ferry to New Jersey, and within hours he was in Newark, looking for his brother. Word spread that the Prophet Matthias was in town, and the first of many mobs began to gather. The Newark authorities played it safe and escorted him out of town.

He walked west into Pennsylvania, but the Spirit stopped him near Lancaster and ordered him back to Babylon (Manhattan). In New Jersey he tried to talk two men into accompanying him on a preaching expedition to the city, and promised one of them a miracle: "Let you and I jump from the deck of the steamboat into the North River, and verily I will save thee and me from the waters." At midpoint in the river horrified passengers and crewmen saw two men (one of them "wore a frock coat curiously made, and was slender in his person") leap from the ferry. Boatmen retrieved Matthias' dying companion, but did not find Matthias. "Thus ends," said the *New York Herald*, "the greatest impostor that has appeared for years."

Not yet, though. Over the following weeks, newspapers in New Hampshire reprinted stories about sightings of Matthias in Pennsylvania, heading west. He passed through Myerstown, Reading, Carlysle and Harrisburg. He preached to the Dunkards, a sect that practiced full-immersion baptism, and in which adult male believers wore beards. He journeyed through Pittsburgh and on to the Mormons at Kirtland, guided at every step by the Holy Spirit. He still wore the green frock coat and pantaloons, although he now carried a second coat over his shoulder, and one account spoke of grey as well as green pantaloons. The wardrobe was expanding, his re-grown beard was an inch long, and he was accompanied by a convert who walked behind (not beside) him. Derision and the threat of mobs met him everywhere, and some newspapers hinted that "the stern law of Judge Lynch" might be in order.

The Mormons kicked Matthias out of Kirtland in October 1835, and Matthias disappeared from the newspapers for the next six months. In the spring of 1836 there were sketchy notices about sightings in Maine, New Brunswick, and Saratoga County. More substantial reports place him in Baltimore early in 1837. There he converted a well-off family, again demanding that his followers give themselves and their property up to him. It might be time, said the *Baltimore Atheneum*, for citizens to take the law into their own hands. Matthias then went south and west to Staunton, Virginia, sporting "the smoothly combed beard of a he-goat." A group of "unruly boys" threatened to cut it off, and he left town. He preached near Richmond, Virginia (where he was, according to the *Baltimore Sun*, "decently clad") but refused to continue unless his safety could be guaranteed. There are unlikely reports that he returned to northeastern Ohio to make a second attempt to "regulate the Mormonites." His next appearance was in Rising Sun, Kentucky in November 1837, where the threat of mob violence chased him out of town. A month later he was in Louisville, with the same result. Matthias walked into what had once been the Northwest Territory. At one town, according to the *Milwaukee Sentinel*, a wag demanded that he perform a miracle. Matthias replied that "I have been exhibiting every day, for the last ten years, the greatest miracle ever shown to the world. *I have been telling the truth without being mobbed.*"

In Illinois, Matthias interviewed a clergyman from St. Louis, who wrote up the encounter for the *New York Spectator*. The prophet's beard, he said, now covered his chest. He wore an old camlet cloak over clothes that were "of ordinary style, though not particularly new or cleanly"; the one hint of the old supernatural wardrobe was a red sash around his waist. Matthias stood in the cold and ranted at length on the nature of true religion. Then he asked the parson if there were many Jews in St. Louis.

Early in 1838, still another account claimed, Matthias crossed the Mississippi into Iowa and preached to the Indians. The Indians at Keokuk worried that Matthias would steal their horses, and chased him away. Next, he supposedly met Black Hawk, who in 1832 had fought a sad little war trying to reoccupy the lands of the Sauk and Fox peoples in Illinois. "Mrs. Black Hawk," a reporter wrote, assumed from the Prophet's beard that he was a spirit. She fed him boiled corn and he ate it, thus assuring her that he was not an *evil* spirit. Matthias then talked with Black Hawk, and tried to explain Native Americans' descent from the lost tribes of Israel. He stayed with the Indians until August 1838, when armed Texans, fighting one of their many little wars with the native peoples to their north, found Matthias and took him to Nacogdoches, deep in Texas. (It is not certain that he wanted to go. A newspaper talked of him "having been taken while coming from the Indians"; another disclosed that his departure from his new Hebrew hosts was "not altogether voluntary.") Matthias stayed in Texas for a few months, preaching that the present border war would be the last before the Millennium. He left Texas and walked into the village of Little Rock, Arkansas early in 1839. A few hours later a mob held him down, cut off his foot-long beard, and rode him out of town on a rail. Matthias then disappeared.

During the summer of 1841, after a two-and-a-half-year absence from the newspapers, a southern paper reported that Matthias had died in upcountry North Carolina a year earlier. Not true, said an editor from Albany. He had seen the prophet, "beard and all," on a steamboat a few days earlier. It was the last time that anyone claimed to have seen Matthias alive.

Some of these reports ring truer than others, but it is ultimately impossible to tell the true stories from the fictions. Plainly, though,

Matthias remained a notorious character in all parts of the nation for several years after his release from Sing Sing prison. Interest in him remained strong enough to lead some newspapers to spread rumors—and perhaps entirely fabricate stories—about his comings and goings. There also may have been some Matthias imitators wandering about, claiming the original prophet's lineage and powers. All of which affirms how deeply the cracked prophet and his kingdom impressed themselves on the American popular imagination in the 1830s and 1840s. The mystery of Matthias' ultimate fate is no closer to being solved today than in was in 1994, although the story is thicker and more detailed. But more than we could have known, Matthias was a well-known character in his own time—and so his story will always be worth pondering, for what it tells us about the hurts, hopes, and yearnings of the America in which the story unfolded.

Paul E. Johnson
Sean Wilentz
November 12, 2011

A NOTE ON SOURCES

Taking the full measure of the history of Matthias and his followers requires consulting numerous sources, many of which tell conflicting stories. The most important of these are: William Leete Stone's *Matthias and His Impostures,* Margaret Matthews's ghostwritten pamphlet *Matthias. By His Wife,* and Gilbert Vale's *Fanaticism.*

Stone's account, published shortly after Matthias's conviction is 1835, recounts the events from the point of view of Benjamin and Ann Folger. Margaret Matthews, with the aid of Origen Bacheler, published her riposte to Stone in August 1835; while telling of her own experiences, Mrs. Matthews was particularly interested in attacking Stone and Benjamin Folger, and in upholding the good name of the Finneyite evangelicals (including Edward N. Kirk). Vale's two volumes, the last of the works to be completed, relied, as Vale wrote, "in the first place through Isabella, a coloured woman"—but he also claimed "that EVERY MATERIAL POINT of her evidence has been verified by other respectable witnesses in connexion with the party." (Conceding to popular prejudice, Vale elsewhere remarked that he always obtained "white evidence" to corroborate Isabella Van Wagenen's claims.)

Margaret Matthews's effort is valuable mainly for its wealth of information about the life of Robert Matthews before he became Matthias and for its corrections of some errors in Stone's book. Even so, it must be used with caution. Mrs. Matthews was faulty and at times self-contradictory in her dating of certain key events; where her dating is consistent other reliable sources sometimes show she was mistaken. Her presentation of still other matters (above all her dealings with Benjamin Folger and her account of her daughter Isabella's involvement in the Kingdom) is highly suspect.

Otherwise, students of the Matthias affair must choose between the sometimes starkly different presentations of William Leete Stone and Gilbert Vale. Wherever possible, we have sought independent verification for every detail of their accounts. Our findings appear in the footnotes. More often than not, the evidence shows that Stone and Vale were both reasonably accurate about the main outline of events. (Vale himself, despite the vituperation he aimed at Stone's book, acknowledged that its account was mainly true.) But on two crucial points, there is no agreement: first, Stone presents the evidence in ways that implicate Matthias and Isabella Van Wagenen in Elijah Pierson's alleged murder; and second, Stone says nothing about the Kingdom's sexual life.

Regarding the death of Elijah Pierson, we are largely persuaded that no poisoning occurred. Folger's retreat in the face of Isabella Van Wagenen's slander suit is one reason for our belief; another is the series of results from the autopsies on Pierson's body. Still, when presenting these matters, we have deliberately avoided making any accusations and stuck strictly to the facts that Stone and Vale agree upon, as further confirmed in the transcript of Matthias's trial in April 1835.

As for the Kingdom's sexual arrangements, we are more prepared to side with Vale and to discount Stone. Above all, Stone's heavy-footed effort to sidestep the matter and protect his friends, the Folgers, is inadvertently damning: instead of refuting the rumors of "licentiousness and lust"—indeed, instead of even denying them—Stone obfuscates. In recounting this side of the Kingdom's history, however, we have highlighted those episodes which Stone and Vale agree occurred (such as the incident at the Yonkers tavern and Benjamin Folger's melodramatic attack on the Prophet) but from which Stone omits any sexual references.

As complex as the story is, we inevitably have had to pass over completely some interesting details, while consigning other matters (such as Matthias's eldest son's flight from Mount Zion) to the footnotes. To include every last bit, we are certain, would have made our telling cumbersome, a trap that Gilbert Vale, a relentless pursuer of facts, too often fell into. Nevertheless, we have tried not to exclude, elide, or demote anything of central importance to the Kingdom's rise and fall.

NOTES

Prologue: Two Prophets at Kirtland

1. This description of Smith and Matthias's conversations is drawn from Dean C. Jessee, ed., *The Papers of Joseph Smith: Volume Two: Journal, 1832–1842* (Salt Lake City, 1992), 68–74; and *Painesville* [Ohio] *Telegraph*, November 29, 1835. On Kirtland, see *Latter Day Saints' Messenger and Advocate*, July 1836. For Matthias's earlier uses of Daniel's vision, see William L. Stone, *Matthias and His Impostures: or, the Progress of Fanaticism. Illustrated in the Extraordinary Case of Robert Matthews, and Some of His Forerunners and Disciples* (New York, 1835), 162, 167. Joseph Smith chose his interview with Matthias to provide one of the first accounts of his first vision. As a result, Smith's interview with Matthias remains important to modern Mormonism. See James B. Allen, "The Significance of Joseph Smith's 'First Vision' in Mormon Thought," in D. Michael Quinn, ed., *The New Mormon History: Revisionist Essays in the Past* (Salt Lake City, 1990), 37–52.

2. On the market revolution, its religious connections, and the other major themes in the remainder of this prologue, see Sean Wilentz, "Society, Politics, and the Market Revolution, 1815–1848," in Eric Foner, ed., *The New American History* (Philadelphia, 1990), 51–71; Paul E. Johnson, "The Market Revolution," in Mary Kupiec Cayton et al., eds., *The Encyclopedia of American Social History* (3 vols.; New York, 1992), I: 545–60; and especially Charles Sellers, *The Market Revolution: Jacksonian America, 1815–1846* (New York, 1991), as well as the voluminous literature cited in these works. For an intelligent recent overview of the Second Great Awakening, see Mark A.

Noll, *A History of Christianity in the United States and Canada* (Grand Rapids, Mich., 1992), 165–244. The richest local history of the Awakening remains Whitney R. Cross, *The Burned-Over District: The Social and Intellectual History of Enthusiastic Religion in Western New York, 1800–1850* (Ithaca, 1950).

3. There have been a number of scholarly attempts to name the revival tradition associated with Finney, Lyman Beecher, and others who preached to middle-class Yankee evangelical congregations from the 1820s onward. Timothy L. Smith settles on the accurately descriptive "Revival" Calvinism; Nathan O. Hatch prefers the more generalized "Moderate" Calvinism; while Byron Cecil Lambert resurrects the evocative contemporary term "Effort" Calvinism. See Smith, *Revivalism and Social Reform: American Protestantism on the Eve of the Civil War* (New York, 1965); Hatch, *The Democratization of American Christianity* (New Haven, 1989); Lambert, *The Rise of the Anti-Mission Baptists: Sources and Leaders, 1800–1840* (New York, 1980). We will use the term "Finneyite evangelicalism" in the hope that it will connote the relatively dignified use of Methodist revival techniques, the Arminianized plan of salvation, the perfectionist reform implications, and the new middle-class constituency associated above all with Charles G. Finney. As Mark Noll has recently suggested, it makes sense to identify the movement with Finney, its leading light: "Because of his dominant role in the revival tradition, and the dominant place that revivalism assumed in the antebellum period," Noll writes, "a good case can be made that Finney should be ranked with Andrew Jackson, Abraham Lincoln, and Andrew Carnegie (or some other representative industrialist) as one of the most important figures in nineteenth-century America. Beyond doubt, he stands by himself as *the* crucial figure in white American evangelicalism after Jonathan Edwards." Noll, *A History of Christianity,* 176–77.

By distinguishing Finneyites from other evangelicals, we do not wish to imply that everyone touched by Finney or one of his allies thought identically. Finneyites often came to different conclusions about specific issues, especially in politics. Yet even here, they generally gravitated to reformist Whig principles, and opposed anti-reformist Whigs and Jacksonian Democrats. On revivalism and politics (which we will return to momentarily), see Daniel Walker Howe, "The Evangelical Movement and Political Culture in the North During the Second Party System," *Journal of American History* 77 (1991): 1216–1239. Howe's "evangelicals" correspond with those we call "Finneyite evangelicals."

4. For contrasting approaches to early nineteenth-century plebeian reli-

gion, both of which emphasize its importance, see Hatch, *Democratization of American Christianity;* and Jon Butler, *Awash in a Sea of Faith: Christianizing the American People* (Cambridge, Mass., 1990). For yet another approach, which details how plebeian evangelicalism contributed to the rise of labor protest in the 1830s and 1840s, see Teresa Anne Murphy, *Ten Hours' Labor: Religion, Reform, and Gender in Early New England* (Ithaca, 1992), esp. 73–100. On related plebeian religious movements in England, see J. F. C. Harrison, *The Second Coming: Popular Millenarianism, 1780–1850* (New Brunswick, N.J., 1979).

5. Frances Trollope, *Domestic Manners of the Americans* (1832; London, 1984), 122; David L. Rowe, *Thunder and Trumpets: Millerites and Dissenting Religion in Upstate New York, 1800–1850* (Chico, Calif., 1985), 72–77; Richard L. Bushman, *Joseph Smith and the Beginnings of Mormonism* (Urbana, 1984); Jan Shipps, *Mormonism: The Story of a New Religious Tradition* (Ubrana, 1985); Kenneth H. Winn, *Exiles in a Land of Liberty: Mormons in America, 1830–1846* (Chapel Hill, 1989). An earlier version of this discussion appears in Paul E. Johnson, "Democracy, Patriarchy, and American Revivals, 1780–1830," *Journal of Social History* 24 (1991): 603–10.

6. [Anon.], "Matthias and His Impostures," *North American Review,* No. 89 (1835), 307.

One. Elijah Pierson

1. William L. Stone, *Matthias and His Impostures: or, the Progress of Fanaticism. Illustrated in the Extraordinary Case of Robert Matthews, and Some of His Forerunners and Disciples* (New York, 1835), 53.

2. On Abraham Pierson and the founding of Newark, see [Frank John Urquhart], *A History of the City of Newark, New Jersey: Embracing Practically Two and a Half Centuries, 1666–1913* (2 vols.; New York, 1913), I, 78–81 (quotation on 79); and John E. Pomfret, *The Province of East Jersey, 1609–1702: The Rebellious Proprietary* (Princeton, 1962), 47–52, 371–72. One of the original Abraham's sons, also named Abraham, returned to Connecticut in 1692, and in 1701 became the first rector of Yale University, where today Pierson College honors his memory. On the Pierson family history in Morristown, see *History of the First Presbyterian Church, Morristown, N.J., Combined Registers from 1742 to 1845* (2 vols.; Morristown, 1885), II, 181–83, 191. On farm size and valuations, see "An Account of the Taxables in the County of Morris in the State of New Jersey taken in the Months of July &

August 1796," microfilm, Family History Library of the Church of Jesus Christ of Latter-day Saints, Salt Lake City [hereafter SLC].

3. Morris County Clerk's Office, Book of Deeds, Book G, p. 134, microfilm, SLC.

4. *History of the First Presbyterian Church,* I, 26, 27, 30, 31, 38, 44, 45, 47; *The Record of the First Presbyterian Church of Morristown, N.J.* (n.p., 1880–85), 5 vols., I, 12, 68.

5. On late eighteenth-century northern Calvinism as it was presented to children, see Philip Greven, *The Protestant Temperament: Patterns of Child-Rearing, Religious Experience, and the Self in Early America* (New York, 1977), 21–148; and Anne M. Boylan, "Sunday Schools and Changing Evangelical Views of Children in the 1820s," *Church History* 48 (September 1979): 320–33.

6. *Record of the First Presbyterian Church,* I, 146–47, II, 26–30; *History of Morris County, New Jersey, with Illustrations and Biographical Sketches of Prominent Citizens* (New York, 1882), 135–36; Jotham H. Condit and Eben Condit, *Genealogical Record of the Condit Family* (Newark, N.J., 1885), 175–76; *History of the First Presbyterian Church,* I, 26.

7. "An Account of the Taxables in the Township of Morris"; *History of the First Presbyterian Church,* I, 22 ("wife of Mr. C."), 27 (Mr. Hyer); widows: I, 22, 23; Crane: I, 26; and see II, 183. The will of Elijah Pierson (Elijah's grandfather, d. 1795), Surrogate's Court, Morris County, Record of Wills, 1740–1900, File No. 890N, microfilm, SLC, provides the use of a room, firewood, and a cow for his daughter Sarah (Usual Crane's wife) because of "her present destitute condition unsupported by her husband." The will then mentions her possible widowhood.

8. Stone, *Matthias,* 52; Tax Assessment Lists, New York County, 1820, Municipal Archives and Records Center, New York City [hereafter MARC].

9. On Pearl Street, see Robert Greenhalgh Albion, *The Rise of New York Port, 1815–1860* (New York, 1939), 43, 63, 280; John A. Kouwenhoven, *The Columbia Historical Portrait of New York* (Garden City, N.Y., 1953), 132; Stuart M. Blumin, *The Emergence of the Middle Class: Social Experience in the American City, 1790–1900* (New York, 1989), 78–83, 86; Bertram Wyatt-Brown, *Lewis Tappan and the Evangelical War Against Slavery* (New York, 1969), esp. 41–77. On the rise of wholesalers generally in these years, see Glenn Porter and Harold Livesay, *Merchants and Manufacturers: Studies in the Changing Structure of Nineteenth-Century Marketing* (Baltimore, 1971), 13–36. Indicative of the middle-class character of Pearl Street and of merchants

engaged in evangelical reform is the fact that of the elite reformers who called themselves the Association of Gentlemen, only Arthur Tappan appears on Edward Pessen's painstaking lists of the city's richest men. Compare Pessen, *Riches, Class, and Power Before the Civil War* (Lexington, Mass., 1973), 320–27, and Wyatt-Brown, *Lewis Tappan,* 61. At the height of his career, Elijah Pierson was "supposed to be worth $80,000," which, if true, would place him at an economic level near the Tappan brothers. Pierson's wealth is estimated in G[ilbert] Vale, *Fanaticism; Its Source and Influence, Illustrated by the Simple Narrative of Isabella, in the Case of Matthias, Mr. and Mrs. B. Folger, Mr. Pierson, Mr. Mills, Catherine, Isabella, &c. &c.* (2 vols.; New York 1835), II, 19.

10. *History of the First Presbyterian Church,* II, 181–83.

11. Shepherd Knapp, ed., *Personal Records of the Brick Presbyterian Church in the City of New York, 1809–1908* (New York, 1909), 181; Stone, *Matthias,* 325–27, 52–53.

12. Ward Stafford, *New Missionary Field: A Report to the Female Missionary Society for the Poor of the City of New-York and Its Vicinity, at Their Quarterly Prayer-Meeting, March, 1817* (New York, 1817), 41 (quotation). On the beginnings of New York City missions to the poor, see Raymond A. Mohl, *Poverty in New York, 1783–1825* (New York, 1971), 203–8; Carroll Smith-Rosenberg, *Religion and the Rise of the American City: The New York City Mission Movement, 1812–1870* (Ithaca, 1971), 52–60; Anne M. Boylan, "Women in Groups: An Analysis of Women's Benevolent Organizations in New York and Boston, 1797–1840," *Journal of American History* 71 (December 1984): 497–523; idem, "Timid Girls, Venerable Widows and Dignified Matrons: Life Cycle Patterns Among Organized Women in New York and Boston, 1797–1840," *American Quarterly* 38 (Winter 1986): 779–97; M. J. Heale, "Humanitarianism in the Early Republic: The Moral Reformers of New York, 1776–1825," *Journal of American Studies* 2 (October 1968): 161–75; idem, "Patterns of Benevolence: Charity and Morality in Rural and Urban New York, 1783–1830," *Societas—A Review of Social History* 3 (Autumn 1973): 337–59; idem, "From City Fathers to Social Critics: Humanitarianism and Government in New York, 1790 to 1860," *Journal of American History* 63 (June 1976): 21–41; and, especially, Christine Stansell, *City of Women: Sex and Class in New York, 1789–1860* (New York, 1986), 30–37, 63–75.

13. *Proceedings of the First Anniversary of the New-York Evangelical Missionary Society of Young Men, Together with the Annual Report of the Board of*

Directors, and the Speeches Delivered on the Occasion (New York, 1817), 31 (italics in original).

14. On Bancker Street, see *Proceedings . . . of the New-York Evangelical Missionary Society of Young Men,* 5. The quotation is from Matthew LaRue Perrine, *Women Have a Work to Do in the House of God: A Discourse Delivered at the First Annual Meeting of the Female Missionary Society for the Poor of New-York and Its Vicinity, May 12, 1817* (New York, 1817), 16.

15. Perrine, *Women Have a Work to Do,* 4, 11 (italics in original); *Proceedings . . . of the New York Evangelical Missionary Society of Young Men,* 27.

16. We use the word "perfectionism" advisedly. Historians of antebellum reform have used it to describe persons who rejected Calvinist determinism and engaged in reform movements intended to improve the world through individual spiritual transformation. Narrower (and more accurate) accounts by historians of religion discuss Wesleyan perfectionism and doctrines of entire sanctification (the attainment of perfect sinlessness in this life) in more formally theological terms. Finally, a few scholars reserve "perfectionism" to describe only those who believed that the Second Coming had occurred, that the kingdom of God on earth was begun, and that believers could share in apostolic sinlessness and partake of spiritual gifts. At various points in his career, all three definitions apply to Elijah Pierson: he was a leading "perfectionist" reformer, he claimed perfect sinlessness for himself in the late 1820s, and between 1830 and 1832 he exercised apostolic gifts and expected to join in the second resurrection without passing through death. Discussions of perfectionist reform in the broadest sense include, David Brion Davis, "The Emergence of Immediatism in British and American Antislavery Thought," *Mississippi Valley Historical Review* 49 (1962): 209–30; John L. Thomas, "Romantic Reform in America, 1815–1865," *American Quarterly* 17 (1965): 656–81; and Carroll Smith-Rosenberg, "The Cross and the Pedestal: Women, Anti-Ritualism, and the Emergence of the American Bourgeoisie," in Smith-Rosenberg, *Disorderly Conduct: Visions of Gender in Victorian America* (New York, 1985), 129–64. Accounts that pay more formal attention to theological matters include Timothy L. Smith, *Revivalism and Social Reform: American Protestantism on the Eve of the Civil War* (New York, 1965), 103–47 and *passim;* Lewis Perry, *Radical Abolitionism: Anarchy and the Government of God in Antislavery Thought* (Ithaca, 1973); and Lawrence Foster, *Religion and Sexuality: The Shakers, the Mormons, and the Oneida Community* (Urbana, 1984), 72–122.

17. On Sarah Stanford, see Stone, *Matthias,* 53–55. On John Stanford, see

Charles G. Sommers, *Memoir of the Rev. John Stanford, D.D., Late Chaplain to the Humane and Criminal Institutions of New York* (New York, 1835). Sarah Stanford was not an officer of the Female Missionary Society, and may not have been directly involved with the Bancker Street Chapel. Stone tells us that she was an active member of the missionary community, both as her father's daughter and in her own right; very few unmarried women held office in the organizations, however, and the record of her participation increased after her marriage. Between 1823 and 1828 she helped lead the Asylum for Lying-In Women, which provided midwifery and post-partum care for poor but respectable (that is, married) women. From 1826 to 1829, she was an officer in the Female Tract Society, which extended the program of home visits and concentrated on the poor black community. For discussions of these organizations, see Smith-Rosenberg, *Religion and the Rise of the American City*, 74; and Stansell, *City of Women*, 70–71. Beginning in 1828, Sarah Stanford moved on to the perfectionist reforms discussed later in this chapter.

18. [New York] *Evening Post*, May 25, 1822.

19. Stone, *Matthias*, 53; Sommers, *Memoir of the Rev. John Stanford*, 244.

20. New York County Register: Conveyances, 1654–1866, Lib. 264, p. 281, microfilm, SLC. Assuming that the Pierson house, as was standard for such houses, included a basement kitchen and dining room, and that the third floor was in fact a half-floor with garret bedrooms, the house on William Street included about 4000 square feet of living space. Thus the Pierson house cost twice as much and occupied about 25 percent more space than the housing that Stuart Blumin identifies as middle class. See Blumin, *The Emergence of the Middle Class*, 151–55.

21. Stone, *Matthias*, 76.

22. Stone, *Matthias*, 63–64, 79, 83, 84, 85. The most helpful study of middle-class, evangelical romantic love is Karen Lystra, *Searching the Heart: Women, Men, and Romantic Love in Nineteenth-Century America* (New York, 1989).

23. Knapp, ed., *Personal Records of the Brick Presbyterian Church*, 80, 219; Stone, *Matthias*, 35; Gardiner Spring, *The Excellence and Influence of the Female Character: A Sermon Preached in the Presbyterian Church in Murray-Street, at the Request of the New-York Female Missionary Society* (New York, 1825), 4, 11. Vale, *Fanaticism*, I, 33–35n, and I, 84n, identifies Susannah Wayland Stone as the victim of Folger's attack. Gardiner Spring's sermon does not mention Folger by name, but Stone states that Spring responded to

Folger in print, and this is his one published statement on retrenchment—pointedly addressed to the more radical retrenchers.

24. Stone, *Matthias,* 35–37.

25. Ibid., 46–47. Benjamin Folger is identified as a hardware merchant, in Vale, *Fanaticism,* II, 20, and in his city directory listings in the middle and late 1820s. Ten years after these events, a reporter described Ann Folger as "rather above the middle size, of an elegant figure, and extremely genteel and lady-like," with "a highly intelligent and interesting expression of countenance," and "exceedingly regular" features, "of the Grecian caste, with the nose slightly acquiline." At one point Gilbert Vale rendered her maiden name as Desbrosse. Vale, *Fanaticism,* I, 71.

26. Stone, *Matthias,* 39–45.On Wesley's Holy Club, see Albert C. Outler, "'Biblical Primitivism' in Early American Methodism," in Richard T. Hughes, ed., *The American Quest for the Primitive Church* (Urbana, 1988), 132.

27. Stone, *Matthias,* 59–60.

28. Ibid., 55–59.

29. Sarah R. Ingraham, *Walks of Usefulness; or, Reminiscences of Mrs. Margaret Prior* (New York, 1843), 20ff; Joel Parker, *A Farewell Discourse to the Free Presbyterian Churches; Delivered in the Chatham Street Chapel, on Sabbath Evening, October 27th, 1833* (New York, 1834), 19; Wyatt-Brown, *Tappan,* 65, 114; Stone, *Matthias,* 49, 61–62.

30. Stone, *Matthias,* 49–51; [Olive Gilbert], *Narrative of Sojourner Truth,* (1850; New York, 1993), 76–77. The Retrenchment Society carried such things further than others, but diet, sexuality, and household furnishings were crucial and closely linked in the process of self-definition among the emerging middle class. For examples, see Stephen Nissenbaum, *Sex, Diet, and Debility in Jacksonian America: Sylvester Graham and Health Reform* (Westport, Conn., 1980); Carroll Smith-Rosenberg, "Sex as Symbol in Victorian Purity," *American Journal of Sociology* 84, Supplement (1978): 212–47; Katherine C. Grier, *Culture & Comfort: People, Parlors, and Upholstery, 1850–1930* (Amherst, Mass., 1988).

31. Stone, *Matthias,* 64–66, 328; [Gilbert], *Narrative of Sojourner Truth,* 95–96 (quotation).

32. On Folger and the Free Church, see Stone, *Matthias,* 48; Parker, *A Farewell Discourse,* 18–20; Wyatt-Brown, *Tappan,* 65, 114; Charles C. Cole, Jr., "The Free Church Movement in New York City," *New York History* 34 (1953), 284–97. On Pierson and the Sabbatarians, see Tappan, *Life of Arthur Tappan,* 97; Bertram Wyatt-Brown, "Prelude to Abolitionism: Sabbatarian

Politics and the Rise of the Second Party System," *Journal of American History* 63 (1971): 316–41; Paul E. Johnson, *A Shopkeeper's Millennium: Society and Revivals in Rochester, New York, 1815–1837* (New York, 1978), 83–94; Richard R. John, "Taking Sabbatarianism Seriously: The Postal System, the Sabbath, and the Transformation of American Political Culture," *Journal of the Early Republic* 10 (1990): 517–67.

33. New-York Magdalen Society, *First Annual Report of the Executive Committee of the New-York Magdalen Society, Instituted January 1, 1830* (New York, 1831), recites these stories (quotation on 3); Stansell, *City of Women,* excavates the social situations in which the stories were constructed. The Pierson quotation appears in Stone, *Matthias,* 60. (Here, as subsequently, all direct holy quotations, whether described as from God, Jesus, or the Holy Ghost, appear in italics.) Sitting at a scholarly intersection of class, gender, religion, and sexuality, the mission to the prostitutes has been a focal point of feminist historical scholarship. As a result, the Magdalen Society and its successors are among the best-studied of antebellum reform movements. See Smith-Rosenberg, *Religion and the Rise of the American City,* 97–124; Barbara Berg, *The Remembered Gate: Origins of American Feminism* (New York, 1978), 176–222; Mary P. Ryan, "The Power of Women's Networks: A Case Study of Female Moral Reform in Antebellum America," *Feminist Studies* 5 (1979): 66–85; Smith-Rosenberg, "Beauty, the Beast, and the Militant Woman: A Case Study of Sex Roles and Social Stress in Jacksonian America," *American Quarterly* 23 (1971): 562–84; idem, "Writing History: Language, Class, and Gender," in Teresa de Lauretis, ed., *Feminist Studies/ Critical Studies* (Bloomington, 1986); and Stansell, *City of Women,* esp. 63–75, 171–92. More generally on New York City prostitution, see Timothy J. Gilfoyle, *City of Eros: New York City, Prostitution and the Commercialization of Sex, 1790–1920* (New York, 1942), 29–178.

34. Larry Howard Whiteaker, "Moral Reform and Prostitution in New York City, 1830–1860" (Ph.D. diss. Princeton University, 1977), 97; Stone, *Matthias,* 62.

35. Vale, *Fanaticism,* I, 20–21.

36. Ibid., 18–19; [Gilbert], *Narrative of Sojourner Truth,* 68. On James Latourette, see George W. Noyes, ed., *Religious Experience of John Humphrey Noyes, Founder of Oneida Community* (New York, 1923), 89–92, 133–34, 186–87; Vale, *Fanaticism,* II, 122n; and Whitney R. Cross, *The Burned-Over District: The Social and Intellectual History of Enthusiastic Religion in Western New York, 1800–1850* (Ithaca, 1950), 240.

37. Stone, *Matthias,* 80.

38. Ibid., 67–68.

39. Ibid., 68–69; City of New York, Department of Health, Borough of Manhattan, Register of Deaths, Liber. No. 7 (Oct. 11, 1829–Jan. 1, 1832), SLC.

40. The account of the funeral and the attempt to raise Sarah that follows is from Stone, *Matthias,* 69–77. While it was certainly deranged, the attempt to raise Sarah made perfectionist sense: Elijah Pierson had moved into apostolic times, and as the Prophet Elijah/John the Baptist he had the power to raise the dead. For other perfectionist attempts to restore the dead, see Rowe, *Thunder and Trumpets,* 64–65, 101, 150. A helpful discussion of the theological questions involved is Cross, *Burned-Over District,* 238–51. On the other hand, most evangelicals branded the apostolic gifts of Pierson and other perfectionists as delusions. More than thirty years after the event, the Rev. Gardiner Spring, in a chapter entitled "Fanaticism in Revivals," cited Elijah's attempt to raise Sarah as his one concrete example. See Spring, *Reminiscences of the Life of Gardiner Spring, Pastor of the Brick Presbyterian Church in the City of New York* (New York, 1865), I, 229.

41. Stone, *Matthias,* 79–80.

42. Ibid., 83.

43. This and subsequent quotations from Pierson's diary are from long passages quoted in Stone, ibid., 83–93.

44. Sommers, *Memoir of the Rev. John Stanford,* 68; Diary of John Stanford, entries for April 18, 1830, May 28, 1830, June 8, 1830, June 29, 1830 (quotation), New-York Historical Society.

45. Diary of John Stanford, July 1, 1830. The Stanford family's rejection of Elijah Pierson extended to beyond the grave. At Pierson's death in 1834, Sarah's brother was asked to help administer the estate. According to the lawyers, "He refused having anything to do with it." Untitled document in the Elijah Pierson Estate Papers, County of Westchester, State of New York: Probate, Administration, Guardian, and Estate Tax Files, Yrs. 1834–up, File stamped 1834–47, microfilm, SLC.

46. New-York Magdalen Society, *First Annual Report,* 2–5; Tappan, *Arthur Tappan,* 110–25; L. J. Brown to Charles G. Finney, January 6, 1831, Finney Papers, Oberlin College Library; Joshua Leavitt, *Memoir and Select Remains of the Late Reverend John R. M'Dowall* (New York, 1838), 100ff (quotation on 100); Whiteaker, "Moral Reform and Prostitution in New York City," 101.

47. Wyatt-Brown, *Tappan,* 70.

48. Leavitt, *Memoir of M'Dowall,* 178–79; [John R. McDowall], *Magdalen Facts* (New York, 1832), 98–99.

49. Stone, *Matthias,* 94–95, 100–103; Vale, *Fanaticism* I, 27, 43. In some sources, Rosetta Dratch's surname is rendered as Drach.

Two. Robert Matthews

1. The best source on the birth date of Robert Matthews is "The Examination of Robert Mathews otherwise called 'Mathias the Prophet,'" in *People v. Robert Matthias,* October 15, 1834, Indictment Papers, Court of General Sessions, MARC. On Cambridge, the most helpful sources are Allen Correy, *Gazetteer of the County of Washington, N.Y.* (Schuylerville, N.Y., 1849–50), 71–85; [Crisfield Johnson], *History of Washington Co., New York* (Philadelphia, 1878), 252–82; William Leete Stone [Jr.], *Washington County, New York: Its History to the Close of the Nineteenth Century* (n.p., 1901), 442–57; Amos DeLany Moscrip, *Old Cambridge District: A Historical Sketch of the Region Composed of the Present Towns of Cambridge, Jackson, and White Creek* (1941; Eagle's Bridge, N.Y., 1969); Islay V. H. Gill, *A History of the Argyle Patent* (n.p., 1956), 16–18, 43–51. On the Scots' migration, see Ian Charles Cargill Graham, *Colonists for Scotland: Emigration to North America, 1707–1783* (Ithaca, 1956), esp. 26–32; Ned C. Landsman, *Scotland and Its First American Colony, 1683–1765* (Princeton, 1985), esp. 251–54; Bernard Bailyn, *Voyagers to the West: A Passage in the Peopling of America on the Eve of the Revolution* (New York, 1986), esp. 45–49, 573–637. On the cultural history of the Scots' settlements, see the helpful synthesis in David Hackett Fischer, *Albion's Seed: Four British Folkways in America* (New York, 1989), 605–782.

2. On Coila, see especially Stone, *History,* 456; [Johnson], *History,* 261–62; Royden Woodward Vosburgh, ed., "Records of the First Presbyterian Congregation in Cambridge," 1917, typescript at New York State Library, Albany [hereafter NYSL]; Gill, *History,* 47–51. See also Thomas Beveridge to A. Bruce, January 30, 1784, in James P. Miller, *Biographical Sketches and Sermons of Some of the First Ministers of the Associate Church in America* (Albany, 1839), 488–90.

3. According to [Johnson], *History,* 261, a Mrs. Mathews attended the Lord's Supper of the Coila Associate Presbyterian Church in August 1785; the Coila Associate Church records show that a Mary Mathews was a

member in 1787, Communicants, Parish Register, Church Records, United Presbyterian Church (Coila, New York) [hereafter CCR], microfilm, SLC. Almost certainly this was Robert Matthews's mother. The apparent absence of the father raises the interesting possibility that the Matthews household was not united in the Anti-Burgher faith—and that Mary Matthews may have been the central figure in the family's religious life. As we shall see, however, Robert moved into a conventional Anti-Burgher household after his parents died in about 1795.

4. On the rise of the Scots Anti-Burghers, the classic and still useful works of J. McKerrow, *History of the Secession Church* (Glasgow, 1841); and Alexander H. B. Balbour, *An Historical Account of the Rise and Development of Presbyterianism in Scotland* (Cambridge, 1911), 118–33, may now be supplemented with J. H. S. Burleigh, *A Church History of Scotland* (Oxford, 1960), esp. 210–62, 277–85; William Ferguson, *Scotland: 1689 to the Present* (New York, 1968), 111–12, 115–27; Andrew L. Drummond and James Bulloch, *The Scottish Church, 1688–1843* (Edinburgh, 1973), esp. 110, 151; and Callum G. Brown, *The Social History of Religion in Scotland Since 1730* (London and New York, 1987), 35–37, 62–63, 105–12. Brown draws attention to the "uncompromising" Anti-Burgher strength in rural Lowland districts, and contends that "in most parishes they were in the vanguard of social and religious dissent from the rule of the gentry" (105). On the Anti-Burghers in America, see James Price, "Origin and Distinctive Characteristics of the United Presbyterian Church of North America," *Journal of the Presbyterian Historical Society* I (1901): 87–110; Randolph A. Roth, "The First Radical Abolitionists: The Reverend James Milligan and the Reformed Presbyterians of Vermont," *New England Quarterly* 55 (1982): 542–45. The remark about "Simon-pure" believers is borrowed from Gill, *History*, 45–46, regarding the Coila Anti-Burghers.

5. Correy, *Gazetteer*, 81–83; Vosburgh, "Records," iii; Gill, *History*, 45–51 (quotation on 48).

6. [Johnson], *History*, 262; John M. Newton, *Memoirs of John Marshall Newton* (n.p., n.d. [1913]), 19. Newton, the son of a Presbyterian pastor, recalled his boyhood days in Cambridge in the late 1830s. The basic outline of American Anti-Burgher doctrine appears in the Associate Synod platform written in 1784 by Thomas Beveridge; Associate Presbytery of Pennsylvania, *Declaration and Testimony for the Doctrine and Order of the Church of Christ, and Against the Errors of the Present Times* (Philadelphia, 1784). New

England Calvinists were amazed at the depth of the Scots' piety, which extended to the enforcement of strict bans on Sunday travel. There are numerous reports of how, because of the bans, travelers wound up stranded in some Scots' village inn from Saturday evening until Monday morning. See Timothy Dwight, *Travels in New England and New York*, ed. Barbara Miller Solomon (4 vols.; Cambridge, Mass., 1969), III, 163–64; Roth, "First Radical Abolitionists," 546.

7. On the Scots' Presbyterian Lord's Supper, the essential source is Leigh Eric Schmidt, *Holy Fairs: Scottish Communions and American Revivals in the Early Modern Period* (Princeton, 1989), esp. 69–168. Schmidt draws heavily on both Scots and American sources, with special reference to the session records by John Beath of the Presbyterian Church of Booth Bay, Maine, from the 1760s. On the Lord's Supper in Coila, see Session Minutes, September 15, 1798, June 10, 1800, April 29, 1805, August 24, 1808, November 27, 1810, CCR. On the parallel between the Lord's Supper and Passover, see Roth, "First Radical Abolitionists," 547. The Scots' rituals were the basis for the revival in Cane Ridge, Kentucky, in 1801, one of the key episodes of the Second Great Awakening. See Schmidt, *Holy Fairs*, 64; Paul Conkin, *Cane Ridge: America's Pentecost* (Madison, 1990).

8. Session Minutes, January 19, 1809, January 24, 1811, and passim, CCR.

9. Ibid., September 17, 1804.

10. Miller, *Biographical Sketches*, 187–95.

11. Ibid., 189. William L. Stone, *Matthias and His Impostures: or, the Progress of Fanaticism. Illustrated in the Extraordinary Case of Robert Matthews, and Some of His Forerunners and Disciples* (New York, 1835), 18; and G[ilbert] Vale, *Fanaticism; Its Source and Influence, Illustrated by the Simple Narrative of Isabella, in the Case of Matthias, Mr. and Mrs. B. Folger, Mr. Pierson, Mr. Mills, Catherine, Isabella, &c. &c.* (2 vols.; New York, 1835), I, 37, report the blessing.

12. Schmidt, *Holy Fairs*, 76–83, quotation on 77.

13. Ibid., 69–114, quotations on 101, 103.

14. Ibid., 145–53, 162–68, quotation on 162–63.

15. *Memoirs of Matthias the Prophet, with a Full Exposure of His Previous Impostures and of the Degrading Delusions of His Followers* (New York, 1835), 3.

16. Miller, *Biographical Sketches*, 204, 208.

17. [Margaret Matthews], *Matthias. By His Wife* (New York, 1835), 5; Vale, *Fanaticism,* I, 37. John Maxwell was first listed as a ruling elder of the Coila church on June 10, 1800. Four years later, Maxwell fell into a dispute with the church, which led him to withdraw from membership, but he returned a little over a year later and regained his position as ruling elder. Session Minutes, June 10, 1800, June 11, 1804, November 4, 1805, January 6, 1806, CCR.

18. [Matthews], *Matthias,* 5–7; *Memoirs,* 3–4; Stone, *Matthias,* 18; Vale, *Fanaticism,* I, 37. On Matthews's height and build, see Stone, *Matthias,* 120–21. On Edward Cook, see Session Minutes, January 10, 1814, CCR. There is some confusion in these sources about when, exactly, Matthews departed for Manhattan. Margaret Matthews reports that he moved in with Cook when he was eighteen (which would have been in 1806), but then claims that he came to New York in 1805. (Elsewhere in her narrative she is equally unreliable about dates.) According to Stone, he came to New York "at the age of about twenty years," which would be about 1808; Vale says only that Matthews "was brought up by a farmer till nearly eighteen years of age." Matthews first showed up in a Manhattan street directory in 1808/09, listed as a carpenter living at 32 Henry Street. *Longworth's Directory,* 1808/09. Most probably, he arrived in New York about 1808, having spent two years living with Cook.

19. [Matthews], *Matthias,* 5–6 (quotation on 6). On the New York Seceder church, see Jonathan Greenleaf, *A History of the Churches of All Denominations in the City of New York* (New York, 1846), 212–13. On Andrew Wright as elder, see Thomas E. V. Smith, *The City of New York in the Year of Washington's Inauguration, 1789* (New York, 1889), 155–56. On Matthews's skills, see Stone, *Matthias,* 19; Vale, *Fanaticism,* I, 37.

20. *Memoirs,* 4. On artisan drinking in New York in the Jeffersonian period, see Raymond A. Mohl, *Poverty in New York, 1783–1825* (New York, 1971), 210–21; Howard B. Rock, *Artisans of the New Republic: The Tradesmen of New York City in the Age of Jefferson* (New York, 1979), 295–98; Sean Wilentz, *Chants Democratic: New York City & the Rise of the American Working Class, 1788–1850* (New York, 1984), 53–54. More generally, see William J. Rorabaugh, *The Alcoholic Republic: An American Tradition* (New York, 1979), esp. 15, 131–32.

21. *People v. Robert Matthews,* June 7, 1811, Indictment Papers, Court of General Sessions, MARC. We have been unable to determine whether

Robert Matthews's older brother James (whom we will meet later) ever married a woman named Hester, or was ever a grocer in New York.

22. Session Minutes, January 29, 1812, CCR; Indenture, Robert Thompson to Robert Matthews, February 29, 1812, Deeds, Book L, 56–57, County Records, Washington County, Hudson Falls, New York. Vale, *Fanaticism,* I, 37, reports that Thompson was Matthews's uncle.

23. [Matthews], *Matthias,* 6; Communicants, 1812 (Robert Matthews), 1814 (Margaret Matthews), Baptisms, December 4, 1814 (Robert Matthews son of Robert Matthews), Parish Register, CCR.

24. Stone, *Matthias,* 19. The Cambridge town meeting elected Matthews as an overseer of highways in 1813, further confirming his respectable social position; New York State Daughters of the American Revolution, "A Copy of the Original Town Clerk's Book of Cambridge District, Old Albany County now Washington County, New York, 1773–1814," n.d., typescript, New York Public Library [hereafter NYPL]. There is a large literature on land scarcity and its effects in the rural North during the eighteenth and early nineteenth centuries. For a case study of a man who failed to secure a landed competency, see Paul E. Johnson, "The Modernization of Mayo Greenleaf Patch: Land, Family, and Marginality in New England, 1766–1818," *New England Quarterly* 55 (1982): 488–516. The exact size of the Matthews family varies according to different sources. For example, *The Sun* [New York], October 2, 1834, reported that Mrs. Matthews gave birth to eight children, five of whom survived infancy. From the account in [Matthews], *Matthias,* it appears that she gave birth to seven children, four of whom survived, although she also mentions having five surviving children. By all accounts, however, the Matthews family was large.

25. [Matthews] *Matthias,* 7; Stone, *Matthias,* 19.

26. [Matthews] *Matthias,* 6; Stone, *Matthias,* 20; Vale, *Fanaticism,* I, 37. On the long-term effects of the market revolution in Cambridge, see [Johnson], *History,* 252, 264.

27. [Matthews], *Matthias,* 6–7. On child mortality and health conditions in early nineteenth-century New York, see Mohl, *Poverty in New York,* 10–12; John A. Duffy, *A History of Public Health in New York City, 1625–1866* (New York, 1968), esp. 101–232, 515–40, 579. Between 1817 and 1819, the New York City directories listed Matthews at three different addresses: 440 Greenwich Street, Watts Street near Greenwich, and 3 St. John's Alley. In 1819, he made his first appearance on the city's jury lists, recorded as a

builder on St. John's Alley with more than $150 in personal estate, eligible to serve as a juror; Jury Lists, 1819, New York County, MARC. According to Margaret Matthews, the family moved to Anthony Street later in 1819; [Matthews], *Matthias*, 8.

28. [Matthews], *Matthias*, 7–8 (quotations on 8). On the Matthews household, see Jury Lists, 1819, MARC. According to Margaret Matthews (8), her husband visited "the African church in Anthony-street." The African Methodist Episcopal Zion Church was located at 156 Church Street, just north of Anthony Street; without any doubt, this is the church in question.

29. On the rise of African Methodism in New York City, see Christopher Rush, *A Short Account of the Rise and Progress of the African Methodist Episcopal Church in America* (New York, 1843); and Rhoda G. Freeman, "The Free Negro in New York City in the Era Before the Civil War" (Ph.D. diss., Columbia University, 1966), 380–86. A full history of slaves and free blacks in New York in these years has yet to be published, but see, in addition to Freeman's dissertation, Leo H. Hirsch, Jr., "The Negro and New York, 1783 to 1865," *Journal of Negro History* 6 (1931): 382–473; and, especially, Shane White, *Somewhat More Independent: The End of Slavery in New York City, 1770–1810* (Athens, Ga., 1991). Elijah Pierson's servant Isabella Van Wagenen was a member of this congregation somewhat later. See below, 116. For a general appraisal of plebeian Methodism, see Nathan O. Hatch, *The Democratization of American Christianity* (New Haven, 1989), 103–10.

30. On the Anti-Burghers and slavery, see Associate Presbytery of Pennsylvania, *Declaration*, 33–47; Roth, "First Radical Abolitionists," 549. On black membership in the Coila church, see Session Minutes, January 26, 1817, CCR.

31. [Matthews], *Matthias*, 8–9.

32. Ibid., 9.

33. The standard life of Noah is Jonathan D. Sarna, *Jacksonian Jew: The Two Worlds of Mordecai Noah* (New York, 1981). On Noah's political career, see also Jerome Mushkat, *Tammany: The Evolution of a Political Machine* (Syracuse, 1971), 58–114 passim.

34. In addition to Sarna, *Jacksonian Jew*, 61–75; see Lewis F. Allen, "Founding of the City of Ararat on Grand Island by Mordecai M. Noah," *Buffalo Historical Society Publications* I (1879): 305–28.

35. [Matthews], *Matthias*, 7–9. On Moses as a figure in Anti-Burgher sermonizing, see Miller, *Biographical Sketches*, 197–98, 205, 216.

36. [Matthews], *Matthias,* 9–10. On Matthews's brother James living in Sandy Hill, see James Mathies, *Rochester, a Satire; and Other Miscellaneous Poems* (Rochester, 1830), 107.

37. Sarna, *Jacksonian Jew,* 65–67, quotations on 67.

38. Ibid., 72–75. See also *National Advocate* [New York], October 4, October 31, 1825; *Evening Post* [New York], October 6, 1825.

39. [Matthews], *Matthias,* 10. Margaret Matthews says her husband departed in the spring of 1825, but her dates (here as elsewhere) are unreliable. Matthews first appeared in the Albany city directory in 1827, living at 37 Chapel Street; *T. V. Cuyler's Albany Directory for the Year 1827* (Albany, 1827). In 1829 he was living on Washington Street, and in 1831, on Spring Street near Washington; *Albany Directory for the Year 1829–1830* (Albany, 1829); *The Albany Directory, and City Register for 1831–32* (Albany, 1832). According to Margaret Matthews, the family lived in "a small chamber in State Street" in about 1830, which *is* consistent with the other evidence. [Matthews], *Matthias,* 13.

40. The most comprehensive history of Albany is still Arthur James Weisse, *History of the City of Albany* (Albany, 1884). See also William Esmond Rowley, "Albany: A Tale of Two Cities, 1820–1880" (Ph.D. diss., Harvard University, 1967), ch. 1; David G. Hackett, *The Rude Hand of Innovation: Religion and Social Order in Albany, New York, 1652–1836* (New York, 1991), 57–58, 69–75, 78–82. On the Albany Regency, see Robert V. Remini, *Martin Van Buren and the Making of the Democratic Party* (New York, 1959); and Michael Wallace, "Changing Concepts of Party in the United States—New York, 1815–1828," *American Historical Review* 74 (1968): 453–91.

41. [Matthews], *Matthias,* 10; Stone, *Matthias,* 20.

42. On the North Dutch Church, see Joel Munsell, *The Annals of Albany* (10 vols.; Albany, 1850–59), I, 86–122; VIII, 93; IX, 210, 354; Gorham A. Worth, *Random Recollections of Albany, from 1800 to 1808* (Albany, 1866), 20–27, 59–60, 71–74; Robert Alexander, *Albany's First Church and Its Role in the Growth of the City* (Albany, 1988).

43. Hackett, *Rude Hand,* 82–88.

44. [John Ludlow], "The 1st, 2nd, 3rd, 4th, & 7th Lectures on Peter. Delivered by the Pastor of the Reformed Protestant Dutch Church of Albany, New York, during the months of March and April of the year 1826," Ms., NYSL. On Ludlow, see also William B. Sprague, *A Sermon Preached in the Second Presbyterian Church, Albany, Sunday Afternoon, September 21, 1857,*

on Occasion of the Death of the Rev. John Ludlow, D.D. (Albany, 1857); William J. R. Taylor, *Sermon on the Life, Character, Services, and Death of the Rev. John Ludlow, LL.D.* . . . (New York, 1857).

45. [Matthews], *Matthias,* 10–11; Stone, *Matthias,* 20–21; Vale, *Fanaticism,* I, 38.

46. [Matthews], *Matthias,* 11, 13–14.

47. Ibid., 12; Stone, *Matthias,* 21; Vale, *Fanaticism,* I, 38.

48. E. N. Kirk to Charles Finney, April 14, 1829, Charles Finney Papers, Oberlin College Library.

49. On Kirk, see David O. Mears, *Life of Edward Norris Kirk* (Boston, 1878), esp. 38–99. There is also an excellent discussion of Kirk and the Albany revival in Hackett, *Rude Hand,* 123–52. On Finney and Kirk, see also Keith J. Hardman, *Charles Grandison Finney, 1792–1875; Revivalist and Reformer* (Syracuse, 1987), 174, 206, 250, 399, 423. On James Chester, see also Edward N. Kirk, *A Memorial of the Rev. James Chester, D.D.; and an Appeal to Those Who Enjoyed His Ministry* (Albany, 1829); *Obituary Notices of the Rev. James Chester, D.D., Late Pastor of the Second Presbyterian Congregation in the City of Albany* (Albany, 1829); William B. Sprague, *Annals of the American Pulpit; or, Commemorative Notices of Distinguished American Clergymen of Various Denominations* (6 vols.; New York, 1857), IV, 401–10.

50. Mears, *Life of Kirk,* 45, 62, 65; Hackett, *Rude Hand,* 126.

51. Kirk, *Memorial,* esp. 18; Mears, *Life of Kirk,* 49–50; Hackett, *Rude Hand,* 126–28. Mears reports that Van Buren, after hearing one of Kirk's sermons, remarked to a friend, "I am accustomed, when men are preaching, to occupy my mind with my political schemes; but politics appeared to me very folly that day. I had to hear the preacher" (Mears, *Kirk,* 49). The quotation may be apocryphal.

52. Mears, *Life of Kirk,* 50.

53. Ibid., 51–63; Hackett, *Rude Hand,* 128–29; Edward Norris Kirk, *Sermons on Different Subjects* (New York, 1841), 312; Records of the First (Reformed) Church of Albany, Minutes (Part A), Vol. 7, December 31, 1828, NYSL. See also *A Confession of Faith, Comprising an Outline of the Doctrines of the 4th Presbyterian Church in the City of Albany* (Albany, 1833), 4.

54. Kirk, *Sermons,* 304; Hackett, *Rude Hand,* 128–35.

55. Kirk, *Sermons,* 105; Hackett, *Rude Hand,* 135–44.

56. E. N. Kirk to A. W. Ives, May 2, 1835, in Stone, *Matthias,* 343–44.

57. [Matthews], *Matthias,* 17, 22; Stone, *Matthias,* 21–23.

58. [Matthews], *Matthias,* 12. On Beman's sermonizing, see E. N. Kirk

to Charles Finney, March 22, 1829, Finney Papers, Oberlin College Library.

59. [Matthews], *Matthias,* 13; Stone, *Matthias,* 21–24, 343–44. According to Stone (21), Kirk's congregation asked the Coila Anti-Burgher church for a certificate on Matthews, but the certificate was withheld. No Margaret Matthews turns up on the list of members of Kirk's church. See *Members of the Fourth Presbyterian Church, in the City of Albany 1836* (Albany, 1836).

60. [Matthews], *Matthias,* 14–15, Stone, *Matthias,* 24.

61. [Matthews], *Matthias,* 16–17. On Charles Finney in Albany, see E. N. Kirk to Charles Finney, July 29, 1829, Finney Papers, Oberlin College Library; Hardman, *Finney,* 174. Finney had long been in touch with Nathaniel Beman, and had first preached in Troy in October 1826. See Hardman, *Finney,* 104–32. It is almost certain that Matthews heard one or more of Finney's sermons the previous July. Both William Leete Stone and Gilbert Vale claimed that Matthews had been much moved by the sermons and sang Finney's praises; Margaret Matthews denied this, and claimed that her husband despised Finney. It is likely, however, that Mrs. Matthews was talking of Robert's later views of Finney and the Finneyites; without question (as a convert to Finney's crusade, out to undo Stone's charges that the Finneyites were "ultraists") she had good reason to distance Finney as far as possible from her husband's religious searchings. Cf. Stone, *Matthias,* 21; Vale, *Fanaticism,* I, 38; and [Matthews], 43–44; and see below, pp. 166–67.

62. [Matthews], *Matthias,* 16–17; Stone, *Matthias,* 24–25; Vale, *Fanaticism,* I, 38. Among the papers of Elijah Pierson, William Leete Stone later found a series of Biblical citations against shaving, notably Leviticus: 19.27 and 21.5. Matthias may well have been convinced by one of these passages. See Stone, *Matthias,* 332–34.

63. [Matthews], *Matthias,* 17–19.

64. Ibid., 19–20. The italicized passage appears on 20; apart from changing Margaret Matthews's pronouns, it is a verbatim transcription. Margaret wrote that Mr. F came to her—her shorthand for Charles Finney.

65. [Matthews], *Matthias,* 20–21; Vale, *Fanaticism,* I, 38. It is far from clear whether Finney actually was in the pulpit that night. At the time, Finney was living in New York City; in September, he would head for Rochester, where he would undertake one of his greatest revivals. About a month before these events, Nathan S. S. Beman did write to Finney, bidding him to leave New York as soon as possible and to "preach in various places in this part of the country"—but Beman and others were always inviting Finney to

preach, and there is no evidence that Finney accepted the invitation. (See Nathan S. S. Beman to Charles Finney, May 17, 1830, Finney Papers, Oberlin College Library.) Margaret Matthews, whose pamphlet is consistently inaccurate when it comes to dates, may have conflated Finney's appearance the previous July with these events. On the other hand, there is no reason to doubt her claim that she *told* her husband that Finney was going to preach that night.

66. *Albany Evening Journal,* June 21, 22, 23, 24, 1830; *Albany Argus,* June 22, 23, 24, 1830; [Matthews] *Matthias,* 21–23; Stone, *Matthias,* 26–27; Vale, *Fanaticism,* I, 38–39.

67. *Albany Argus,* June 25, 1830; *Albany Evening Journal,* June 24, 1830; [Matthews], *Matthias,* 23–25; Stone, *Matthias,* 27–28.

68. [Matthews], *Matthias,* 25–26. On divorce laws in this period, with direct reference to New York State, see Hendrik Hartog, "Marital Exits and Marital Expectations in Nineteenth Century America," *Georgetown Law Journal* 80 (1991): 95–129. Margaret Matthews could have sought a divorce *á mensa et thoro* (from bed and board) on the grounds of extreme cruelty, but the process would have been costly and gained little or nothing in property, given her husband's state. In any event, the possibility apparently did not arise at this time. Later, however, when Robert's circumstances had changed dramatically, Margaret would (as we shall see) consider pursuing full divorce proceedings.

69. [Matthews], *Matthias,* 27. On Matthews's resemblance to the Bible engravings of Jesus, see Vale, *Fanaticism,* I, 40.

70. William Robertson, *The History of the Reign of the Emperor Charles V* (1769; Boston, 1857), 11, 295–304, quotation on 298. Earlier American editions of the work appeared in Philadelphia in 1770 and New York in 1810. There is a large historical literature on the Münster events. For a recent summary with a provocative social interpretation, see Po-chia Hsia, "Münster and the Anabaptists," in Hsia, ed., *The German People and the Reformation* (Ithaca, 1988), 51–70.

71. [Anon.], Matthias and His Impostures," *North Anerican Review,* No. 89 (October 1835): 317–18. William Leete Stone also noticed the parallels between Robert Matthews's beliefs and the Münsterians'; Stone, *Matthias,* 293–96. On the Münsterian legacy, with special reference to sixteenth- and seventeenth-century England, see Christopher Hill, *Puritanism and Revolution: Studies in Interpretation of the English Revolution and the Seventeenth Century* (1958; London, 1968), 312–13. Gilbert Seldes played up the possible

Matthias-Mathys connection in his discusssion of the Prophet. Seldes, "A Messianic Murderer," in his *The Stammering Century* (New York, 1928).

72. Stone, *Matthias*, 30; Vale, *Fanaticism*, I, 39. On Rochester and the revivals, see Johnson, *A Shopkeeper's Millennium*.

73. For details on J. L. D. Mathies life and art, see Herbert A. Wisby, Jr., "J. L. D. Mathies, Western New York State Artist," *New York History* 39 (1958): 133–50. See also Mathies's obituary in *Albany Evening Journal*, December 1, 1834. His full name was John Lee Douglas Mathies. In 1832, Mathies placed an advertisement for the Clinton House in the deist newspaper, *The Liberal Advocate* [Rochester], October 13, 1832, strongly indicating his affinity for free-thought.

74. Wisby, "Mathies," 137–39, 143–48. On Mathies's display of the Red Jacket portrait, see Henry O'Reilly, *Sketches of Rochester* (Rochester, 1838), 383. On natural terror and the sublime in early American painting, with special connection to this part of New York State, see Elizabeth McKinsey, *Niagara Falls: Icon of the American Sublime* (Cambridge, 1985).

75. On James Mathies, the most informative source is his brother's introduction to Mathies, *Rochester*. See also Wisby, "Mathies," 140. On James's support for Jackson, see his poem, "A Song, For the Eighth of January, 1828. Old Hickory," ibid., 95–104.

76. Mathies, *Rochester*, 19, 37–39, 114. On James's death, see *Rochester Daily Advertiser*, May 7, 1830. James purportedly died of "dropsy," a strong (and common) hint that he drank himself to death.

77. Stone, *Matthias*, 30; Vale, *Fanaticism*, I, 39. Both Stone and Vale mistakenly reported that Matthias met with his "mechanic" brother, which would have been James.

78. Ibid., 30; Mathies, *Rochester*, 19. The most recent interpretive history of Anti-Masonry is Paul Goodman, *Towards a Christian Republic: Antimasonry and the Great Transition in New England, 1826–1836* (New York, 1988), which has implications beyond the New England states. On the origins of the movement, see above all Ronald P. Formisano and Kathleen S. Kutolowski, "Antimasonry and Masonry: The Genesis of Protest, 1826–1827," *American Quarterly* 29 (1977): 139–65.

79. [Matthews], Matthias, 27; Stone, *Matthias*, 31; Vale, *Fanaticism*, I, 39.

80. For superb descriptions of New York's growth in these years, see Elizabeth Blackmar, *Manhattan For Rent, 1780–1850* (Ithaca, 1989).

81. Stone, *Matthias*, 31; Vale, *Fanaticism*. I, 39–40.

Jack Larkin writes:

> As they had been since the late seventeenth century, virtually all American men were clean-shaven until the late 1820s, when "a portion of young men," as Felt recalled, primarily city gentlemen of fashion, began to sport mustaches. . . . Beards remained far less acceptable, customarily worn only by a tiny minority of Orthodox Jews. Those few men daring enough to wear beards at this time, two or three decades before their widespread adoption in the 1850s, actually suffered abuse and persecution. When Joseph Palmer of Fitchburg, Massachusetts, appeared at church with a beard in 1830 he was denied communion and later assaulted by a group of men armed with soap and razors who tried to shave him forcibly.

Larkin, *The Reshaping of Everyday Life, 1790–1840* (New York, 1988), 184. Among evangelical Christians, in particular, beards appear to have had dark associations with a heathen patriarchy. Probably the outstanding literary example of the link between shaving and genteel Christian manhood before the Civil War appears in Harriet Beecher Stowe's *Uncle Tom's Cabin,* where in a scene describing an Ohio Quaker household, Stowe writes of how Simeon the elder "engaged in the anti-patriarchal operation of shaving," Stowe, *Uncle Tom's Cabin* (1852; Harmondsworth, 1981), 223.

82. Vale, *Fanaticism,* I, 39.

83. Stone, *Matthias,* 32–33. This is a verbatim transcription with two minor ellipses at the beginning.

84. W. E. Drake, *The Prophet! A Full and Accurate Report of the Judicial Proceedings in the Extraordinary and Highly Interesting Case of Matthews, alias Matthias* (New York, 1834), 8.

85. Vale, *Fanaticism,* I, 39–40.

86. Ibid., I, 40; Stone, *Matthias,* 104.

Three. The Kingdom

1. The account of the first meeting of Matthias and Elijah Pierson in this and the succeeding two paragraphs is from William L. Stone, *Matthias and His Impostures: or, the Progress of Fanaticism. Illustrated in the Extraordinary Case of Robert Matthews, and Some of His Forerunners and Disciples* (New York, 1835), 104–7, 129; G[ilbert] Vale, *Fanaticism; Its Source and Influence, Illustrated by the Simple Narrative of Isabella, in the Case of Matthias, Mr. and*

Mrs. B. Folger, Mr. Pierson, Mr. Mills, Catherine, Isabella, &c., &c. (2 vols.; New York, 1835), I, 40–42.

2. Gilbert Vale states that Matthias moved out of Pierson's house because of disagreements with a man who operated a school in part of the house. Perhaps more important, another part of the house was occupied by Reuben and Frances Folger, and was often visited by Pierson's old perfectionist followers. The information in this and the following paragraphs is from Stone, *Matthias*, 111–12, 107–8, 131, 132, 140, 160, 161n.; Vale, *Fanaticism*, I, 43. The Prophet's reference to Passover in a lower room (like many of his uses of scripture) is from the Last Supper, which was taken in an *upper* room (Mark: 14.15).

3. The account of Matthias's teachings in the following seven paragraphs is from the testimony of Ann and Benjamin Folger published in Stone, *Matthias*, 153–63, 105–6, 160–61, 134–35; and "The Examination of Robert Mathews otherwise called 'Mathias the Prophet,'" in *People v. Robert Matthias*, October 15, 1834, Indictment Papers, Court of General Sessions, Municipal Archives and Records Center, New York. On the Apostle Matthias, see Acts: 20. 1–3.

4. The accounts of the Prophet's furnishings, clothes, shopping trips, and promenades in the next four paragraphs are from Stone, *Matthias*, 136–38, 122, 120, 126. The Bible references to the Prophet's tools are from Revelation: 12.5 and 19.15 (iron rod); Revelation: 20.1–3 (chain and key); Amos: 7.7–8 (plumb line); Revelation: 1.16 (two-edged sword). Stone, *Matthias*, 120 states that it was the children of Elijah Pierson whom Matthias led through the park. Vale, *Fanaticism*, I, 47, insists that they were the children of Sylvester Mills.

5. The account of Elijah Pierson which ends this section is from Stone, *Matthias*, 120, 108, 132–33, 136, 113–14.

6. Ibid., 109, 127–28; Vale, *Fanaticism*, I, 43, 44, 52, 21.

7. Stone, *Matthias*, 139; Vale, *Fanaticism*, I, 49–51. *People v. Robert Matthews*, Indictment Papers, December 10, 1832, Court of General Sessions, MARC, list Levi Andrew Mills, Thomas M. Hooker, and Alexis L. Dias as participants and witnesses to Matthias's oaths during the assault. Mills was an auctioneer, Hooker and Dias were merchants, all of 151 Pearl Street. A list of ten names accompanying the indictment for blasphemy includes, along with the Prophet's brother George, seven merchants, a law clerk, and a J. B. Mills who was not traceable through city directories. All addresses and occupations: *Longworth's American Almanac, New-York Register, and City*

Directory for the Fifty-Eighth Year of American Independence (New York, 1833). The watch is mentioned in an untitled document in the Elijah Pierson Estate Papers, County of Westchester, State of New York: Probate, Administration, Guardian, and Estate Tax Files. Yrs. 1834–up, File stamped 1834–47, SLC.

8. The following account of the Kingdom's career in New York between the arrests and the move to Sing Sing is reconstructed from Stone, *Matthias,* 139, 141–44, and Vale, *Fanaticism,* I, 53–55, 48. It is unclear when Katy left Pierson's employ; it may have been as early as the autumn of 1830, long before Matthias arrived on the scene. An undated memorandum later found in Pierson's papers hints at how he purchased her freedom for $400 so that she could live in Virginia as a free woman. See Stone, *Matthias,* 81–82.

9. Stone, *Matthias,* 95, 149, 183–84. Stone says that the Folgers moved to Sing Sing as early as April 1832. The Westchester County Registry of Deeds, Deedbook 47, p. 148, SLC, records the purchase of Heartt Place from Abraham Heartt in September 1832, for the price of $6,000, and describes the house and land. But other Sing Sing purchases begin, as Stone would have it, in Spring 1832: Books 45–402 (May 1832); 47–146 (September 1832); 48–80 (December 1832); 51–314 (June 1833). J. Thomas Scharf, *History of Westchester County, New York* (2 vols.; Philadelphia, 1886), II, 364, locates the Folger house in the hamlet of Sparta, a mile south of Sing Sing.

10. The account of the Folgers' introduction to Matthias in the next two paragraphs is from Stone, *Matthias,* 148–52, 170–71, 183.

11. The move to Sing Sing recounted in the next two paragraphs is from ibid., 152–53, and Vale, *Fanaticism,* I, 55.

12. Vale, *Fanaticism,* I, 60, II, 36–37; [Anon.], *The Very Interesting and Remarkable Trial of Matthias, at White Plains, Westchester County, New-York, for the Alleged Murder of Elijah Pierson* (New York, 1835), 4. For more on Lewis Basel and Henry Plunkett, see Vale, *Fanaticism,* II, 72–73. Basel's name appears in some sources as Basil.

13. For descriptions of the Prophet's dress, see Stone, *Matthias,* 122, 126; W. E. Drake, comp., *The Prophet! A Full and Accurate Report of the Judicial Proceedings in the Extraordinary and Highly Interesting Case of Matthews, Alias Matthias, Charged with Having Swindled Mr. B. H. Folger, of the City of New-York, Out of Considerable Property* (New York, 1834), 3–6, 9; *Remarkable Trial,* 2; Dean C. Jessee, ed., *The Papers of Joseph Smith: Volume Two: Journal, 1832–1842* (Salt Lake City, 1992), 68; *The Sun* [New York], November 12, 1834; *Evening Post* [New York], November 12, 1834; *National Daily*

Intelligencer [Washington, D.C.], November 11, 1834, April 21, 1835; *The Man* [New York], April 16, 1835. The value of the green cloth was estimated by the *New York Daily Advertiser,* as reprinted in the *Massachusetts Spy,* November 19, 1834. The Prophet's insistence on a new watch to replace the one taken from him by Sylvester Mills's brother is recalled in Benjamin Folger's deposition in *People v. Robert Matthias,* October 15, 1834, Indictment Papers, Court of General Sessions, MARC. Though the sources center on clothing, the Prophet's new possessions included household furnishings. When Mount Zion's furniture was auctioned off after the cult's demise, the lawyers remarked that it was "new principally," and that it "sold extremely well." Untitled document, Pierson Estate Papers.

14. The fashion in coats, waist coats, cravats, pantaloons, and boots can be followed in Norah Waugh, *The Cut of Men's Clothes* (London, 1964), 113–17; C. Willett Cunnington and Phyllis Cunnington, *Handbook of English Costume in the Nineteenth Century* (London, 1959), 64, 80, 82, 101, 103, 105, 128–29; Elisabeth McClellan, *History of American Costume, 1607–1870* (New York, 1904; reprint, 1969), 546. For the Prophet's explanations about his clothing and tools, see Stone, *Matthias,* 168–69. On beards and the clean-cut military style, we are indebted to Sarah W. Le Count, personal communication to Paul E. Johnson, June 22, 1993.

15. See Stone, *Matthias,* 164, 132; Vale, *Fanaticism,* I, 44, 58.

16. Stone, *Matthias,* 112; Drake, *The Prophet!,* 3; Vale, *Fanaticism,* II, 36–37. On the prohibition on strangled fowl, see Acts: 15.20.

17. The literature on American foodways in these years is nicely surveyed in Jack Larkin, *The Reshaping of Everyday Life, 1790–1840* (New York, 1988), 169–82; still useful is Richard Osborn Cummings, *The American and His Food: A History of Food Habits in the United States* (Chicago, 1941), 10–52; Susan Strasser, *Never Done: A History of American Housework* (New York, 1978), 32–38, discusses the implications of ovens; the most detailed study of urban foodways in these years is Barbara G. Carson, *Ambitious Appetites: Dining, Behavior, and Patterns of Consumption in Federal Washington* (Washington, D.C., 1990); the foodways of rural Scots-Americans are described in David Hackett Fischer, *Albion's Seed: Four British Folkways in America* (New York, 1989), 727–31. Isabella Van Wagenen remembered a feast at which a fatted calf was killed and stewed, boiled, and "roasted" out of doors (Vale, *Fanaticism,* II, 36–37). The Prophet's strict ban on roasting, then, applied to *oven*-roasted meat.

18. Noah Webster, *A Dictionary of the American Language* (New York,

1828), definition of "supper." (See also "dinner" and "dining.") Stone, *Matthias,* 173–74: "supper (as the third meal was always called). . . ." On the rise of "dining," see John F. Kasson, *Rudeness & Civility: Manners in Nineteenth-Century Urban America* (New York, 1990), 182–214.

19. Stone, *Matthias,* 132; Vale, *Fanaticism,* II, 37; *Remarkable Trial,* 8–9; Kasson, *Rudeness & Civility,* 205–7. The Judas reference is from the Last Supper, where Jesus predicted that his betrayer would dip his hand into Jesus' dish, a prediction that Judas fulfilled. Matthew: 26.23; Mark: 14.20.

20. Stone, *Matthias,* 130.

21. The decline of external worship and the rise of supper-table terrorism described in the next two paragraphs is from Stone, *Matthias,* 111, 127, 152, 172, 173–74, and Vale, *Fanaticism,* I, 59–60, 66.

22. For Matthias's pronouncements on sickness, see Stone, *Matthias,* 162–65, 179–80; Vale, *Fanaticism.* I, 158. On folk beliefs ascribing illness to a foreign presence (usually a devil or evil spirit) that must be exorcised or conjured, see Keith Thomas, *Religion and the Decline of Magic* (New York, 1971), 177–92; David D. Hall, *Worlds of Wonder, Days of Judgment: Popular Religious Belief in Early New England* (Cambridge, 1989), esp. 189–204; Jon Butler, *Awash in a Sea of Faith: Christianizing the American People* (Cambridge, Mass., 1990), 23, 67–97, 231–33; D. Michael Quinn, *Early Mormonism and the Magic World View* (Salt Lake City, 1987).

23. [Olive Gilbert], *Narrative of Sojourner Truth* (1850; New York, 1993), 3–4, 5–6, 14–17.

24. Ibid., 22–23, 24. Thomas, who had been married twice before being paired with Isabella, was described as "quite advanced in age" in 1828, when Isabella was about thirty years old (p. 54).

25. Vale, *Fanaticism,* I, 18; [Gilbert], *Narrative of Sojourner Truth,* 6–7, 51–52.

26. [Gilbert], *Narrative of Sojourner Truth,* 62, 50–51, 67–68; Vale, *Fanaticism,* I, 18–19. Various recent works have noted the simplicity, humility, and openness to popular/personal religious experience that drew the poor, and particularly blacks, to Methodism in the early nineteenth century. See Nathan O. Hatch, *The Democratization of American Christianity* (New Haven, 1989), 103–10, and Margaret Washington Creel, *"A Peculiar People": Slave Religion and Community-Culture Among the Gullahs* (New York, 1989), 145–47. On Methodist acceptance of dreams and other personal experiences, Butler, *Awash in a Sea of Faith,* 236–41.

27. [Gilbert], *Narrative of Sojourner Truth,* 54, 62, 55. While Isabella's relations with kin remained partial and intermittent far beyond the period of our story, she did rescue those relations late in life. In the late 1850s she bought a house in Battle Creek, Michigan, and all of her surviving children and their families joined her there (ibid., xxiv, 109n.).

28. Ibid., 30–40, 56–61.

29. Vale, *Fanaticism,* I, 40ff. The account of the Matthias cult in [Gilbert], *Narrative of Sojourner Truth,* 69–76, is cribbed from the earlier and more detailed account that Isabella provided Gilbert Vale.

30. Vale, *Fanaticism,* I, 41, 63; II, 24.

31. Ibid., I, 61–62.

32. Ibid., 63–66, 67; *Remarkable Trial,* 4; Stone, *Matthias,* 171–72.

33. Vale, *Fanaticism,* I, 64.

34. Ibid., 63. On fears of feminine seduction in societies where men monopolize power, see Mary Douglas, *Purity and Danger: An Analysis of the Concepts of Pollution and Taboo* (London, 1966), 149–54, and I. M. Lewis, *Ecstatic Religion: A Study of Shamanism and Spirit Possession* (2nd ed.; London, 1989).

35. Vale, *Fanaticism,* I, 67–69.

36. Ibid., II, 10–14; Stone, *Matthias,* 166. There are discussions of American bathing practices in Richard L. Bushman and Claudia L. Bushman, "The Early History of Cleanliness in America," *Journal of American History* 74 (1988): 1213–38; and Jane C. Nylander, *Our Own Snug Fireside: Images of the New England Home, 1760–1860* (New York, 1993), 144–48.

37. Vale, *Fanaticism,* II, 44–52; Stone, *Matthias,* 184–87; *Remarkable Trial,* 13. The patent for the globe stove, held by Walter Hunt, states explicitly that the stove was for use in heating, as a "radiator," and not for cooking. Hence the stove scheme did not compromise Matthias's evocations of the old rural cooking hearth. See United States Senate, *Executive Documents, 23rd Congress, 2nd session (1834–35), Document No. 55* [Patents], 16. On the transfer of Heartt Place, see also Westchester County Registry of Deeds, Deedbook 53–368, microfilm, SLC. On the Third Street house, see Vale, *Fanaticism,* I, 65.

38. Vale, *Fanaticism,* I, 69–71.

39. Ibid., 71–72.

40. Ibid., 75–78; [Margaret Matthews], *Matthias. By His Wife* (New York, 1835), 29–32. Vale, who had little regard for Margaret Matthews,

challenged her claim that she did not tell Folger of her daughter's marriage, on the basis (Vale said) of an interview with an eyewitness to the departure, a friend of Isabella's husband.

41. Vale, *Fanaticism,* I, 78–79; [Matthews], *Matthias,* 33–34, 45. Ann Folger's participation in the beating was witnessed by Isabella Laisdell, Benjamin Folger, and the servant Isabella Van Wagenen. According to Margaret Matthews (33), Matthias beat their daughter because she had married Charles Laisdell without receiving his permission.

42. Vale, *Fanaticism,* I, 79; II, 14–17, 26.

Four. The Downfall

1. G[ilbert] Vale, *Fanaticism; Its Source and Influence. Illustrated by the Simple Narrative of Isabella, in the Case of Matthias, Mr. and Mrs. B. Folger, Mr. Pierson, Mr. Mills, Catherine, Isabella, &c., &c.* (2 vols.; New York, 1835), II, 17.

2. Ibid., 17–18.

3. Ibid. It is possible that Catherine asked on a different occasion about someone going to Benjamin and finding out whom he preferred.

4. The information in this and the following two paragraphs is from Vale, *Fanaticism,* II, 22–24.

5. Ibid., 26–28; [Margaret Matthews], *Matthias. By His Wife* (New York, 1835), 32.

6. Vale, *Fanaticism,* II, 28–29; William L. Stone, *Matthias and His Impostures; or the Progress of Fanaticism. Illustrated in the Extraordinary Case of Robert Matthews, and Some of His Forerunners and Disciples* (New York, 1835), 226.

7. Vale, *Fanaticism,* II, 29; Stone, *Matthias,* 227–28.

8. Vale, *Fanaticism,* II, 30–31 (quotation on 31); [Matthews], *Matthias,* 32–35.

9. Stone, *Matthias,* 188; Vale, *Fanaticism,* II, 30.

10. Vale, *Fanaticism,* II, 31.

11. Ibid., 33, 36.

12. Ibid., 33–35 (quotations on 34, 35).

13. On this incident, cf. ibid., 37–39, and Stone, *Matthias,* 188–89. The version in Stone, part of the Folgers' narrative of their life in the Kingdom, naturally includes nothing about the sleeping arrangements at the tavern, but corroborates other details.

14. Vale, *Fanaticism*, I, 32, 37–42 (quotations on 32, 39).

15. Ibid., 51–54; Stone, *Matthias*, 189–91.

16. Vale, *Fanaticism*, II, 54.

17. Aside from some minor alterations, the following dialogue is taken verbatim from Vale, *Fanaticism*, II, 54–57. In Vale's version, Benjamin appears as Mr. B. Folger, and Ann appears as Mrs. B. Folger. The stage directions (in italics) are our own rewording of the somewhat more prolix directions in Vale's book. The substance is unchanged. Almost certainly it was Vale, and not Van Wagenen, who rendered the scene in theatrical form, but he did so based on her re-creation of what occurred. For the Folgers' account of the confrontation, see Stone, *Matthias*, 190–91, 230–31.

18. Vale, *Fanaticism*, II, 56–58 (quotation on 57).

19. Ibid., 59–60; Stone, *Matthias*, 230.

20. Vale, *Fanaticism*, II, 60; Stone, *Matthias*, 231. On Elephant Taylor's election, see *Westchester Herald and Putnam Gazette*, November 18, 1834.

21. Vale, *Fanaticism*, II, 60–61.

22. On Pierson's physical condition, see Stone, *Matthias*, 192–93, 225. On the dealings with Hunt, see Vale, *Fanaticism*, II, 64–68. According to Vale, Hunt eventually became convinced that Folger, his ex-partner, had lost all his money, and then pressed Matthias unsuccessfully for a settlement. Finally, Hunt undertook a suit in Chancery court to force the Kingdom's hand; he settled out of court with Pierson and Folger (for whom he had more sorrow than anger), agreeing to receive his back salary in connection with the Kingdom stove plus something less than one thousand dollars, in exchange for his total release from the enterprise.

23. Vale, *Fanaticism*, II, 61, 70–71. On the Folgers in Oyster Bay, see ibid., I, 84. Stone confirms the story of Pierson's visit, based on an interview between Matthias and one of Benjamin Folger's attorneys some weeks later; Stone, *Matthias*, 236.

24. Vale, *Fanaticism*, II, 74–75. Benjamin Folger's business trip almost certainly included Albany among its stops; Margaret Matthews later wrote that he visited her several times during the spring and summer of 1834. Each time he turned down her requests to return her children. Mrs. Matthews also stated that at some point over the summer, her eldest son, William, ran away from Mount Zion and returned to her safely, saying that "he could stay no longer with them, on account of their tyrannical treatment toward him," [Matthews], *Matthias*, 36.

25. The most exact account of this incident appears in Ann Folger's

testimony in *The Very Interesting and Remarkable Trial of Matthias, at White Plains, Westchester County, New York, for the Alleged Murder of Mr. Elijah Pierson* (3rd ed.; New York, 1835), 8–9 (quotations on 8). See also Stone, *Matthias,* 134, 193–94; and Vale, *Fanaticism,* I, 15–16; II, 76.

26. *Remarkable Trial,* 9; Vale, *Fanaticism,* II, 77–78; Stone, *Matthias,* 194–96. The Folgers' narrative, included by Stone, claims that Catherine Galloway also fell ill with similar symptoms.

27. *Remarkable Trial,* 10–11; Vale, *Fanaticism,* II, 78–81; Stone, *Matthias,* 196–206.

28. Vale, *Fanaticism,* II, 81; Stone, *Matthias,* 206–7.

29. Vale, *Fanaticism,* II, 81–83; Stone, *Matthias,* 207–9. News of Pierson's death and the coroner's inquest appeared in the local newspaper, *The Westchester Herald,* and was quickly picked up by religious newspapers in New York City. See *New-York Observer,* August 23, 1834.

30. Vale, *Fanaticism,* II, 83–86; Stone, *Matthias,* 209–10; *Remarkable Trial,* 13.

31. Stone, *Matthias,* 210.

32. Ibid., 257–58; *Remarkable Trial,* 5–7.

33. Vale, *Fanaticism,* II, 85–89.

34. Ibid., 89–91; [Matthews], *Matthias,* 45. Vale, basing his account on Isabella's testimony, observed that Ann Folger was fond of Matthias for his personal qualities, "[b]ut when she became the object of his resentments, her love for a moment appeared to turn to hatred."

35. Vale, *Fanaticism,* II, 91–93 (quotation on 92).

36. Ibid., 93–94. Cf. [Matthews], *Matthias,* 45; Stone, *Matthias,* 231–32.

37. Vale, *Fanaticism,* II, 107–8. Cf. Benjamin Folger's deposition in *People v. Robert Matthias,* October 15, 1834, Indictment Papers, Court of General Sessions, MARC, which claims that Matthias defrauded him of the money, a portion of Ann Folger's estate. The mention of Durando is the first in any of the sources on the Kingdom, and his connection to Matthias remains mysterious. Perhaps he was one of those who had attended the Prophet's public sermons in 1832–33 without actually joining the group at Mount Zion or Third Street. Perhaps he was one of the tailors who outfitted the Prophet.

38. Ibid., 108–9; Stone, *Matthias,* 232; *Commercial Advertiser* [New York], September 20, 1834.

39. Ibid.; [Matthews], *Matthias,* 36–39.

40. The information in this and the next two paragraphs is drawn from

Stone, *Matthias,* 233–34; *The Sun* [New York], September 27, October 1, 1834; *The Man* [New York], September 27, 1834; *New-York Observer,* September 27, October 4, 1834; Drake, *The Prophet!,* 3–6.

41. "The Examination of Robert Mathews, otherwise called 'Mathias the Prophet,'" in *People v. Robert Matthias,* October 15, 1834, MARC. In the Old Testament, Abraham receives the priesthood from Melchizedek, who had received it through the lineage of the fathers back to Adam. In his revelation at Kirtland given on September 22 and 23, 1832, Joseph Smith developed the theme of the Melchizedek priesthood; it remains today the basis of Mormon conceptions of the priesthood handed from father to son—and thus a foundation of Mormon patriarchal religious and social organization. See *The Doctrine and Covenants of the Church of Jesus Christ of Latter-day Saints: The Pearl of Great Price* (Salt Lake City, 1985), 153–54. Matthias's reference to Melchizedek almost certainly indicates that at some point he had come into contact with Smith's teachings and recognized their affinities with his own. This is also, however, the earliest such reference in the sources on Matthias, which should dispel any suspicion that Matthias simply plagiarized Smith from the very start of his mission.

42. On the police exhibitions, see Stone, *Matthias,* 168. On the rise of the penny press, see Dan Schiller, *Objectivity and the News: The Public and the Rise of Commercial Journalism* (Philadelphia, 1981); David S. Reynolds, *Beneath the American Renaissance: The Subversive Imagination in the Age of Emerson and Melville* (New York, 1988), 171–75; Alexander Saxton, *The Rise and Fall of the White Republic: Class Politics and Mass Culture in Nineteenth Century America* (London, 1990), 95–108. On earlier modes of crime narrative, see Karen Halttunen, "Early American Murder Narratives: The Birth of Horror," in Richard Wightman Fox and T. J. Jackson Lears, eds., *The Power of Culture: Critical Essays in American History* (Chicago, 1993), 67–101: and for a different view focused on New England, Daniel A. Cohen, *Pillars of Salt, Monuments of Grace: New England Crime Literature and the Origins of American Popular Culture, 1674–1860* (New York, 1993), 3–194.

43. For a sampling of reports in newspapers outside New York City on the Prophet, see *Pennsylvania Reporter* [Philadelphia], November 14, 1834; *Democratic State Journal* [Harrisburg], April 25, May 2, 1835; *Harrisburg Chronicle,* April 27, 1835; *Daily National Intelligencer* [Washington, D.C.], October 6, November 11, 1834; April 20 (quoting *Philadelphia Inquirer*), 21, 23, 24, 1835; *United States Telegraph* [Washington, D.C.], April 24, 1835; *Richmond Enquirer,* April 28, 1835.

44. Vale, *Fanaticism,* II, 109–12; *Sun,* October 2, 1834; [Matthews], *Matthias,* 46.

45. Vale, *Fanaticism,* II, 113; [Matthews] *Matthias,* 34, 39–40, 42, 46–47.

46. Vale, *Fanaticism,* II, 112. The testimonials appear in ibid., I, 10–12. Folger asked that his notice be published by all papers that regularly carried the police blotter; see *Commercial Advertiser,* October 4, 1834; *Working Man's Advocate* [New York], October 4, 1834. The text also appears in Stone, *Matthias,* 241–42.

47. Vale, *Fanaticism,* II, 113–14; Drake, *The Prophet!,* 11–14; *Commercial Advertiser,* November 8, 1834. The texts of Folger's note to the district attorney and his newspaper notice appear in Stone, *Matthias,* 244–45.

48. Drake, *The Prophet!,* 13–15; *Sun,* November 12, 1834; *Evening Post,* November 12, 1834; *Man,* November 12, 1834 (quotation); April 17, 1835.

49. Vale, *Fanaticism,* II, 112.

50. Ibid., 113–14.

51. [Anon.], "Matthias and His Impostures," *North American Review,* No. 89 (October 1835), 323.

52. *Sun,* October 2, 1834. In the coming months, the Boston materialist Amariah Brigham would scandalize religious opinion with his claim that pious fanaticism caused insanity. See Brigham, *Observations on the Influence of Religion upon the Health and Physical Welfare of Mankind* (Boston, 1835). But for some years before this, medical doctors, moral philosophers, and theologians had been debating related issues, particularly the origins and effects of intense religious belief. Although much commented upon and deplored, fanaticism's alleged links to specific forms of religious experience became a particularly important topic of discussion. High-church anti-Finneyites, for example, were prone to view the Finneyites and perfectionist extremists as fanatics; radical deists and Jacksonian Democrats agreed (although they were also likely to find fanaticism lurking in all forms of Christianity); Finneyites (including Finney himself) regretted any fanaticism they may have caused, but insisted that their labors were worth the price, and that, furthermore, by bringing wavering, mentally afflicted sinners to peace in Jesus Christ, they probably did more to limit the phenomenon than to cause it. The Matthias case quickly became entangled with these debates, as newspapermen and pundits tried to explain the Prophet's motives. For reviews of the discussion of fanaticism and insanity in the 1830s, see Norman Dain, *Concepts of Insanity in the United States, 1789–1865* (New Brunswick, N.J., 1964), 183–93; and David J. Rothman, *The Discovery of the*

Asylum: Social Order and Disorder in the New Republic (Boston, 1971), 109–29. For a case study of the debate on fanaticism in connection with the Millerites, see Ronald L. Numbers and Janet S. Numbers, "Millerism and Madness: A Study of 'Religious Insanity' in Nineteenth-Century America," in Ronald L. Numbers and Jonathan M. Butler, *The Disappointed: Millerism and Millenarianism in the Nineteenth Century* (Bloomington, 1987), 92–117.

53. *Sun*, November 25, 1834.

54. *Man*, April 22, 1835. On Evans, see Edward Pessen, *Most Uncommon Jacksonians: Radical Leaders of the Early Labor Movement* (Albany, 1967), esp. 71–75.

55. "Matthias and His Impostures," 323–25.

56. *Evangelical Magazine* IV (1835):163–64.

57. *Evening Star* [New York], reprinted in *Daily National Intelligencer*, April 23, 1835.

58. Ibid.

59. The gist of the *Commercial Advertiser*'s stance appears in Stone, *Matthias*, 315–24.

60. *Evening Post*, April 16, 1835; *Man*, April 16, 1835; *Sun*, April 17, 1835; Stone, *Matthias*, 252.

61. The description of Matthias and the following interview originally appeared in the New York *Transcript*, a penny paper, and was later widely reprinted; see, for example, *Democratic State Journal*, April 25, 1835. For a slightly different rendering, see Stone, *Matthias*, 251–52. The italics in the present version have been added.

62. *Remarkable Trial*, 2.

63. Ibid., 2; Stone, *Matthias*, 252.

64. *Remarkable Trial*, 2; Stone, *Matthias*, 253–56.

65. *Sun*, April 18, 1835.

66. *Man*, April 17, 1835.

67. *Remarkable Trial*, 3–7.

68. Ibid., 7–11.

69. Ibid., 11–13.

70. Ibid., 14–15.

71. Ibid., 15–16.

72. Ibid., 16; *Evening Post*, April 20, 1835; Stone, *Matthias*, 267–68.

73. Stone, *Matthias*, 268; *Evening Post*, April 20, 1835.

74. On the alleged deal between Western and the prosecution, see Vale, *Fanaticism*, II, 120. Vale had no hard evidence to support his charge, only a

free-thinker's gut reaction that Western, a Christian, must have worked out some arrangement with the district attorney to protect the Folgers' reputations.

75. This information, and that in the remainder of this chapter, is drawn from *Evening Post,* April 20, 1835; and Stone, *Matthias,* 268–72.

Epilogue

1. *Democratic State Journal* [Harrisburg], April 25, 1835; *Memoirs of Matthias the Prophet, with a Full Exposure of His Previous Impostures and of the Degrading Delusions of His Followers* (New York, 1835), 2; *Evening Star* [New York] reprinted in *Daily National Intelligencer* [Washington, D.C.], April 23, 1835.

2. William L. Stone, *Matthias and His Impostures: or, the Progress of Fanaticism. Illustrated in the Extraordinary Case of Robert Matthews, and Some of His Forerunners and Disciples* (New York, 1835), 221–23.

3. [Margaret Matthews], *Matthias. By His Wife* (New York, 1835), esp. 3–4, 34, 44.

4. G[ilbert] Vale, *Fanaticism; Its Source and Influence, Illustrated by the Simple Narrative of Isabella, in the Case of Matthias, Mr. and Mrs. B. Folger, Mr. Pierson, Mr. Mills, Catherine, Isabella, &c. &c.* (2 vols.; New York, 1835), I, 50.

5. Ibid., II, 116.

6. On Vale, see Horace Traubel, *With Walt Whitman in Camden* (3 vols., 1906–1914; New York, 1961), III, 140; Sean Wilentz, *Chants Democratic: New York City & the Rise of the American Working Class, 1788–1850* (New York, 1984), 154, 337; as well as the works cited therein.

7. Vale, *Fanaticism,* II, 120.

8. Ibid., 9.

9. Writings on Matthias include Theodore Schroeder, "Matthias the Prophet (1788–1837)," *Journal of Religious Psychology* VI (1913): 59–65; Richardson Wright, *Hawkers and Walkers in Early America* (Philadelphia, 1927), 222–23; Gilbert Seldes, "A Messianic Murderer," in Seldes, *The Stammering Century* (New York, 1928); Christopher Ward, "Mr. Pierson and the New Messiah," *The New Yorker,* December 8, 1934; Robert B. Pattison, "Matthias the Imposter," *New York Folklore Quarterly* 3 (1947): 138–41; Thomas M. McDade, "Matthias, Prophet Without Honor," *New-York Historical Society Quarterly* 62 (1977): 311–34.

10. David S. Reynolds, *Beneath the American Renaissance: The Subversive Imagination in the Age of Emerson and Melville* (New York, 1988), 169–210 (quotation on 171); Karen Halttunen, "Early American Murder Narratives: The Birth of Horror," in Richard Wightman Fox and T. J. Jackson Lears, eds., *The Power of Culture: Critical Essays in American History* (Chicago, 1993), 67–101, makes some pertinent observations about the underlying moral tensions in supposedly sensationalist literature.

11. Jay Leyda, *The Melville Log: A Documentary Life of Herman Melville, 1819–1891* (2 vols.; New York, 1969), I, 42–65; Herman Melville, *The Confidence-Man: His Masquerade* (1857; Harmondsworth, 1990), 14, 158. In 1835, the year of Matthias's widely reported murder trial, Melville was clerking for his brother, Gansevoort Melville, who had taken up their now-deceased father's fur business. The brothers resided on Clinton Square, only yards from the North Dutch Church. On Melville and the penny press, see Reynolds, *Beneath the American Renaissance,* 146–47, 169–81.

12. A full and satisfactory history of these cults remains to be published. For a fascinating study of a single example, see Roger Van Noord, *The King of Beaver Island: The Life and Assassination of James Jesse Strang* (Urbana, 1988). Wallace Stegner discusses some of the other more interesting Mormon heretics, in *Mormon Country* (1942; Lincoln, Neb., 1981), 128–35. On changing sexual systems in the United States, see above all John D'Emilio and Estelle B. Freedman, *Intimate Matters: A History of Sexuality in America* (New York, 1988). On the sexualized meanings connected with the recent religious Right, see Sean Wilentz, "God and Man at Lynchburg," *New Republic,* April 25, 1988.

13. Vale, *Fanaticism,* II, 122.

14. *Albany Citizens' Advertiser and General Directory for 1834–35* (Albany, 1834); *Hoffman's Albany Directory and City Register for 1837–8* (Albany, 1837); [Matthews], *Matthias,* 36.

15. [Matthews], *Matthias,* 40, 46–47. A search through the relevant divorce court records at the Old Records Division, Office of the County Clerk, New York County, turned up no evidence of a divorce granted to Margaret Matthews. On several occasions, Mrs. Matthews wrote, Benjamin Folger begged her not to seek a divorce and once offered her $250 if she would promise in writing to desist; ibid., 39–40. Perhaps Folger finally made her a convincing offer.

16. Vale, *Fanaticism,* II, 68. According to the New York City directories, Benjamin Folger lived at 32 Morton Street in 1836–37. His name next

appears in 1842–43, living at 449 Greenwich Street; the following year he moved to King Street, where he remained until 1848–49. For accounts of Folger's continuing real estate dealings, see Westchester County Registry of Deeds, Book 81, p. 247; Book 86, p. 211; Book 93, p. 94; Book 94, pp. 689, 691; book 108, p. 353; Book 111, p. 3; microfilm, SLC.

17. Stone, *Matthias,* 246. The complete file on the legal entanglement over Elijah Pierson's estate is in County of Westchester, State of New York: Probate, Administration, Guardian, and Estate Tax Files, Yrs. 1834–up, File Stamped 1834–47, microfilm, SLC.

18. Frank E. Sanchis, *American Architecture: Westchester County, New York, Colonial to Contemporary* (n.p., 1977), 45–47.

19. [Matthews], *Matthias,* 41–42.

20. Henry Caswall, *The City of the Mormons: or Three Days at Nauvoo in 1842* (London, 1842), 31; *Alton* [Illinois] *Commercial Gazette,* February 19, 1839, cited in Dean C. Jessee, ed., *The Papers of Joseph Smith: Volume Two: Journal, 1832–1842* (Salt Lake City, 1992), 569; on Matthias's death, see, for example, Jessee, ed., ibid.

21. Vale, *Fanaticism,* II, 110, describes Isabella's suit and states that Benjamin Folger was convicted of slander and forced to pay damages to her. [Olive Gilbert], *Narrative of Sojourner Truth* (1850; New York, 1993), 78, says only that Isabella "received a small sum of money from Mr. B. Folger, as the price of Mrs. Folger's attempt to convict her of murder." The case pleading appears as *Isabella Van Wagenen v. Benjamin H. Folger,* in Pleadings, 1754–1837, Supreme Court of Judicature, Old Records Division, Office of the County Clerk, County of New York, V–395, but the records for the Supreme Court sittings in New York City and Albany show no evidence of the case actually coming to judgment.

22. [Gilbert], *Narrative of Sojourner Truth,* 77–101; Vale, *Fanaticism,* I, 82 (quotation).

23. [Gilbert], *Narrative of Sojourner Truth,* 80.

ACKNOWLEDGMENTS

We are grateful to several institutions for vital financial assistance: the American Council of Learned Societies, the John Simon Guggenheim Memorial Foundation, the National Endowment for the Humanities, and the University of Utah Humanities Center. The commentators and audiences at various seminars and lectures asked instructive (if sometimes discomfiting) questions; above all, we wish to thank our listeners at Princeton University, the University of Utah, Harvard University, the Johns Hopkins University, the University of California at Irvine, and the New York State Historical Association (which generously invited one of us to give a preliminary version of the entire story as the Alexander C. Flick Memorial Lecture in 1988). Our research began at Sterling Memorial Library at Yale University; since then, we have benefited from the help of the librarians and their staffs at various repositories, above all the Family History Library of the Church of Jesus Christ of Latter-day Saints, the American Antiquarian Society, the Henry E. Huntington Library, the Library of Congress, the New York City Archives and Record Center, the Old Records Division of the County Clerk's Office of New York County, the New-York Historical Society, the New York Public Library, the New York State Library, the Oberlin

College Library, Marriott Library of the University of Utah, Firestone Library of Princeton University, and Speer Library of the Princeton Theological Seminary. Colleagues, friends, and family gave us invaluable aid by answering our questions, reading portions of the manuscript, or both. We are especially indebted to Kasey Grier, Christine Stansell, Peter Brown, Jon Butler, Anne Boylan, Tom Dunnings, Janet Ellingson, Gerald Geison, Anthony Grafton, Dirk Hartog, Sarah Le Count, Nell Painter, and Margaret Washington. For their research assistance, we wish to thank Marriott Dougan Barthalomew, Karen Carver, Jonathan Earle, and Jeffrey Merkowitz. Sheldon Meyer was, as ever, a patient, perceptive, and endlessly encouraging editor. Leona Capeless improved the manuscript greatly, with her usual thoroughness, grace, and wit.